ITHAKA

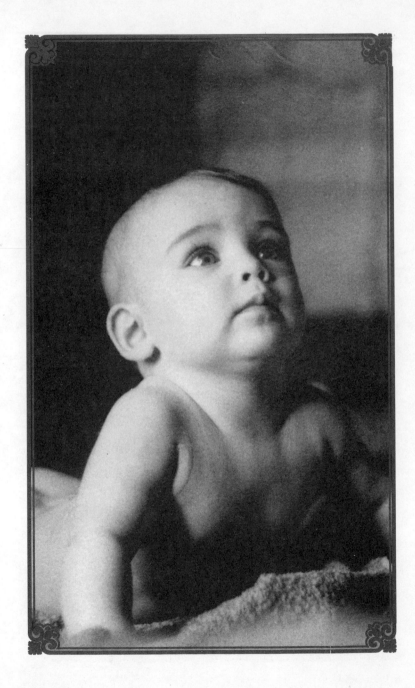

ITHAKA

A DAUGHTER'S MEMOIR
OF BEING FOUND

SARAH SAFFIAN

BASIC
BOOKS

A Member of the Perseus Books Group

The frontispiece photograph of the author, age approximately six months, was taken by her father, Marvin Saffian.

The names and some identifying characteristics of the author's birth family, as well as of certain friends and members of the adoption field, have been changed to protect their privacy. Any resemblance between these pseudonyms and real people, living or dead, is coincidental.

SOURCE NOTES

Grateful acknowledgment is made for permission to quote from the following sources:

The lines from "i am so glad and very," copyright 1940, © 1968, 1991 by the Trustees for the E. E. Cummings Trust, from *Complete Poems: 1904–1962 by E. E. Cummings*, edited by George J. Firmage. Reprinted by permission of Liveright Publishing Corporation.

"Windy" by Ruthann Friedman © 1967 (Renewed) Irving Music, Inc., All Rights Reserved, Used by Permission, Warner Bros. Publications U.S. Inc., Miami, Florida 33014.

"Casey Jones," lyrics by Robert Hunter, music by Jerry Garcia © Ice Nine Publishing Company.

"Glory of Love," Words and Music by Billy Hill, Copyright ©1936 Shapiro, Bernstein & Co., Inc., New York, Copyright Renewed, International Copyright secured, All Rights Reserved, Used by Permission.

Keeley, Edmund and Philip Sherrard, translators; *C. P. Cavafy/Collected Poems*. Copyright © 1972 by Edmund Keeley and Philip Sherrard. Reprinted by permission of Princeton University Press.

Tao Te Ching by Lao-tzu, A New English Version, with foreword and notes by Stephen Mitchell; translation copyright © 1988 by Stephen Mitchell; reprinted by permission of HarperCollins Publishers, Inc.; also reprinted by permission of Macmillan Magazines Limited ©1988.

The New Mahzor courtesy of Walter B. Stern.

Speak, Memory by Vladimir Nabokov ©1967 by Alfred A. Knopf.

The WINS News motto courtesy of WINS News.

FIRST EDITION

Designed by C. Linda Dingler

Library of Congress Cataloging-in-Publication Data
Saffian, Sarah.
  Ithaka : a daughter's memoir of being found / Sarah Saffian.
    p. cm.
  ISBN 0-465-03618-X
  1. Saffian, Sarah. 2. Adoptees—United States—Biography.
3. Birthparents—United States—Identification. I. Title.
HV874.82.S24A3 1998
362.82'98'092—dc21   98-38955
[B]   CIP

98 99 00 01/v 10 9 8 7 6 5 4 3 2 1

To Mom and Dad
with love
for being all that parents can be

Keep Ithaka always in your mind.
Arriving there is what you are destined for.
But do not hurry the journey at all.
Better if it lasts for years,
so you are old by the time you reach the island,
wealthy with all you have gained on the way,
not expecting Ithaka to make you rich.

Ithaka gave you the marvelous journey.
Without her, you would not have set out.
She has nothing left to give you now.

And if you find her poor, Ithaka won't have fooled you.
Wise as you will have become, so full of experience,
you will have understood by then what these Ithakas mean.

–from "Ithaka," *C.P. Cavafy/Collected Poems*
translated by Edmund Keeley and Philip Sherrard

Contents

ix

1994

1995

1996

x

PROLOGUE

Aperture

It is less than a month until my twenty-fourth birthday. It's
Friday, and I'm looking forward to the weekend. As on most
mornings before heading to the office, I go to the gym and then
return home to shower, dress, eat breakfast. At nine-fifteen,
after taking a last sip of orange juice and double-checking that I
have everything I need for the day—datebook, journal, notes for
an article I'm writing, cash—I'm ready to go.

The telephone rings.

"Hello?"

"Hello, is Sarah Saffian there?"

"This is Sarah." I guess that it's a magazine editor, calling
about work.

"Sarah, my name is Hannah Morgan. I think I'm your birth
mother."

1993

A good traveler has no fixed plans
and is not intent upon arriving.

—from *Tao Te Ching*
by Lao-tzu, adapted by Stephen Mitchell

1

Awakening

I remember being seven years old. It was not long after my mother Nancy had died. I was alone in the living room of our old apartment, poking around in the leather-topped desk by the windows that overlooked Lexington Avenue, or "Lex," as my father coolly said to cab drivers. The yellow light in my memory is of late afternoon, early evening, and the bustle-free air suggests a weekend, a Sunday. I pulled open the wooden drawer to find a black datebook with the year "1969" embossed on the front in gold. Curious, and still young enough to think unfailingly of myself first, I looked up my birthday and was proud to see, penciled in my father's rushed but tidy hand on February 23, "Sarah Ruth is born." I continued to flip through the book and was startled to find written sometime in late April, "Sarah Ruth comes home."

I mulled over the two-month discrepancy for several seconds before calling to my father to ask why I had taken so long to come home from the hospital. I perched on the leather hassock, facing him as he sat in the large red armchair, his slender legs crossed with an easy elegance, his brown hair curling with a weekend unruliness (to go to his Wall Street office on week-days, he tended to slick it down with Dep, matching the slick-ness of a tailor-made suit, a polished Gucci loafer). Even when I was young, he took me seriously, was attentive to my ques-tions and straightforward in his answers. He explained that I had been jaundiced as a newborn, assuring me that this was a common condition, that nothing had been seriously wrong with me, but that I'd had to recover before I could leave the hospital. Then, for the first time, he told me the story of my adoption.

"Mommy and I tried to have you on our own, but we weren't able to," he began. I didn't yet know exactly how babies were made, but I had seen pregnant women before—on the street, mothers of friends. "So we adopted you, which means that someone else gave you to us to be our daughter." He went on to talk about filling out the forms.

"Most people are so desperate for a child, they say they'd be overjoyed with *any* baby, and don't put down preferences." He smiled then, brown saucer eyes glimmering behind round glasses, and smugly recalled, "But Mommy and I looked at each other and said, 'Well, we really want a little girl.'" He said they had also requested that the birth parents be college graduates, or at least in college—as much as my father has always been steadfast in proclaiming me his *true* daughter, "birth" daughter or no, he must have believed that intelligence is somewhat genetic.

"We were asking for you in particular—you were meant to be with Mommy and me," he said, and I did have the sense of being carefully selected, deliberately ordered, as if I were a Saffian because I met their specifications. The message that I was supremely wanted overrode any potential feelings of being unwanted by my original set of parents. We discussed how I had been chosen and brought home, not how I had been abandoned. Mostly, however, I absorbed this new information the same way that I had taken in my mother's death, turning numb in the face of its enormity—as though the revelation belonged to someone else, or were unfolding outside of reality, in a movie or a book. My feelings seeped out, displaced, haphazard (once, when a friend knocked over my Sea Monkeys tank, I burst into a fit of nervous tears, so profoundly did such an accident upset my precariously balanced sense of order).

The impact of this initial conversation about my adoption was gradual. I soon discovered that there was another adopted girl in my class at the Spence School, and that being adopted was regarded as only slightly weirder than having divorced parents, which had become practically as common as having parents who were still together. The fact that my mother had died was deemed exotic, perhaps because it was tragic, while being adopted wasn't necessarily so.

Being a child who spent much of the time in a make-believe world, I responded primarily through fantasy. The news didn't preoccupy my daily life, but whenever I was in the mood, I would let myself drift into imagining who my birth parents might be. As a little girl, I pictured fairy-tale characters—Cinderella and Prince Charming, Snow White and Prince Charming, Rapunzel and Prince Charming. Or modest-living but always very beautiful peasant men and women, ruby-lipped and fair-skinned, frolicking in the glistening green hills of the countryside, fetching water from the winking stream, living life robustly, passionately, purely. As an adolescent, my thoughts turned to the celebrities du jour: Was Marie Osmond my birth mother? Was John Travolta my birth father? As an adult, whenever I passed people on the street with a coloring and build similar to mine, I looked them over closely, or else I catalogued people I knew—teachers, friends of my parents—and wondered.

With a single phone call on an otherwise ordinary morning, this life of vague curiosity was instantly transformed.

"Oh my God," I whispered, receiver clutched in hand. Tears sprang to my eyes as I made my way to a chair. A pause. My birth mother started to speak, her voice soft and shaky, but forthright. She didn't sound like a New Yorker, an uptight urban dweller—underneath the surface unease, I sensed a core of calmness.

"I'm sorry to startle you by calling on the phone," Hannah hesitantly began, "but I worried that if I sent a letter and got no answer, I wouldn't know if you had gotten the letter and didn't want to write back, or if you hadn't gotten the letter, because I'd written to the wrong person."

"Mm hm," I answered, reduced for a while to one-word or one-sound responses. I was so preoccupied with the fact that we were speaking at all, it was difficult to concentrate on what we were speaking about. To ground myself, I grabbed a scrap of notepaper off my desk and scribbled down key facts while we talked. Hannah told me that she had been twenty-one years old when she gave birth to me at Staten Island Hospital, and that I had weighed only five pounds.

"It was an easy pregnancy and an easy delivery, so chances are you will have easy pregnancies and deliveries, too—that is, if you want to have children."

"Oh, I *definitely* want to have children," I gushed automatically, surprising myself.

Hannah said that she and my birth father, Adam Leyder, had attended the University of New Hampshire together, and that I had been conceived soon after graduation. So my father had been granted his wish of college-educated birth parents after all, I thought in passing. The link between this live voice and a preference on a form felt oddly arbitrary. What if Marvin and Nancy Saffian hadn't written that in—would I have been placed with someone else? Hannah went on to admit that toward the end of the pregnancy she had begun having second thoughts about giving me up, but believed it was too late to change her mind.

"I have another shock for you," she said. "I'm married to your birth father, and we have three other children." Renee, age fourteen, Lucy, ten, and Samuel, six—my full biological siblings.

"Oh, that's so wonderful," I heard myself saying, "then I can visit you all at once." Their family lived in Hanover, New

Hampshire, where Hannah worked as a potter and Adam as a draftsman. She mentioned a store in New York called Moonstruck, which sold her pottery. I tried to absorb this barrage of information. The phone call was creating a rift in me: while one part was interacting, the other part was unaffected, on the outside looking in.

Then Hannah revealed the name she had given me, the name that appeared on my original birth certificate: Susan Morgan. I turned the strange name over in my head as if I were meeting a new person.

"Could you tell me about your family?" she asked next. "I feel like I've been doing all the talking." In the split second before responding, I considered how best to relay the most painful piece of the story. I felt oddly protective of Hannah, already. I had no intention of startling or hurting her, and was loath to contribute to any regrets she had about relinquishing me. At the same time, I also felt protective of my family. I didn't want to give Hannah the wrong impression, that I had grown up neglected in a broken household—I had always been cared for, loved without bounds. In answering this woman who had given me life, I had to be gentle, but also direct.

"Well, one important thing you should know," I offered, "is that my mother died when I was six."

Hannah took in a short, sharp breath. "That's one of the things birth mothers always fear, that something happens to the adoptive parents," she said. And then, "Adam's mother died when he was six, too." I was stunned by this unexpected parallel. But I blinked and recovered, going on to explain that my father,

Marvin, had remarried when I was ten, and that he and his new wife, Kathy, had had two children together within two years— my brother, Maxwell, and my sister, Rachel Anne. I reassured Hannah that I loved my family dearly: my father had been and continued to be my anchor, and Kathy, whom I considered Mom, had picked up where Nancy left off and mothered me devotedly, with strength and sensitivity.

"What do you look like?" Hannah asked later in the conversation.

"I have dark brown hair, wavy, about shoulder-length, and green eyes . . . "

"Yes, I think we were told that you had green eyes. All of us but Sam have green eyes—he has blue eyes. Are you left-handed, by any chance?"

"Yes!"

"I'm left-handed, and so are Lucy and Sam!"

"Oh, is that genetic?"

"I think so. You know, your birth father is six-foot-four."

"Six-foot-four? I'm only five-five! What happened?"

"Well, I'm not quite five-three."

"Oh, I see. Thanks a *lot* !" We shared our first laugh.

I told her that I had known I was adopted for almost as long as I could remember, and that I had always planned to seek out my birth parents. She asked if I had ever expressed this interest to my father and if so, how he had reacted. I said that when I had brought it up to him hypothetically, he had answered that he would be as supportive and informative as he could, but that he didn't want to be personally involved.

Hannah gave me their address and phone number, which I jotted on the notepaper. She said I could call anytime.

"Would it be all right if Adam called you? I feel badly that I'm getting to talk to you without him here."

"Why don't I try to call him instead?" I quickly responded. "Maybe over the weekend."

Hannah asked in parting, "Did you ever think you would pick up the phone and it would be me?"

After pausing to think, I replied simply, "No, because I always assumed I would be the one making the call."

I carefully returned the receiver to its cradle and fixated on it for a beat. Still sitting, I took a deep breath and switched my gaze to a point on the wall for several seconds. The room was very quiet, in that palpable way that comes after there has been loud noise. Unclear of my emotions in this moment—shock? confusion? loss?—I nonetheless felt them physically, tingling through me. After several minutes, not knowing what else to do, I wiped my eyes, pulled on my backpack, and headed out into the cold bright day.

I watched with a mix of envy and amazement the people bustling past—shower-fresh hair still glistening, hands balancing hot paper coffee cups bearing the Greek-lettered declaration "We are happy to serve you"—on their way to work, to appointments, to a normal end of a normal week. Once at the office, I said quick, perfunctory "Good mornings" as I made my way to my desk, where I sat and stared at the articles to be fact-checked, letters turning into hieroglyphics, text blurring into two fuzzy, distant columns before my unfocusing eyes. I finally broke through my trance and called my father, who was home for the day. At the first sound of his voice, all at once I began to cry in earnest. Between sobs I told him about Hannah's phone call, and he said to come right over.

I pleaded "family emergency" to my editor—the emergency being my newfound confusion about the concept of family—and rushed out. As I walked from the subway to my parents' house, I was surprised that their block, the stoop, the tree in front of their brownstone, all looked a bit different, as though I were seeing them for the first time. Through a kitchen window, I saw Dad sitting, waiting. Noticing me, he smiled and got up to let me in. Relief flowed through me as we hugged and I breathed in his warm, fatherly smell of soap and coffee and cig- arettes. I sat down at the table, running my hands along its butcher-block solidity, and gradually began to feel oriented again, in these familiar—familial—surroundings.

My father had a look of concern, but not of surprise. "So, tell me what happened." I took him from the ring of the telephone through the entire conversation in as much detail as I could muster. I was dry-eyed, matter-of-fact, exhausted and wired at once, like the sensation after staying up all night. When I men- tioned my birth name as Susan Morgan, he nodded.

"Yes, I remember. 'Susan' was one of the few things we knew. That, and that the birth mother was Jewish, being that Louise Wise Services is a Jewish adoption agency." The confirmation quelled my fears that this woman might be an impostor, or sim- ply mistaken.

11

As we talked, I felt deeply connected to my father, sure that he was my parent, and not these strangers who had unexpectedly burst into my life. Who were they to me? He and I have always shared an especially close bond, but usually it is simply a silent understanding. Discussing my birth parents and the circumstances of my adoption brought our bond to the surface. Perhaps we were even clinging to our connection, because this new element was potentially threatening—it didn't have a place in our world of father and daughter.

After a while, I called Mom, who was at the school where she taught fifth grade. I had been open with my father, but cautiously so, afraid that he would feel defensive about my birth parents' sudden emergence. With my mother I could speak more freely, because even though the Leyders presented a potential threat to her as well, she wasn't the one who had adopted me. Outwardly, she reacted with curiosity and support. That evening, however, while loading the dishwasher after dinner, she confessed that inside, her immediate response had been, "Oh, shit." After hanging up, she had gone into a friend's office to ask, "Why did she have to call Sarah? Why couldn't she have contacted us instead, so at least we could have acted as an intermediary?" But as my mother was admitting this, I felt glad that Hannah had called me and not them. Each of us wanted to soften the blow for the other.

Mom paused at the sink then, hands inactive in the soapy water. "I appreciate a birth mother's desire to know, but I never would have called my child without warning," she mused. "If you two had met by chance it would have been one thing, but when one person has years to prepare and the other receives the call all of a sudden, it's an unfair advantage."

Because I already liked Hannah from our single half-hour-long interaction, I felt the urge to defend her, to understand her reasons for calling me. "What would you have done if Hannah had contacted you instead?" I asked both my parents, bringing the wine glasses to the counter.

"No opinion," my father answered tersely from the half-cleared table. "I may or may not have talked to her. I would have called you first." Then he added, "I certainly wouldn't have started blabbing to someone who said she was my daughter's mother." Mom said that if Hannah had called her or written her a letter, we as a family could have discussed the possibility of pursuing a relationship, whether I wanted to respond, and how.

Over the weekend, which I spent mostly with my family, I resolved not to tell my brother and sister yet that my birth mother had contacted me. They did know that I was adopted and that my adoptive mother, Dad's first wife, had died when I was little. I had told them during the summer before my freshman year at Brown, when Max was nearly eight years old and Rachel six and a half—right around the ages that I myself had been when these facts had become known to me. It was evening, on a family vacation in Spain. I related my story plainly, and then let them respond. Rachel took in the information with a small smile and a nod, and probably went to mull it over by herself in bed later. Max, on the other hand, began to shudder with sobs of betrayal, hurt that this was the truth and we hadn't told him, he hadn't known. My parents had left it up to me to decide when to tell them, agreeing that they weren't old enough to understand until that summer. Now, however, at thirteen and nearly twelve, Max and Rachel were certainly old enough to be told about Hannah. But this time, my hesitation hinged more on my own emotional needs.

I also decided not to call my birth parents back yet. It was too soon—I needed time to digest what had happened and to decide what I wanted to do about it. But in their eagerness, they didn't afford me that space. On Monday evening, again as I was on my way out, the phone rang. "Hey, Sarah, this is Adam Leyder, your birth father." My stomach leapt in panic. As the impact of both phone calls hit me at once, I felt not just startled, but invaded.

We exchanged much of the same information that Hannah and I had—what we looked like, general overviews of our lives. When I admitted my feelings of shock and self-protectiveness, Adam apologized for prompting these reactions and then stuttered, clearly moved, "I, I can't believe I'm talking to you. I'd drive down to New York to meet you on five minutes' notice and leave after five minutes, if that was what you wanted."

I tried to maintain a pleasant composure on the surface, but inside I was churning. "No, please don't do that, not yet," I answered, drumming my fingers on the kitchen table, laughing shrilly with disbelief at the extreme situation I was being thrust into. "I'd like to meet you someday, but right now, I'm overwhelmed even by these phone calls. Why don't we write instead, for the time being," I continued, choosing my words deliberately, trying to let him down easy. "I can't have an emotional upheaval every time the phone rings. It's hard to be taken by surprise like that. Letters would be much more manageable for me, just while we figure all this out. Would that be okay with you?"

He asked whether I felt comfortable sending photographs along with these letters, but I answered that I wasn't even ready for that yet. He said he understood, stressing, "We want to do whatever is best for you, whatever *you* want," but I thought I could sense his disappointment, his urgency deflated.

After we hung up, I paused long enough for it to dawn on me that this wasn't about a single phone call, an isolated incident, but about an ongoing process. I'd had my fantasy heritage whisked out from under me, like in the old magic trick, only I wasn't left intact as the place setting is supposed to be after the tablecloth has been yanked away. Then, flustered, I rushed out.

At work later in the week, I looked up Louise Wise Services in the phone book. I took down the number on the same piece of notepaper that I had been carrying around with me since Hannah's call, and snuck downstairs to the lobby pay phones where I wouldn't be overheard. I dialed and asked for post-adoption services. Someone with the raspy, singsong voice of a middle-aged Jewish woman answered.

"Hello, this is Millie Burns in post-adoption. How can I help you?"

"Ms. Burns, my name is Sarah Saffian. I was adopted through your agency almost twenty-four years ago." Pause, breath. "And my birth mother just called me out of the blue last Friday."

"Oh, God," she groaned, as though she'd heard this story before. Then, "Do you want to come in and talk about it?"

15

Immediately I felt touched, cared for. A quiet "uh huh" was all I could manage.

A few days later, I walked into Louise Wise, situated in a townhouse on East Ninety-fourth Street, and was shown into a small sunny room to meet Millie Burns. Even though I couldn't remember having been there before, the place felt strangely familiar, as it was partially responsible for my being Sarah Saffian, for my identity.

"Be glad they didn't come and knock on your front door," Ms. Burns said after I had reiterated my story in greater detail, pulling her chair closer and leaning in toward me to whisper conspiratorially, "I've seen it happen." She agreed that starting by writing letters was a good idea. Then we could progress to exchanging photographs, speaking on the phone again and even visiting, if and when I felt ready. But as one apparently disinclined toward reunions, she emphasized that I didn't owe "these people" anything, that I didn't ever have to contact them if I didn't want to. I left with a sense of solace, and also with a somewhat more sympathetic attitude toward Hannah and Adam, if only in reaction to Ms. Burns' unforgiving stance.

The following week, I received a single, white, business-sized envelope, addressed in neat capital letters—an architect's hand, which at first glance reminded me of my grandfather's. After staring at the return address for several moments, I carefully opened the envelope to find two separate letters, both a couple of pages long, typed on a computer and hand-signed. I took a deep breath and plunged in.

Intimate Strangers

Dear Sarah,   *February 8, 1993*

(I have to get used to calling you Sarah after all these years of thinking about you as Susan. Adam says he likes Sarah better anyway.)

I am writing this letter to you to tell you some of my thoughts and feelings and also to reassure you. We are not going to invade your life—we are not going to show up on your doorstep or call you repeatedly, we are going to give you space and time, as much as you need, and we are very patient and understanding. We are also not going to go away.

I can't express how much our phone conversation meant to me. In a sense it was the end of a very long and torturous journey. Every birth parent must dream of finding out that her child is healthy and happy and well taken care of. Our major goal was to find out if you were all right and to let you know that we wanted to find you, that we have always thought about you and longed for you. I know you are overwhelmed, but I do want you to know that there are a bunch of people out here who care about you and long to know you someday. This is something you can add to your already full life, when you're ready. In no way do I want you to feel any pressure or jump every time the phone rings or someone knocks at your door. You are in charge here—finally—and you make the rules. We will do this in whatever way is best for you.

Adam said that you didn't want any pictures yet. I understand and I won't send you any. When you do want some, let me know. If you feel like sending us a picture or two, however, we would love it.

It's so strange to have carried you for nine months, talked to you for those nine months, felt you, given birth to you, and now you are a stranger—and yet you are so familiar. I can't get a handle on all of this. All I know is that the emotions run high and how lucky we are to have found you and that you are the whole and wonderful person you are.

My heart breaks at the thought of all we missed out on—that I didn't get to raise you, to hold you (except in the hospital), to watch you grow, that I was unable to take on the incredible responsibility of having a child in 1969. But how warm my heart feels at the thought of the joy your parents experienced and are experiencing through knowing you. Your wonderful, close relationship with your father fills me with happiness. I am so sorry about so many things, but I have never been sorry that I had you. I thank you for this sense of peace.

Whatever you want, however you want it, we are finally here for you, Sarah, with an unconditional love that's hard to explain or express—

Hannah

P.S. You know that you can call us, write to us, visit us anytime you want to. H.

18

Dear Sarah,   *February 7, 1993*

Over the years or in the last weeks of our search for you, when I've written to you in my journals or my mind, I was writing "Dear Susan," the name we gave you when you were born.

We were told by Louise Wise that once you were 21, if both you and Hannah registered, the agency would arrange a reunion. After registering we hoped, even naively expected, to hear from them soon with news of you. We worried about imposing on your privacy and that of your parents. Over the past 8 months, we learned some new things. We learned why an adoptee might want to search for her birth parents but not do so. She might fear another rejection from her birth mother. She might worry about hurting her adoptive parents or siblings by showing interest in her birth parents. Of course there are some adoptees who don't want to search, who are so angry at their birth parents that they have no desire to see or know of them. Even in these cases, the adoptee benefits from knowing she was searched for and that information is available.

We learned of the rootlessness that adoptees often feel. This was familiar. When I was 2 weeks old, in Los Angeles in 1946, my father, then in his late thirties, was killed in a hunting accident. When I was six, like you, my mother died. She was 40 and had breast cancer. I was taken in by the Smiths, a kind family, friends of my mother, who became my guardians and raised me along with their son, Mike, six months older than me. I avoided asking about my parents for fear of hurting my guardians, making them feel they weren't giving me everything I needed, seeming ungrateful or unloving. Not until years later, when I was in my 30s, was I able to talk openly with them, to know my parents some, to grieve for them at last as well as I could. Two years ago, my Aunt Meg, my father's only sister, died in Ohio. We had exchanged Christmas cards over the years, but I had met her only once, when I was 14. She knew more about my father than anyone, but I had resisted visiting her. When her cousin called to tell me she had died, I was overwhelmed with fear and guilt (guilt that I had never visited her, but why had she never visited me, particularly when I was a child?). It seemed unbearable to go to the funeral. But I knew I would regret not going for the rest of my life. Then a therapist friend of ours suggested simply that Hannah go with me, something I hadn't considered. That made it possible. My aunt's cousin met us at the airport, gave me cartons of photos and letters, told stories about my father, introduced more distant relations. The time was transforming in a way I could not have imagined. I was glad for these connections to where I came from.

In the years after your birth, Hannah and I were apart but would see each other. We grew closer again and eventually married. It gave us great joy to have Renee, a child to love, but it seemed then even more tragic that you were not with us. We had ended up together after all. We were loving parents. As we've raised your sisters and brother, I've often despaired, not knowing how you were, helpless to offer you anything. Ironically, it is comforting to remember how confused and frightened we were in 1968 and 69, to speculate that if we had married then and kept you, we might not have provided as stable a home as we hoped you would have and did have, we might have split up and never had Renee, Lucy and Sam, who are now here for you.

You said that someday you'd like to meet all of us. That would be wonderful. If it starts to feel like too big a first step, please know that we are open to any first steps. You can visit bringing friends or family. All or one of us can visit you in NYC. Any way of meeting that would make it most comfortable for you, any scenario you can imagine. Please don't hold back on initiating contact with us, fearing we'll take it as license to open up the floodgates and keep coming at you.

You said you'd always thought you'd be the one to find us. I'm sorry this caught you unprepared, but having given you up, it seems right this way. I'm glad you were spared some of the anxiety of wondering what you would find. We took away your search. This may sound silly, but maybe you want to do some of the things you might have done in your search, like calling Louise Wise or visiting the Genealogy Room of the Public Library to examine the 1969 New York City Birth Book.

Sarah, although these are all things I've considered doing, these are things we will not do: We will not ring your bell. We will not come up to you as you walk out of your building. We will not hang out outside your apartment, waiting to catch a glimpse of you. We will not call you. We will not call your number during the day when you are likely to be gone, to hear the voice on your answering machine (I don't even know if it's your voice). We may write from time to time. I hope this is all right. You can decide if and when you want to read the letters. Photos will not spill out of the envelope when you open it. Remember that our thoughts are with you constantly, and that the reason you're not hearing from us is out of respect for your wishes.

I believe you told Hannah that your father was ready to support you if you wanted to search, but that he had no desire to meet or know about us. We can understand how he might feel this way. We would welcome the opportunity to get to know him and all your family, particularly if that would make you happy, and because it would help us to know you better. If you wish, please tell them that we are completely accessible to

21

them. *The degree of our communication is entirely up to you and them. The closeness with your family you've described is all we've hoped for. It's wonderful you were able to go to them in the hours after Hannah called you.*

Sarah, this is not a newsy letter to tell you all about us. What I want you to understand is that we found you not only for selfish reasons but because, after much research and soul-searching, we concluded it would be the best thing for you. If we did not believe this, and even though we have been desperate to find you, we would not have searched. We would have simply registered and waited. This letter is to assure you that we will intrude no further. You are in charge. Please do what you want. Don't worry about us. We are blessed to find you as you are.

There is an unconditional love that parents have for their children. In 1969 we didn't know this until it seemed too late. I've felt this for you all these years, although I only saw you for a few moments as a tiny, dimpled newborn in Staten Island Hospital. You were the prettiest baby in the nursery. I regret that we didn't search for you right after your 21st birthday. I regret that I haven't been telling you I love you every day of your life.

Sarah Ruth Saffian is a beautiful name. I've been trying to think of how to tell you how wonderful it was to talk with you, but I give up. I can't do it justice. Since then, I was able to locate a copy of the 1991 Brown yearbook. Your face is magic. I look at it 20 times a day. You are right——photos are powerful. I wasn't going to tell you I had done this, for fear it might feel like one more invasion. Then I remembered you said it was nice that we'd searched for information about you. The reason I am telling you is that it seems deceptive not to. I'm trying to be as absolutely honest as I can. Learning your name, hearing the details of your conversation with Hannah, talking with you and listening to your voice, seeing your face. My goodness. Take care. I love you very much.

> *Your birth father,*
> *Adam Leyder*

I read the letters repeatedly over the next several days, slowly, quickly, slowly. I carried them around with me, committed information to memory, analyzed the tone of certain phrases and comments. Sometimes the sheer act of reading them made me cry—in bed, on the subway—leaving me exposed, raw, vulnerable.

I was touched by Hannah and Adam's generosity in being encouraged rather than threatened by my close relationships with my parents. Grateful that they had lovingly given birth to me and just as lovingly surrendered me, I had the impulse to thank them—from my parents, as well.

On the other hand, both Hannah's "We . . . are not going to go away" and Adam's "We took away your search" sounded more ominous than reassuring to me. While I was glad to have been spared the anxiety and frustration of detective work, I couldn't help but hear his statement as saying that they had robbed me of an opportunity rather than alleviated a burden. His claim that their making contact was "the best thing" for me rang presumptuous, even though I knew it came with good intentions. The litany of "things we will not do" raised suspicion in me, too; judging from the length and detail of the list, these acts had been more than mere passing notions. And then,

23

after Adam's repeated assurances that they wouldn't invade my life, he turned around to tell me that he had looked up my photograph! The prickly sensation that I had unwittingly shared myself crept over me like a rash.

My birth father's background was also completely overwhelming, its similarities to my own at turns startling and soothing. He was a stranger, I thought defensively, and thus had no right to be connected to me in these ways—my adoption and my mother's death were *mine*. Yet I yearned for the connections as much as I resisted them.

About a week later, I was ready to respond.

Dear Hannah and Adam,   *February 17, 1993*

Thank you for your letters. You expressed so much of what I was planning to write in my letter to you, which has been brewing in my head since we spoke. I appreciate your patience and sensitivity so much, your understanding my desire to take it slowly and just write until I feel comfortable enough to do more.

I am pretty sure that I would someday like to visit all of you. My curiosity is now all the more piqued by being aware of your existence, learning a bit about you. But I have no idea when I will be ready. It could be in a month, it could be in ten years, it could be (though I doubt this) never. But I know that I would want to come to you in Hanover, and not have you come to me—to my life, to my familiar surroundings. It would be too invasive.

Please don't take this badly, Adam, but I felt a bit intruded on that you looked up my photo in the Brown yearbook. The reason I didn't want to send pictures yet was not only because I wasn't ready to see all of you, but also because I wasn't ready to have you see me, either. I think I should be allowed the privacy to share myself with you at my own pace.

In fact, the only thing that I resent (probably even too strong a word) about you calling is having the control of knowledge taken away from me. It's not that I didn't want to know—on the contrary, I have always been curious—but I had planned on setting out to find you when I was ready.

I understand your eagerness, but by the same token, you should appreciate my caution. After nearly twenty-four years, I am not looking for another family. I have parents and a brother and sister whom I love and feel extremely close to, bonded with, even. I am happy, and I don't feel incomplete. And yet there is this intrinsic connection between us that has always intrigued me. We have gone for so long without being in one another's lives—now that we are, let's do it carefully, as it is a delicate and special and powerful thing. Please know that my hesitancy is not a rejection. It is rather a positive reaction, in that I take this sudden introduction very seriously, and it means more to me than I can even fully understand, yet.

I am confused, excited, scared, feeling new, unfamiliar feelings that I can't label. I want to pour my heart out to you, but I want to protect myself. I long to know you, but I don't know where to put you. I need some time.

Sarah

3

Eros

The September before Hannah's phone call, I met Chris. He was two years my junior, the younger brother of Jennifer, a friend from Brown. My first glimpse of him was at a theater benefit in Chelsea, standing in a shadowy corner: long fingers encircling a green beer bottle, lanky frame draped with a flannel shirt, straight brown hair falling across his forehead, open blue-green-eyed face smiling. "Sarah," said Jennifer's boyfriend, David, also a college friend, "this is Chris." He was the funniest, most inquisitive, most insightful person I had ever met. We spent the night laughing.

I had recently returned from a cross-country voter registration drive prior to the 1992 presidential election—the little sleeping we did was on floors of YMCAs, and the rest of our time was spent sitting in air-conditioned buses, standing on sweltering street corners for hours at a stretch, eating fast food and chain-smoking. So I wasn't surprised when I contracted a mild case of pneumonia soon after meeting Chris. The upside to this development was that our relationship neatly skipped over the traditional stiff date phase—dressing up, making an effort to impress and allure—and cut right to the familiar hanging-around-at-home-in-sweatpants phase. A philosophy major in his senior year at New York University, Chris came to me each day after class, often grasping a bunch of deli–bought daisies, naked of fussy paper, as though he had yanked them out of the ground himself. Being forced to wait to sleep together tantalized us, as we spent our time instead drinking Earl Grey tea, listening to Miles Davis tapes, talking incessantly.

Once I had recovered, about a month later, we continued this easy, sprawling way of falling in love. I read him essays and poetry I had written and he played the guitar for me, but neither of us ever took ourselves too seriously. Afternoons turning to nights, we ate cheeseburgers in East Village diners, saw movies and went to hear live music, walked in the cold twilight around Washington Square, kissed under SoHo street lamps, made love finally and with tears in our eyes.

There was a graceful simplicity, a freshness, to our togetherness, and we held it lightly. I felt I was awakening when I was with him.

27

4

Tiptoeing

After Hannah's and Adam's phone calls and our first exchange of letters, I went back to my life, as if it remained the same. I continued to function within the reality that I had constructed for myself: living in my apartment, hustling for freelance jobs at magazines, spending time with my friends and family. I didn't talk with my parents much about the Leyders, only when my mother occasionally asked if I'd "heard from Hanover lately?" My father never introduced the topic, and I was wary of bringing it up with him. I didn't tell any friends what had happened. I didn't write in my journal about the phone call and the letters. I processed them privately, almost unconsciously. My split state persisted—on the inside, my secret changed self, and on the outside, my public self, denying this change.

Chris was the only person besides my parents whom I told about the Leyders. Around noon the day of Hannah's call, he had phoned me at work and, concerned when my editor said I had left, called my apartment and then my parents' house, where he caught up with me. I spoke from the phone in the library, looking out the window onto the street below, with a detached awareness that I was dropping a bomb. Somewhere inside I gleaned pleasure from the shock value—almost bragging, "look what happened to me," as one might parade around a gory but superficial injury after an accident—not yet considering that there could be any deep, long-lasting repercussions. Chris responded with surprise, curiosity, sympathy. "A whole family? Did you cry? How do your parents feel about it? What happens next?" There was a whirlwindedness, a playful insanity to the situation as we talked—a reunion with the Leyders even felt imminent in this initial realm of possibility.

Three days later, however, Adam's phone call had compounded the shock of Hannah's. Afterward, I met Chris at a bar, showing up late and obviously distraught, the bruise from the blow beginning to show slowly. As my life-with-birth-parents began to unfold, I shared my inchoate feelings about them at length with Chris alone. From everyone else, I guarded the fact of the Leyders' existence in a grasping, almost paranoid way.

And so it surprised me one day at work to receive a call from Jennifer, excitedly asking about my birth parents' phone calls. It turned out that Chris had told his parents, who had in turn told Jennifer. Chris and his parents had talked about my birth parents; his parents and Jennifer had talked about them; Jennifer and David had undoubtedly talked about them. I went

29

along with the conversation, giving her an abridged version of the story, all the while feeling abruptly exposed. It wasn't that I wanted to keep this information from them in particular; I just wanted to be in charge of it and where it went. Now it was out there, on display, beyond my reach. I immediately called Chris, who had an internship at another magazine. We couldn't talk at length, but my anger and anxiety came out in hushed jabs, and he was quietly apologetic. We hung up with the matter unresolved. A few minutes later he called back from a pay phone on the street, crying, sorry that he had told something private without asking me, worried that I would no longer trust him. Touched by his emotional response, and knowing that he had acted out of interest and love, I forgave him. And while I maintained that I had a right to protect details about myself as closely as I chose to, I was also aware that my reaction to this natural grapevine occurrence had been extreme.

I began keeping a tiny paperback English-language copy of the *Tao Te Ching* in my pocket, occasionally pulling it out and opening to a random page—at my desk at the office, while walking down the street. I was inevitably soothed and enlightened by what I read. Sometimes feeling the book's small weight was solace enough. One day I came across this passage:

> She who is centered in the Tao
> can go where she wishes, without danger.
> She perceives the universal harmony,
> even amid great pain,
> because she has found peace in her heart.

I longed for that discovery of peace, that perception of harmony. I was experiencing the exact opposite of what the Tao described in such simple, streamlined language: I was skewed, I sensed impending danger, my reality was in flux and my spirit was like a tranquil sea turned stormy.

The Leyders responded promptly to my initial letter. "We not only understand your closeness with your family, we appreciate and are grateful for it," Hannah wrote on February 21. "We do not want or expect to replace or crowd anyone in any way." Then she confessed, "I sometimes thought if I knew, if someone could have told me, that my birth daughter would call me in x many years, I would have waited. But, of course, there was no way of knowing, so we moved ahead."

Our respective desires for control were at odds. Upon learning the benefits of reunion for adoptees, they had felt restless sitting passively, waiting for me to contact them, which might never have happened as far as they knew, or else contacting me with a letter and then waiting for a response that might never have come. By being found, I could have been reassured that people who leave can return; but I was also unnerved by having my sense of identity and reality suddenly thrown into question. As much as it broke the cycle of abandonment, being found also aggravated the cycle of powerlessness: just as I hadn't decided to be given up, I hadn't had the opportunity to decide to be found, either. So my empathy for my birth parents' desire for control was exactly my reason for resenting it.

"What comes across in your letter, as it did in our conversation," wrote Adam, "is intelligence, sensitivity, strength and honesty."

It's heartbreaking to know you're on this emotional rollercoaster and not to be able to help you, not to be there for you, to be in fact the problem and not the solution. You wrote beautifully of wanting to proceed carefully in our relationship. We respect that. Please know that anything about yourself that you choose to share with us is precious. There is a great deal of love and deep feeling, history and current events, that we ache to share with you, if and when and however you want.

I wasn't sure if I wanted them to ache to share with me, if they had the right to ache to share with me. But remarkably, I was also concerned that I wasn't reacting in the "right" way, that I was letting them down by not providing the immediate, joyous reunion that they clearly longed for.

On my twenty-fourth birthday, I received my first card from the people who had given birth to me.

Dear Sarah,   *February 23, 1993*

I want so much to write to you on your birthday—to let you know that we have noticed every February 23 for the last twenty-four years, and it feels right and necessary to let you know this now.

I have so much I want to share with you, to tell you about the past, the present, all the years in between. I'd like to suggest books for you to read that might help you understand all the emotions you are feeling. I want to hold you and hold you and tell you everything is going to work out okay.

I am not clear on all my emotions—I'm sad, I'm happy, I'm wist-ful, I'm worried, I'm anxious, I'm exhausted. The sadness I know about. I've felt it for a very long time. But all emotions are intensified now.

I wish I knew what I could do for you, could offer you, besides my patience. I wish I knew what you wanted now, and eventually, in terms of a relationship.

I look forward to knowing you.

I hope you have a very happy birthday, Sarah. We're thinking of you and loving you.

Hannah.

Me too—Happy Birthday. Much love, Adam.

Reading their words gave me chills—a couple hundred miles north were two strangers who not only knew my birthdate but thought about me on that day every year. My guard was up this time, however, so Hannah and Adam's sentiments—recommending books to me, loving me—had almost no effect. Nevertheless, I couldn't help but feel a small, inexpressible, almost guilty desire for my birth mother to hold me and hold me.

After the card, Hannah took my cue, pulling back somewhat. Adam, on the other hand, turned more effusive. I received a letter from him just two days later.

A lot of what I've written to you, or written and thrown away, have been attempts to describe emotions in words. Is that what I (we) should be doing? If I weren't trying desperately to communicate with

33

you, I don't know if I'd be analyzing my emotions so meticulously. I'd probably do my best just to let them flow, not bottle them up like I would have done in the past. That weekend after you spoke to Hannah and I was waiting for you to call, agonizing over if and when to call you, I was working all weekend, but I was essentially catatonic (as it sounds like so were you). After I hung up with you that night, I curled up on the living room floor and cried for a while. It was nice. Joy. Love. Identifying with you. Wonder. Sadness. Much more. The emotion seems to spill out whenever it will. I'm open to it. But 24 years of defenses against pain, guilt, worry, anger, loss, etc. don't come down easily or all at once. Frankly, we can tiptoe around and try to ease into this, but I have a feeling that when and if we ever meet, it's simply going to be very heavy, wonderful and perhaps terrible. I'm sure you'll like us and we'll like you, but in the beginning anyway, I don't even know if that matters much.

I'd love to know about your writing. Not just what you write, but how you feel about it. Same with your acting. Same with whatever is essential to you. This has been fun. Now I'll try to send it without rewriting it five times. Tell me if I'm writing too often, and I'll back off. I love you.

I was bowled over by Adam's expressiveness: The words he used to describe his actions—"desperately," "meticulously." The image of him, a grown man, six-foot-four by Hannah's description, weeping in the fetal position. His emotion "spilling out." His already somewhat impatient tone, in indirectly referring to my caution as tiptoeing. Even concluding with "I love you." Did he just love the image of the daughter he had lost? Didn't he love Susan—a name on a birth certificate identifying a five-pound newborn—not *me?* I cringed as I read, putting the letter down every now and again to take a breath. I didn't respond.

Meanwhile, on the outside I was thriving, and Chris along with me. His graduation in early May was a rainy but lively affair, a sea of purple-robed students leaping into Washington Square Park's fountain with their diplomas and whoops of triumph. We took a hot-air balloon ride over the New Jersey countryside that weekend to celebrate, kissing as we floated, glowing from the setting red sun—the pilot, elderly woman and grandson also on board making us laugh self-consciously in the midst of our romantic moment. The following week, I was hired to write about the arts for the *Daily News* and Chris landed a marketing position in the music industry. We ran around the city, from concerts to movie screenings to theater and dance performances, happily shortsighted, reveling in the present.

When Adam's next letter arrived, I didn't open it immediately. I put it on the corner of my desk, where it caught my eye each morning. A few days later, after returning home from work, I felt calm and curious enough to read it.

It's easy to get self-conscious in re-reading the letters we've written, grateful for things properly expressed, cringing at things that seem too glib, didactic, sophomoric, self-indulgent. As you get little glimpses of us, I worry about distorted impressions. For example, you might think I am pushy (or at least outgoing), am obsessive about the deaths of my parents, and love to talk about myself. I'm not, and I don't. So it goes.

We're operating under the premise that for us to meet and know one another, to deal with all the emotional issues, is a good thing for everyone involved. How do you think we can best help you now? I'm sure your strongest and most complex feelings and questions must be for Hannah, and she so desperately wants to know you. But she thinks you'd appreciate the space of not hearing from us at all for a while. I can only be direct. If you'd prefer we not write, just let us know and we'll (I'll) stop. I'm writing simply because it's wonderful to be able to do so after all these years, just as it is and would be wonderful to read letters from you, to talk to you, or to see you. I'm not writing because I necessarily think it will make you want to see us sooner. I can't know. So I try not to worry too much and just openheartedly blunder on.

Until we hear from you again, Sarah, I want you to know that finding you has left me feeling reborn, raw, full. Every time the phone rings, or I check the mail, hear most music, walk out of a building, turn a corner, I think of you. It is such a relief to feel this way. You are wonderful.

Adam's words led me to appreciate Hannah's sensitivity, and think that perhaps her experience was more similar to mine: after our surprisingly normal phone conversation, the significance of our contact had been sinking in, daunting both of us. Contrastingly, Adam's gushing made me squirm again: that he felt "reborn, raw, full," that he thought of me practically all the time, that he found me "wonderful" without knowing me. This piling on of twenty-four years of pent-up love was succeeding more in smothering than in reassuring me. And by repeating in this letter that I could ask them to stop writing, he put me in the position of being the bad guy. I didn't want to hurt their feelings, I didn't want to reject them, abandon *them*. All I could do was choose not to open a letter immediately if I didn't feel like reading it, choose not to write back until I wanted to.

I did like the word he used to describe himself, however: "openhearted." Peaceful, perceiving the universal harmony, like the master of the Tao, whom I wished to emulate. My own heart was closed now, protective, cautious. As much as I resisted, I gradually began to collapse inward, feeling lonely and listless, but also distracted, unmotivated. "What is wrong with me?" I asked in my journal. "Oh, I long to be taken care of. But I don't think I want to be a person who longs for that."

5

Fresh-Washed Face

Hannah finally wrote again in May. I opened her letter immediately—as I hadn't heard from her since the February birthday card, I was now ready, eager even, to read her words to me.

Dear Sarah,   *May 17, 1993*

I've been thinking about writing and wanting to write and ready to write for several days. It just feels like it's time.

I'm anxious about your state of mind and hope that you have found help to begin to understand what is happening in your life now. It's still so hard to believe, so strange to know that you are out there and that we are so connected in some ways, and yet we don't know each other at all. I don't think I really expected it would be you picking up the phone on the other end, and obviously you never expected it would be me; and yet our conversation seemed to flow so easily and touch on so many different things. Maybe that's because we were both caught off-guard. Now I don't know how to proceed—I want to communicate with you again, so I'm writing, but it's hard, because I'm trying to figure out how to move on from my first few letters and get to know each other little by little in our correspondence.

I would love to know everything about your life—your family, your job, what you do on weekends, what you eat for breakfast, whether you're a morning person or a night person, what movies and books you like, what your friends are like, every little thing you've done since I last saw you. Most of all, I would like to know how you are feeling and what you are thinking right now. I would love it if you wrote and asked me a million questions. But instead, I will tell you about me and my life, because you said you were curious, and it's the only thing I can do.

Hannah wrote that she had been born in Manhattan on May 27, 1947. The family's name was Morgan—as a young Jewish man breaking into the engineering industry, Hannah's father, Morris Morgenstern, had changed his name to avoid discrimination. When Hannah was four years old, her middle-class family moved from the Bronx to Queens, where she lived until she went to college. Her grandparents, aunt and uncle and cousins all lived nearby, and she saw them often. Hannah took piano lessons and went to Hebrew school and had a *bat mitzvah,* as her two brothers had *bar mitzvahs.* But she suspected that she took the spirituality of it all more seriously than they did. "I was a sensitive, wanted-everyone-to-be-happy, aware-of-everyone's-feelings kind of kid. I was the sweetheart, the peacemaker, and never liked any strife in the family." Smart and pretty, Hannah always did what was expected of her. She had two best friends growing up, one of whom would be her confidante when she became pregnant with me. She went to sleep-away camp in New Hampshire every summer, "which I loved, but I got homesick a lot, too."

I had also gone to sleep-away camp in New Hampshire, from ages eight through eleven, for two months each summer. Mornings at Camp Walt Whitman had been the hardest. I often awoke before reveille, a warbling bugle call broadcast from a record player. No matter what I had been dreaming about, or whether I had been dreaming at all, the moment I became fully conscious of my surroundings the tide of homesickness, which had ebbed in slumber, flowed over me again. I lay in the cold stillness of the New England morning among the sleeping girls, pulled my itchy navy wool blanket up to my chin and smelled my little cloth cat stuffed with pine needles for comfort. On the bus ride home each August, though, the summer would seem altogether wonderful in retrospect. I chatted with friends about things that had happened and people at camp, exchanged addresses and feigned melancholy about our impending separation. But at the first glimpse through the window of my father and Kathy—my mother-to-be, and then mother—I brimmed with relief and contentment. The homesickness was worth enduring for such a sublime feeling.

In high school, Hannah had been a cheerleader and gotten good grades because she wanted to be accepted at the University of New Hampshire, where her older brother Jacob was a student. "I wanted to go there more than anything in the world." Arriving in Durham as a freshman in the fall of 1964, however, Hannah found the university remote and cold. But "I adjusted—I was always a very adaptable kid." She double majored in psychology and studio art, making average grades. She knew many people and was social, but also shy. "I always felt as if I looked at things a little differently, took things a little more seriously, thought about things a little more deeply than other people. I meant what I said, and I assumed other people did, too. I was a romantic, or maybe I was simply naive."

After dating a few men, Hannah met Adam in March 1966, during their sophomore year. Hannah thought her parents would prefer him to her previous, more wayward boyfriends, but that was not the case, at least initially. When they met him for the first time, he had just come from fixing a friend's car and was wearing an old, grease-smeared T-shirt, which prompted them to take Hannah aside and comment, "*That's what he's wearing to take you out?*" She tried to explain that the two of them were going back to his apartment first where he would shower and change, but this only made matters worse, as it highlighted their intimacy. The Morgans' unsavory impression of Adam was enhanced when he dropped out of college during senior year.

Hannah graduated in May 1968. In June, she and Adam spent a weekend back in New Hampshire, for a friend's wedding. They had no plans for a future together: Adam was thinking of heading back out to California; Hannah was taking a summer trip to Europe, a graduation present from her parents, and then moving to Manhattan to live with a friend and find a job. While traveling, her period was late, but so were her friends',

41

because of the fluctuations in time, climate and diet. Returning to the States in September, Hannah was unsure of how she felt about Adam and eager to begin her new, independent life in New York.

When I found out that I was three months pregnant, I was confused, terrified and absolutely certain that I couldn't cope and that I did not want to get married. At that point, before I had any feeling of or any connection with a life growing inside me, it seemed that the only solution for you, me and Adam was to have you and give you up for adoption, so that you could have a complete and loving family to raise you, as I had.

I told my parents I was pregnant one evening in October. I even thought about telling them it was someone else so that they wouldn't hate Adam so much, but I didn't. Their reaction basically was, "How could you have done this to us?" My mother strongly felt, actually, that I should get married and keep the baby. Then, if (when) it didn't work out, get divorced. But there was no mention or thought of keeping the baby and not getting married, no offer of help or support in that scenario, and I was scared to death and desperate. My mother said, "If you give this baby up, you will never get over it." She was right.

I also told my brother Jacob, who was twenty-four and thought himself the only sane one in the group of us. I felt that I could talk to him, but this was actually out of his league. He had always been the black sheep, and here I was, doing him one better, the last thing I ever intended to do, always having been the good girl. Stewart, my younger brother, was fourteen at the time, and my parents decided not to tell him, thinking he was too young to understand.

Stewart had been fourteen when Hannah became pregnant, and Max, my own brother, would turn fourteen this year of Hannah's phone call to me. Both my birth mother and I had opted not to tell our younger siblings of these profound occurrences in our lives. Could it also have been for her that she was reluctant to come to him from such a bewildered place?

When my parents realized my decision was unswayable (at that time), we got in touch with Louise Wise. They would have a new, white, Jewish baby to put up for adoption—a valuable commodity—and I would be rid of my "problem." Just before I began to show, I moved into a relative's vacant apartment in the Bronx where there weren't any people around who knew me. My parents were eager for me to go, because my grandmother was staying with us, and they were afraid she would soon be able to guess what was going on. I moved the weekend after Thanksgiving. My friends and extended family thought I was going to California to visit people and have adventures. That Monday, I called my boss at the publishing house where I was working and told him I had hepatitis and would not return to work. I never knew what he, or anyone else at work, thought, but he was very sweet, concerned and understanding.

I remember very well making that call from the apartment, and then my mother calling to see how everything was. I got very emotional for a moment—unusual for me, especially with my mother—partly with fear and sadness, I think, that this was really happening, but also with relief that I was out of their house and alone and could stop worrying about the way I looked.

Adam stayed with me at the apartment just about all of the time. There, in spite of my sadness and fears and feelings of isolation, we

43

formed a close and warm cocoon for ourselves. I think of that time and place as a little island amidst a lot of external craziness.

As the pregnancy progressed, though, I began to realize the seriousness of what I had decided to do, and started to feel, little by little, what it would be like actually to give you up. But I tried to shut out those feelings, because I thought that the wheels were already set in motion for your adoption, that I was bad, guilty and had no rights. A kind of numbness was the result.

I promised my parents that I would go to the home for unwed mothers for the last month, because they were so worried about my physical well-being. They had wanted me to go for the whole pregnancy, but I'd refused. I said I would go at the end, because it seemed that the end would never come. The idea of the home was like prison to me. I dreaded leaving Adam—my only support, really—and I was scared to go off and have my baby among strangers. Then, there was a blessed snowstorm, a record breaker, and my move was postponed for a week. Adam and I were ecstatic, feeling like we'd been given some kind of reprieve, and we took a walk in the snow that night. It was beautiful. Since then, I have always loved taking walks in snowstorms, and I always think of you when I do. Writing this, I realize how able I was to live in the moment, pushing away any thoughts of the reality that would come down on us in a few days. At those times, I was able to experience complete happiness.

I looked up from the letter and saw an image of myself as a little girl in the wintertime, sitting on the hot radiator and looking out one of the living room windows at the street below, covered in a glistening silence. Sometimes the snow seemed to fall upwards. I would draw little pictures with my finger in the mist that my breath created on the cold pane and put a Dixie paper cup out on the sill to catch the falling snow, which I'd then drench in Aunt Jemima maple syrup and eat with a spoon. I liked being warm and inside while it was cold outside.

Hannah had eventually gone to the home for unwed mothers, but as I was born three weeks early, she stayed there only one week.

The people at the home were fine, for the most part. The doctors and nurses at the hospital were not. They were disdainful toward the birth mothers, treating us like we were the scum of the earth, tramps. They put me out for the delivery, they gave me a milk inhibitor shot after I gave birth to you to make me stop lactating. They didn't even ask me if I wanted them to do these things. I know now that we birth mothers could have demanded better treatment, but we didn't know our rights then. I didn't have to be afraid to ask to hold you, Adam didn't have to be afraid for the hospital staff to discover who he was. I hadn't signed any papers yet.

My parents came to visit me once in the hospital, which was very uncomfortable. They never saw you as a newborn. My mother and father told me later that she had asked him, "Do you want to see the baby?" and he had answered, "Are you crazy?" It surprised me that they had even talked about it, even considered it. That time was so tense for us, and there were probably a lot of misunderstandings, I realize now. But at the time, my mother seemed so cold and unreachable that I felt I couldn't talk to her at all. My father was so worried about her that I felt I couldn't talk to him, either.

But when I woke up and realized that you were born, it was the most glorious feeling I had ever had. Totally forgotten, or blocked out again, was the reality of giving you up. I was absolutely euphoric. You were perfect—Adam and I agreed at the nursery window that you were the most beautiful baby there. I found that I loved the sense of responsibility that I felt for you. Nothing can describe the love. While in the hospital, I got to hold you and look at you. Leaving you and driving away from Staten Island was the hardest thing I have ever done. I felt as though I were leaving a part of my life, a physical part of my body, behind. I was.

The doctor told me that they were keeping you to run some tests. "You know, when babies are this small, they can go just like that," he said, snapping his fingers. I was sure that he made this offhanded comment because he assumed I didn't care. Whenever anyone reacted to me in that way—like when I asked the nurse whether I'd had a boy or a girl and she didn't answer me at first—I thought it was because I was giving you up.

Adam and I returned to Staten Island once to check on your progress. I loved the opportunity to be your parent still. I remember seeing a Band-Aid on the heel of your tiny foot, where they had taken blood. It's funny, because I recall so little from that time, but I can remember small details like that.

When I signed the surrender papers six weeks later, I think I was a basket case. I cannot remember it at all. For quite a while after that—years, probably—I felt so changed, so altered, years older. No one knew, and certainly no one could understand.

46

Adam retreated to Durham, while Hannah lived with a friend in Manhattan for a couple of years and worked at a literary agency. She visited Adam on some weekends and tried to "date" on other weekends. But in January 1971, she moved to New Hampshire to be near him. She started making pots, and the following fall she began graduate school in education. After completing her thesis and receiving a master's degree, she nonetheless decided to become a full-time potter. "Adam and I had our ups and downs for the next several years. I think it was hard to imagine staying together after having given you up. It seemed like such a tragedy."

But in May 1976, they decided to make a commitment and bought some land in the woods. Adam spent seven years single-handedly designing and building their house and they inhabited whatever section was completed. With so few expenses—no mortgage, using wood for heat—they subsisted on their modest income from Hannah's pottery sales, Adam's carpentry gigs and other odd jobs. In March 1977, they were married, "a joyous, joyous occasion," and in July 1978, Renee was born. "Those were very, very happy years for me." Adam was redeemed in Hannah's parents' eyes, as they saw what a caring, responsible husband and father he was. The young couple even decided to raise their children Jewish, because Adam, who had been born Protestant, now considered himself an agnostic. When Lucy was born in April 1982, Hannah stopped working to take care of her daughters. "I loved being home full-time." The next year, the growing family sold the house and moved to Hanover. "We started going to therapy and dealing with some issues we had apparently not dealt with—the major one for me being the loss of you. It felt so good to talk about it with someone knowledgeable. Over the next few years, we learned a lot about ourselves, and we're still learning." In 1985, they bought the house that they lived in still, and Sam was born in May 1986.

After what had turned into a ten-year break, Hannah started making pots again. Adam built her a studio in the basement, where she gave lessons and worked on her own pots to sell. "I also teach women's self-defense and swim laps and play tennis and cross-country ski, and love to read novels and see movies, and have very dear friends. Adam's at the top of that list. I consider myself extremely lucky. I love my family and I love what I do."

But I have always longed to know about you: if you're happy, if you're healthy, if you're being raised by the wonderful family I fantasized about for you and if I would ever get to see you again and know you. Following our phone call, I was elated. After so much worrying, could it really work out this well? Knowing that you were okay. Hearing your open and honest voice. Hearing how good you feel about your life. I kept thinking of you as sounding like a fresh-washed face—whatever that means, but that's what kept coming to mind.

I'm sorry you are uncomfortable that we have your yearbook picture. But if you'd like to know sometime who you look like, let me know. I would love to tell you anything, if you would just ask. I worry so much about reassuring you: that there is no pressure on you in any way, and also that we are not going to disappear and, in a sense, give you up again. I worry about coming on too strong, yet I do not want to appear not to care enough. We care so very deeply. We are patient people, and we are not invasive people. We are here when and if you want us, in whatever capacity you want us.

Unless you tell me not to, I will continue to write to you now and then, and when you're ready, I hope you will feel comfortable writing to me. Perhaps we can get a dialogue going and get to know each other in some way. I would like to know how you are doing. It's just the way I feel. That's all.

Much love to you, Sarah,
Hannah.

There was also a handwritten postscript: "Sarah—Now that I've spent days writing this letter, I re-read my others to you and found that I said I would tell you about us when you asked. You haven't actually asked, and here I am sending you a long letter about myself. I feel a little (very?) self-conscious, but I'm going to take the plunge. I hope it's okay."

It was okay. I welcomed Hannah's letter, in spite of its length and density, because her words seemed to be there for me to take in but not to ask anything of me in return. Learning about the facts of her life and her thoughts and feelings helped me flesh out the abstract idea of "birth mother" into a tangible person with depth, ideas, fears, pain. The story of Hannah's pregnancy, my birth and the aftermath made me ache, and yet I read that section over again and again—never completely able to grasp that I was the baby whom she had loved so unconditionally those first few days in the hospital, the baby whom she had left behind with her heart breaking.

Her Eyes Have Seen the Glory

"NANCY"

by Maude Dickinson

Her voice is hushed . . .
All music else be still.

She has no need
Of roses blooming,
Nor glory of the moonlight,
Nor gold nor gem . . .

She knows
The perfect waking.

— *written for my mother after her death by her Aunt Maude*

I recall her hands. Pale, delicate but with slightly gnarled knuckles, a smooth half-moon at the base of each tapered nail.

Her left hand's slim ring finger adorned, silver-laden. Triangular filter of True cigarettes, lipstick-stained. Scent of Ponds cold cream. Graceful, loopy handwriting on shopping lists and backs of photographs.

In a silver frame, a photograph. She looks like a movie star, a sultry Snow White—milky arms, raven hair, cleft chin below pouting red lips. Wearing a strapless bathing suit the colors of the sea, she is posed on a pool's step ladder, holding onto the railing and leaning back as though about to let herself fall into the water.

One morning during kindergarten, I woke up feeling peculiar. When I turned my head to the side I felt a pulling, as if my skin were too tight for my face. Touching it gingerly, I found it caked, puffy. I climbed out of bed and padded over to the closet door mirror. It was shadowy in my room, more like right before night falls—barbeque time, bath time, Daddy-comes-home-from-work time—than morning. I sat "Indian-style" on the floor and looked at my face, but it wasn't fully there. I saw myself, but not well enough to tell what was wrong. Maybe what was wrong I could not see.

I heard Mommy in the bathroom, next to my bedroom. I decided to go to her, and felt the smooth wood of the hallway floor under my bare feet, the soft flannel of my nightgown against my legs as I walked. She sat on the toilet, facing the door, which was ajar. I silently stood there, waiting for her to see me. She glanced up and shrieked. What could be so wrong with me to make her react that way? I worried, sorry that I had startled her. It turned out that I'd had a nosebleed in the night that had run and then dried all over my face. I don't remember if Mommy held me up to the medicine cabinet to look, or if she thought that would be too disturbing—the mere idea of blood frightened me. But she filled the tub with warm water and put me in, gently, and cleaned me with a warm wet washcloth, carefully. I could feel my face coming back to life, supple again, young.

Around the same age, I posed for a Polaroid photograph in a lavender tutu—right leg pointed out to the side, rounded arms framing my head, Mona Lisa smile demurely revealing my pride. My mother often made costumes for me, sitting on the living room couch with her big old green sewing machine set up in front of her on the marble coffee table. A girly girl—always quick to announce that Sarah meant "princess" in Hebrew—I played dress-up, took ballet lessons and refused to wear pants from early on. I can still feel the coarse taffeta and tulle against my skin, see the glinting braid of pearl-like beads adorning the waist and shoulder straps.

In the thick mist of summer, my father, mother and I were in West Hampton by the side of the road, feeding ducks. We brought our offerings of stale bread to a certain spot where the water receded, leaving a marshy sand bank where we could walk close enough to toss our crumbs in by the handful. The mallards, almost artificial in their beauty, forest green necks and heads, purplish spotted wings spread in occasional gestures of bravado. The flecked brown females, fuzzy gray rows of children trailing after. The duck families noticed the floating food, picking at it neatly with their smooth bills and dipping underwater for any sinking morsels, leaving only their wiggling white tufted tails in view. Sometimes swans glided by in regal, long-necked silence. One day, my mother came very near to the water, and in a single motion, a territorial swan swiftly surfaced and approached her with an awful squawk, pinning her with its menacing black eyes. At first unaware, my mother quickly realized that she was the focus of the swan's attention and rushed, arms flailing, back to us.

Ever eager to perform, I made cassette-tape recordings with my father starting at about age three—singing, reciting addition tables, telling stories, chatting with him. My mother, who was shy about her musical abilities, saying that she "sounded like a hillbilly" (which, though southern, she most certainly did not), was often captured in these recordings nonetheless, if only puttering and conversing in the background. Listening to the tapes now, I can still smell the plastic of the microphone, still see the REC button, which I thought meant that it "wrecked" whatever was previously on the tape (which, in a way, it did). Hearing my mother's voice is eerie, because she isn't frozen in time, as in a photograph, but rather exists in the past and the present simultaneously.

On one tape from October 1975, two months before her death, I finally coerced her to sing, but not before she had put up some gentle resistance.

"Mommy never sings," she says good-naturedly. Her voice is soft and lilting, a bit weary, with the slightest tinge of a drawl, remnant of her upbringing.

"Why don't you sing?"

53

"We *have* to get you some new ribbons."

"Come on, you were singing fine when you were singing around the house."

"Well, it may sound fine to you, because it's your mother's voice," she allows. "Like my mother's voice sounded great to me, but not to anyone else in the world."

But then, "You know what she used to sing?" And my mother begins, tentatively, "Give a little, take a little, let your poor heart break a little . . ." She pauses to laugh, embarrassed, forgetting the words. But my father, a show person like me, comes to her aid, and she turns pluckier, singing together with him: "That's the glory of, that's the story of love." Then they really give it their all, belting boisterously: "You've got to give a little, take a little, and let your poor heart break a little, that's the story of, that's the glory of love."

"That's one of the songs that my mother used to sing to me," she explains after the performance is over. "It was popular in those days."

"Hey, sing it alone," I protest, not about to give up on my crusade because of a mere duet. "I didn't hear it when Daddy was screaming." Both father and mother chuckle.

Once more, she withdraws. "You know Mommy can't sing. That's one thing she can't do. I can make ballet tutus, and I can draw pictures, and I can do various other things. But I *cannot* sing." But after a beat, she is again tempted. "You know what my favorite song is?"

I do. "Sing it," my father and I chime. And she gives in at last, launching into "Battle Hymn of the Republic," more boldly than she did her previous outing. "Mine eyes have seen the glory of the coming of the Lord! He is trampling out the vintage where the grapes of wrath are stored."

She falters, trying to recall the words again, then proceeds shakily, slowly picking up steam, "He hath loosed the fateful lightning of his terrible swift sword! His truth is marching on." My father and I join in for a robust round of, "Glory, glory, hallelujah! Glory, glory, hallelujah! Glory, glory, hallelujah! His truth is marching on."

I piece together my mother's history. Nancy Elaine Dickinson grew up in Bradenton, Florida, the elder child of Don Pedro Dickinson, Jr.—an owner of trailer trucks that hauled fruits, vegetables and semi-tropical plants up north for sale—and Mary Ina Dickinson, a housewife. Teenaged Nancy often had crushes on the truck drivers, thinking they resembled Elvis Presley. The derivation of my grandfather's name is a story in itself. One day during the land rush following the Civil War, my great-great-grandmother, very pregnant with my great-grandfather, had sat in her comstock wagon heading west, reading a novel about a dashing romantic figure named "Don Pedro." She had named her newborn son after this literary hero, taking "Don" to be the character's first name, rather than an honorific. In the second generation of the name, some people called my grandfather "Don," while others referred to him by the Americanized nickname "Pete." Despite the misnomer, the name has stuck for a third generation, down to my Uncle Pete, Don P. Dickinson, III; but Uncle Pete has two daughters, so it ends there.

Bellowing and ornery, my grandfather Don Jr. was imposing at six feet, four inches in his workboots, army-green chinos and shirt and wide-brimmed straw hat—or pointy-toed snakeskin boots, bolo tie and cowboy hat for special occasions—driving around in his red pickup with his CB and plastic mug of Mountain Dew, his two hound dogs, Pud and Nancy, in the back, howling. I was always afraid of them when I visited, but tried to hide it, because Grandpa would tease me for being a sissy. But like the dogs, his bark was worse than his bite, and he softened more often than not when faced with a beguiling little granddaughter—I could usually charm the crankiness right out of him by climbing into his large lap, kissing him on his leathery cheek and sighing, "Oh, Grandpa." One of my favorite games was to sit on his extra-long bed at night and draw with him—one of us starting a picture in an effort to "stump" the other person, who would try to finish it. "Aw, that's a stumper, Sarah Ruth, you got me!" he would hoot in mock frustration. This didn't happen very often, though, as he was a skilled artist with an active imagination—he had even designed a picture of a naked woman to decorate his shower stall door. As he drew, I would look around his room—my grandparents slept in separate rooms next to each other—noting such details as his gun collection stored in the hutch against the wall.

A diminutive, round, soft-skinned and soft-voiced woman, my grandmother was a true southern lady, always smoothing things over, having nothing but kind words for everyone, seeing the good. Her bedroom and bathroom were all in pink, right down to the pink bar of Dove soap in the pink tub where I often took baths—"I can do it myself," I'd insist, but Grandma would still call decorously from the other room, "Be sure to wash all the nooks and crannies!" Squeezing fresh juice each morning from oranges Grandpa had picked in the grove behind their house, she would chirp cheerfully, "You're a Yankee, Sarah Ruth, and we're Crackers!" She and I had a habitual exchange, whereby she sang to me, tiny pink-lipsticked mouth in a mischievous grin, watery eyes drooping, "I love you so much, I can't conceal it. I love you so much, it's a wonder you don't feel it," to which I responded, squealing with delight, "But I *do* feel it, Grandma!" At bedtime, she gave me backrubs, powdering me with her big puff, relating anecdotes about her childhood and our sprawling extended family. She did this until we both were probably too old, but I couldn't help yearning for the security of her lilting voice telling stories I'd heard a million times before, her small velvety hand caressing my adolescent back.

Nancy was intelligent and rebellious—graduating from Florida State and heading north to Carnegie Mellon to study acting, performing in summer stock productions, eventually moving to New York City with a friend. There she became a fashion stylist, circulating in a glamorous world of makeup, clothes, appearances. She met my father at a party, when he abandoned his date to introduce himself after overhearing her in conversation. Marvin was a native of Brooklyn, a graduate of Columbia, an engineer who designed rockets for NASA. Nancy married him, converting to Judaism at his request. They were wed at Manhattan's Central Synagogue in June 1962—"Of course," my father would say. "*Everyone* got married in June!" There is the stylish couple, pictured dancing together: Marvin

57

pencil-thin in his morning suit, young behind horn-rimmed glasses; Nancy smiling for the camera, silk gown billowing from her tiny waist, white-gloved hand resting on his arm.

Another photograph, my favorite glimpse of our family, shows us out at the beach one early evening during my fifth summer. We three are dressed in white—apricot-colored collar poking out from my father's jacket and straw fedora angled on his head, embroidered strawberries decorating my sundress as flowers decorate my mother's. My father and I are tan, my mother only slightly pink in the cheeks, as, like her father, she protected her fair skin from the sun. The photo is like a movie still, capturing my parents' theatrical gestures and passionate looks: she, with a questioning hand on its way to touch his face, he, with eyebrows raised, eyes wide to her. There is a yearning in the space between them, almost as though if I looked carefully enough, I might see them moving closer to each other. I am in the middle, little brown arm around my father, gap in front where a tooth has recently been lost, gazing up at my parents with an expression of hope.

Going through boxes of old photographs and papers, I come across a letter Nancy sent to her Aunt Sarah during college in the early 1950s. She writes about how lucky she feels to have all these loving, supportive aunts—her father's sisters, Maude, Ruth and Sarah, and her mother's sister, Daisy. In her large, young-adult hand—a less sure version of the flowing writing with which I am familiar—Nancy wonders, "I really don't see how most girls get along with just one mother!"

58

7

Two Steps Forward, One Step Back

The summer of 1993 was torrid—thick, still air in my small studio apartment barely breathable, manholes in the melting tar streets emitting oily waves of heat, globs of spittle sizzling on the pavement, cooking in the white sunlight like eggs. The sensation of insecurity and depression, though dulled under the surface, was all-encompassing like a weight. I could feel it in my shoulders, my feet. On July 30, I again pleaded in my journal, "I just want to crawl into a corner and be taken care of."

As the weeks wore on, I became increasingly paranoid about the Leyders. Despite their promises to lay low, I would look around every time I left my building for someone who resembled me lurking on the corner or across the street, afraid of being ambushed, particularly by Adam. My shell of self-sufficiency was slowly cracking, leaving me unprotected in this uncharted territory—the adjusted reality of my adoptive family, the newness of my birth family—unguarded against the possibility of being left, yet again.

External pressures frayed my nerves, as well. Very late one night, a call awakened me. In the fog of half-sleep, I could hear the sound of a voice on the machine but not make out what it was saying. I stumbled down from my loft bed to answer the phone, only to reach it a second too late. Playing back the message, I heard a friend who lived a few blocks away say that she had just been raped. I couldn't call back, because she had phoned from a neighbor's apartment and hadn't left the number. So all I could do was sit and wait, hoping that she was being taken care of and would call again. Wide awake now, I stared into the blackness with stinging eyes, aware that I was alone in my apartment, that I had no gate on my fire escape window and only one lock on my door. Even though I was terrified, I resisted calling my parents or Chris, not wanting to alarm them unnecessarily. I eventually fell into a fitful sleep. The next evening, I saw my friend, who was shaken but all right. A few days later, I had a window gate and a Medeco lock installed.

Meanwhile, I began receiving crank calls from someone who always addressed me by name and expressed a peculiar desire to suck on my toes. And there was an old man living downstairs who terrorized me. He shuffled around the building, stooped and chain-smoking in a dirty undershirt, vehemently muttered gibberish whenever I passed and let out blood-curdling howls and bangs on his ceiling if I so much as crossed my living room wearing shoes. I'd had my share of cantankerous neighbors, but never one who managed to scare rather than merely annoy me.

In a physical manifestation of my emotional tumult, my skin erupted into a rash of little red bumps, starting around my mouth and then spreading until it covered most of my face. Disfigured, I felt even more vulnerable, as though everyone were staring at me.

I hadn't written to Hannah and Adam in six months. As I wonder at this hiatus, the recent incredulous words of a friend echo in my ears: "Weren't you curious? Didn't you want to rush out and meet them right away?" Yes, I was curious, had always been, but now that I was actually confronted with my birth parents, my impulse was instead to slow down. I didn't understand my hesitancy at the time, didn't even acknowledge it. But I would come to learn that while birth parents and children usually did reunite soon after their initial contact, in most cases, the adoptee was the one who did the searching.

In August, I sent my second letter.

I've been thinking a lot about what makes a parent. And I really believe that the true parent is the one who raises the child, who teaches her and watches her grow. That's important for me to say. Because I am curious about all of you and feel a necessary tie to you, but I am not your long-lost daughter. I have a father, mother, brother and sister, and I feel very much related to them, that they are my family. I don't need another one. Perhaps that's why I've been cautious in progressing in this new relationship with you—because I don't really have a place for you in my life. Perhaps closure is what we all need (particularly you, I would imagine).

In spite of that, I'd love to see pictures of all of you now. In addition to current ones, could you send me some of the two of you when you were my age and from around the time after you gave me up? I'm also thinking about when I will visit. I might like to come up in the fall, whenever it is convenient for you and whenever we all are ready.

I also have a couple of technical questions: What is my ethnic background? Are there any things about my medical history I should know, things that run in the genes? Specifically, do any of you have a chronic skin condition? Because I have had sensitive skin and eczema for as long as I can remember. And if so, any tips on how to treat it? I have dermatologists baffled!

62

Just over a week later, I found a Federal Express slip in my mailbox, and my heart beat faster as I knew that it must be photographs from the Leyders. It was too late that evening to pick up the package, and while I was eager to see my birth family for the first time, I partially welcomed the enforced delay. The next day after work, Chris and I walked over to the FedEx office by the Hudson River. It was a sunny afternoon, warm, but I shivered as I approached the counter and handed my slip to the woman and she handed me a package, addressed in Adam's now familiar neat block handwriting. We sat on the bench outside the office, the sunlight bouncing off the large white envelope.

Opening it carefully, I felt the photographs, but left them there while I pulled out the letters and read them aloud. After offering a rundown on what they had been doing over the summer, Hannah wrote, "I have a lot to say about a 'true parent,' and for the most part we are in total agreement. Perhaps when we meet we'll talk about it. For now, here are some pictures. I hope they're not too much for you." She told me about her Polish and Russian ancestry and answered my medical questions: "Everyone has (or had) thick hair. We all have low cholesterol, low blood pressure and no heart conditions. Good healthy stock!" What a coincidence, I thought, that not only my father's lineage, but also my mother Kathy's was based in Poland and Russia, as well. I had a brief flash of being roped into one of those grade school discussions about family heritage and claiming I was "Polynesian"—partly because I meant to say "Lithuanian," and partly because I figured that, since I didn't actually know what my genealogy was, I could choose whichever one struck my fancy. But now knowing definitively made me feel grounded, culturally connected. Predictably, Hannah's response to my mention of coming to visit was positive: "We are ready." Adam told me about his Russian and Scottish ancestors and his case of eczema that kept him out of Vietnam, and also expressed his eagerness for a reunion: "We are ready when you are—the sooner the better." Regarding my suggestion about us all needing closure, I thought he bristled a bit:

I'm not sure what you mean by "closure." If you mean that we might meet cordially, exchange photos and addresses, wish each other well and say goodbye until someone needs a kidney transplant, well, that's not what we hope for. It may seem premature to you for me to say this, but I know we would love a close ongoing relationship with you. We

63

totally understand and accept your feeling that you are not our "long-lost daughter." But it would not be true to say we feel the same. We have always thought of you as our long-lost daughter and love you as our child even though we are just getting to know you. When I tell you this, I don't in any way mean to pressure you, and I hope it doesn't make you uncomfortable to hear these things from strangers. I am trying to be honest and to throw the doors open for you, to give you your full range of options as you try to "find a place" for all of us in your life, whether that's a close emotional relationship, a hello and goodbye, something in between, or something that changes with time.

The weight of the photographs in my lap, still inside the envelope, distracted me as I read the letters, and so I didn't absorb much of their content. I did, however, start slightly at the quotation marks that Adam had put around my word "closure," a sarcastic gesture, I thought. And I did feel burdened by the long-lost daughter role, which I had been playing my whole life unawares. Trembling, I slid the photographs out. I held them in my hands, and before registering the image of the top one, I started to cry. It was not out of sadness, or shock, or recognition, because I hadn't even looked yet. The immensity of the situation overtook me—seeing people genetically related to me for the first time. As I cried, with my hands lightly resting on the pictures, hiding them, I laughed at my own reaction. Chris laughed, too, putting a comforting arm around me, searching my eyes for where he could find me.

After pausing once more, I finally began to look at the photographs. There were many of Hannah and Adam, alone and together, during various periods, some from the year I was born and shortly afterward. I pored over these early pictures especially. One from 1971 showed the couple, still in their early twenties, posed by a white station wagon with faux-wood paneling: Adam strikingly tall in a white T-shirt and jeans, arms crossed, squinting against the sun; Hannah barely coming to his shoulder, with long hair and in shorts, standing solidly and smiling for the camera. This woman has already been pregnant and given up a child, I thought. What is really going through both their minds in this instant? I imagined myself as I noted the year on the back of each photo. In 1971 I was two years old, living with my father and mother Nancy in New York City, having playdates with my upstairs neighbor Lisi, going out to West Hampton during the summer, perhaps about to start nursery school at the Ninety-Second Street Y. Our lives had intersected only at the origin of mine, and then had become parallel, existing simultaneously but separately.

There were also several pictures of their three other children at various ages. Looking at these, I felt a barely detectable twinge of being excluded. While I had appreciated the orderliness of my birth family being a single unit, it also meant that I was the lone missing piece, off to the side. I meticulously searched all their images for likenesses, scrutinizing every feature. I'd always thought myself adept at noting resemblances in others, but now, when it was me for the first time, I needed Chris' help to spot them. In her school portrait, Renee's green eyes, full eyebrows and forehead with its prominent widow's peak were familiar. A shot of Lucy, canoeing in a bathing suit, showed similarly square shoulders and muscular arms. Sam, wearing a red T-shirt and smiling impishly for the camera, had my coloring. My favorite photograph was a recent one of Adam and Hannah on the beach. The ocean is behind them, he has his arm around her, and their faces are turned toward each other, both smiling warmly. They appear resplendent, invigorated, in love, genuinely content together—in spite of, or perhaps because of, what they have been through.

However, as I went through the photographs several times, still sitting there on the bench, the initial impact subsided. They began to seem just like pictures of people. I didn't know the people in the pictures, I didn't think I looked remarkably like any of them, not really. Maybe I had thought—hoped? feared?—that I would open them up and see myself looking back at me.

8

The Anchor

Each autumn for as long as I can remember, my father and I have gone to *shul* for the High Holidays, Rosh Hashanah and Yom Kippur, at the Ninety-second Street Y. The red-carpeted aisles sloping down to our velvet seats, the stage where the cantor and rabbi stand white-robed behind draped podiums, the haunting waves of music washing over me as I sing along vigorously, my father by my side in his *talis* and *yarmulke*, swaying, Hebrew-murmuring—the hushed sense of unity, of family, with the other people there.

When I was a girl, Da Da Fred, my father's father, and Uncle Dick, my father's uncle, came in from Queens and Brooklyn for Rosh Hashanah dinner. Sometimes Uncle Dick accompanied my father and me to *shul*, maintaining into his seventies the dashing slimness that my father had inherited, carrying his *talis* in a similar blue velvet pouch inscribed with gold thread. My grandfather stayed at home, where he and my father would call each other "Fred?" and "Mahv?" in the identical singsong that they slipped into together. Shorter, stouter and jollier than his son and brother-in-law, Da Da Fred smelled of aftershave, wore a wide, waxy tie and liked to wiggle his finger into my stomach, chortling, "Pokey in the *beikee!*" with a gap-toothed grin as broad as the ample girth straining underneath his short-sleeved dress shirt.

Over the years at *shul*, I developed a ritual of untangling the tassels on my father's *talis*—he still wears the one he received on his *bar mitzvah* more than fifty years ago—as I sat contentedly next to him. Even now, he often tosses the end of his prayer shawl into my lap with a smirk, and even now I am calmed by fiddling with the delicate silky threads. Despite my diligent maintenance, there are always knots to undo.

On Yom Kippur mornings, my father and I attend the Yizkor memorial service to commemorate my mother Nancy together. We recite the Mourner's Kaddish, with its rhythmic, somber drone:

> *Yit-gadal v'yit-kadash sh'mey raba,*
> *B'alma di v'ra hirutey, v'yam-lih mal-hutey*
> *B'ha-yey-hon uv-yomey-hon uv-ha-yey d'hol*
>   *beyt yisrael*
> *Ba-agala u-vizman kariv, v'imru amen . . .*
> *Oseh shalom bi-m'romav, hu ya-aseh shalom*
> *Aleynu v'al kol yisrael, v'imru amen.*

During the silent individual prayers, as I am reading "In remembrance of a mother" and I know my father is reading "In remembrance of a wife," he always takes my hand, which I hold as much for his security as for my own:

> May God remember the soul of my beloved mother who has gone to her eternal rest. In tribute to her memory I pledge to perform acts of charity and goodness. May the deeds I perform and the prayers I offer help to keep her soul bound up in the bond of life as an enduring source of blessing. Amen.

Afterward, having focused on my mother so pointedly, I am emotionally enervated, drained, lighter. It is the one time that my father and I fully acknowledge our continuing sense of loss, the one time that we mourn together—although it is hard, it is good.

❧⊰⊱❧

69

The spring following my mother Nancy's death, my father and I went on vacation to St. Martin. Seven years old, I danced with my father in the sunshine as a group of men in straw hats played the steel drums and sang "Yellow Bird" and "Jamaica Farewell," which I knew from our Harry Belafonte album. I joined in, two octaves higher than the men, who appeared amazingly tall from my close-to-the-ground perspective, long-legged, stretched out, as though they were reflections in a funhouse mirror.

I rarely had a sense of my father being absent. Of course, he had to go to the office and went out with friends occasionally in the evenings, and I missed him terribly whenever he did, but these times were few. On Saturday mornings while watching cartoons, I would straighten the living room, emptying ashtrays and stacking newspapers as he slept. One rainy weekend afternoon, a Fred Astaire record was playing and I commented that my father reminded me a little of the old-time movie star. All at once, he took my hands and glided in graceful imitation around the living room, all lean limbs, half-closed eyelids and small sure smile, lilting "Stepping Out with My Baby." In the evenings, he would reach up to the high cupboard in the kitchen for the Mallomars, our favorite cookie, which we consumed with mischievous, guilty pleasure before dinner as a shared secret ritual.

Two different women took care of me, one after the other. They each came early in the mornings to take me to school and left when my father returned home from work in the evening, or stayed later, stayed over, if he were going out. "I may have gone out late sometimes," my father would recall, chuckling, "but I was always there for breakfast."

I was a little afraid of my first nanny, Mrs. Edsill, who lived down the block and had started baby-sitting for me when my mother was still alive. She was a crotchety but kind woman with a musty, powdery smell, wrinkled skin that was surprisingly soft, and a tuft of red hair, which I now guess she must have dyed to keep that flaming color. She taught me how to crochet—I began an awful orange scarf for my father that I never completed, but left to unravel in a wicker basket at the foot of my bed.

Mrs. Edsill had identical twin granddaughters, Adele (named after her) and Alicia, who were two years older than I was and constantly hectored me. The four of us spent the summer I was seven at a rented house in West Hampton while my father worked in the city during the week, coming out on weekends. On Fridays, waiting for the train from the city, Mrs. Edsill let me sit on the white poles bordering the tracks, where I had put pennies on the warm metal to be flattened into smooth copper disks. Suntanned and showered, I let the scents of early evening tickle my nostrils: dusty tar from the tracks, clean starch from my father's shirt as I jumped into his arms when he arrived.

On weekdays, though, I yearned for him. Even though I could tell the twins apart easily—there was something a bit harder about Adele, more fully formed, as though she had been born a minute or two earlier—they insisted on pretending that one was the other, which was maddening, because I was positive that I was right. And being older and wiser than I was, they also liked to inform me of various facts—for example, that children who are unattractive grow up to be beautiful, while children who are pretty turn out ugly. "We aren't good-looking now," one of them told me—which was absolutely untrue, with their long legs, smooth tanned skin, straight blond hair, almond cat's eyes—"so we'll be beautiful when we grow up." The other nodded, solemnly deadpan. "But you're pretty now, so you'll be ugly when you grow up." Even though I knew these mind games to be preposterous, Adele and Alicia still succeeded in making me worried, lonely and generally miserable. I couldn't stand up against them—there were two of them to my one, they spoke with the authority of the double, they belonged. I never tattled on them to their grandmother, but tried to go along, weakly resisting their jibes, preferring to play by myself with my dolls and stuffed animals—leading Adele and Alicia to mock me further, for talking to myself.

One night, we watched a scary movie on television. Then the others went right to sleep, leaving me alone to miss my father. I couldn't go to any of them with my fear, because Mrs. Edsill would act tired and impatient, and the girls would tease me for being a baby. As I sat on the carpeted floor in a shadowy corner—perhaps I shared a bedroom with the girls and was trying to keep my crying quiet—the streetlight or moonlight from outside made slanted patterns on the ceiling, breaking up the bleeding navy darkness like watercolors.

Mrs. Creegan started taking care of me after Mrs. Edsill became sick, when I was about eight. She was younger, probably in her early forties, and one of the most warm-hearted people I have ever known. She had a doughy face that still looked as though it were smiling in the rare instances when it wasn't, light brown hair up in a twisted bun, large eyes that always seemed to be asking a question behind large glasses, a mole on her neck that fascinated me. She laughed easily, a throaty giggle, and spoke indirectly, which I thought a pleasant way to communicate: "Mrs. Creegan has to leave early today, because she has a doctor's appointment." "Are we ready for our bath now?" She allowed me practically free rein, and though a particular child, I wasn't demanding and didn't take undue advantage of her tolerance. Perhaps my quirks didn't strike her as unreasonable. For instance, I was a finicky eater and often took breaks in the middle of dinner—Chef Boyardee ravioli, iceberg lettuce, Quik chocolate milk—at the coffee table in the living room while watching reruns of *The Brady Bunch* and *I Love Lucy* on television. "Are we finished?" Mrs. Creegan would inquire, poking her head in to see me lying on the couch. "No, not yet—I'm just resting for a minute," I would answer, sighing contentedly.

My father dated a few women, most of whom I liked, some of whom I didn't. Barbara, with shaggy, dirty-blond hair and an animated face, played circus games with me on my father's king-sized bed, involving much jumping and tumbling. Annabel, a soft-spoken, patrician beauty, was an actress in a Gilbert and Sullivan troupe. We went to see her in *H.M.S. Pinafore,* and my father took Polaroids of us after the performance, with Annabel still in her costume, and my friend Heather and me in our patent leather Mary Janes and spring coats with velvet collars, clowning around for the camera. Melissa, of the dark bobbed haircut and classy clothes, had attended Spence as a child, but despite having this in common I could sense her cold lack of interest in me. She and my father would spend time together in her living room—which I thought resembled a genie bottle, with peach-colored fabric billowing from the ceiling—while I stayed in her blue bedroom, sitting stiffly on her bed, watching *Monty Python's Flying Circus* on a black-and-white television.

73

❧━◁▷━❧

Lying in bed, unable to fall asleep, I call to him. "Now, put your *kepela* on the pillow, Saraleh," he murmurs, "and close your eyes." He brushes a dry, gentle hand over my eyelids several times, intoning low, sonorously, "sleep . . . sleep . . . ," as I first giggle and then fall slowly, lulled by my father's presence.

9

Allies

I kept the Leyders' photographs in my file cabinet with their letters, and pulled them out to look at occasionally, sometimes with Chris, sometimes alone. A week or two after receiving them, when I went to my parents' house for dinner, I brought the pictures along. Throughout the meal I could feel them burning a hole in my knapsack hanging by the front door, and wondered if I would decide to show them to my parents, and if so, how I would suggest it. As I still hadn't told Max and Rachel about Hannah and Adam's existence, I waited until we had cleared the table and they had gone up to their rooms to do homework.

Dad was in the lanai smoking a cigarette, and Mom was standing at the kitchen counter, making a list of things to do the next day. I felt more able to tell her alone first. Pause, breath. "You know what?" I began, simple, straightforward, upbeat. "The Leyders sent me pictures of them."

"Really?" she responded, interested.

"Yeah. You want to see them?" She nodded, and I felt calmer now that I had broached the topic and made my mother my confidante. "Do you think Dad would want to look at them, too?" She thought I should ask him, and we both went into the lanai. "Dad, guess what?" I said, a casual cheerfulness masking my uncertainty. "The Leyders sent me pictures. Do you want to see them?"

"Sure," he answered. Sharing the photographs with my parents, I felt less that this was my secret, that I had to deal with the Susan Morgan side of myself alone—I felt less divided. But as I passed the photographs to my mother and she passed them on to my father, I continually checked for reactions. Mom was curious, comparing features, asking questions; while this was a relief to me, I still worried that she was just being supportive, that it was actually hard for her. Dad remained on the periphery, taking in the pictures halfheartedly. What were they each feeling? When I ask now, my mother says that she was struck by how much the Leyders resembled me, but doesn't recall having any emotional response. My father doesn't remember looking at the photographs at all.

75

Running Between the Raindrops

When I was eight years old, Kathy came along like a bracingly cool breeze, but one that puts things in order when it blows through. Her hearty optimism helped loosen my taut need for order. "Just run between the raindrops," she'd say when the weather took a turn for the worse, and, "If you get lemons, make lemonade," when confronted with less-than-favorable circumstances. Kathy had grown up during the 1950s and 1960s in a working-class Massachusetts town, and then gone to Syracuse, majoring in English, and graduated the year I was born. After college, she moved to Manhattan to work in publishing—coincidentally enough, at the same time and age that Hannah moved from New Hampshire to do the same—and later switched to Wall Street, where she met my father, initially as a colleague only.

She baby-sat for me sometimes. I recall sleepovers at what came to be known as her "single girl apartment" on York Avenue, with a pub on the corner where we went some evenings for chocolate cake. One afternoon, we went to see the movie *Freaky Friday*, and then she took me home, where Dad and Melissa were having a drink in our living room. That strikes me as odd now, considering that Kathy became my father's wife, my mother—I don't know what happened to Melissa, or how much time was in between the two of them, or whether they overlapped. I hugged Kathy goodbye that day, feeling her slender shoulders through her sweater, noting her sporty bowl haircut, dark brown streaked with gray, her toothy smile. I appreciated her practical nature and down-to-earth way of treating me as an equal. It was almost like hanging out with an older sister.

When she started dating my father, Kathy was only twenty-nine, the age that I am now—sometimes she jokes, "So how would you feel if you met a forty-five-year-old man with an eight-year-old daughter?" As my father and I were a package deal, I was included in some of the courtship: bike rides in Central Park, slices at a Third Avenue pizzeria, strolls around the city when I would lag a few paces behind the two of them, equally tall and slim in their jeans, hands in each others' back pockets.

A year into their relationship, Kathy's mother, whom my father and I never had the opportunity to meet, became terminally ill with cancer. Kathy and I talked about the situation one day in my father's bedroom, she sitting in a chair and I on the bed, facing her. "I draw strength from you and your father," she

77

said. "I think to myself, Sarah is so young and has already lost a mother—if she can get through it, Kathy, you can, too." I, a nine-year-old, able to provide solace to an adult! At the time, her mother's death didn't seem premature to me, as Kathy was of that rarefied "grown-up" realm, and grown-ups' parents died (my father's mother, for example, had died before I was born). Soon after this conversation, she let me know that the last thing her mother said to her during their final hospital visit was, "Take good care of Sarah."

At some point, Kathy and her black-and-white cat, Amelia—a stray from an Italian restaurant who was actually male—moved in with us. Mom and Dad later told me about a game whereby he kept proposing and she kept coyly refusing him.

"Will you marry me?" he would ask.

"No, not today," she'd answer. "I'll say yes on New Year's Eve."

On New Year's Eve: "Will you marry me?"

"No, not today. I'll say yes on Valentine's Day." And so on. But finally one evening in the fall of 1978, while I was reading in their bedroom, my father called, "Saraleh, could you come here for a minute?" I went out into the living room, where Dad and Kathy were sitting close together on the couch, holding hands. I remember thinking how peacefully happy they looked. "What would you think if we got married?" he asked me. I felt a rush of unadulterated joy. I didn't compare Kathy to Nancy, didn't worry that Kathy would turn into a fairy-tale evil stepmother or that my father would devote all his attention to his new wife. My immediate thoughts were of security, of family, of mother.

The wedding took place on February 22, 1979, at the Explorers' Club on East Seventieth Street. It was the day before my tenth birthday, a Thursday, the only evening the club was available. Snow fell lightly outside the window, a huge stuffed polar bear loomed in the hallway, a fire burned in the fireplace. Gretchen, Kathy's eight-year-old niece, and I were flower girls. As a pianist played "What I Did for Love" from *A Chorus Line,* Kathy ascended the staircase escorted by her father—who would become my third grandfather, Papa, quizzing me on history and current events, coming for visiting day at school. The bride was calm and radiant in an unadorned, ankle-length, white dress, which, eight years later, I would wear to my high school graduation. My parents were married in the library by a judge; my father hadn't suggested that Kathy convert from Catholicism, but he did uphold his faith in crushing a glass underfoot for good measure. During the reception, three friends and I sat atop the upright piano to sing "The Circle Game." Looking at pictures from the wedding, I see my father with glinting eyes, playful, revitalized and very much in love.

In the weeks before the wedding, I had assumed that I could accompany my father and Kathy on their honeymoon to California and Mexico. But when, toward the end of the reception, it became clear that they were leaving that night without me and I was going home with Mrs. Creegan, I panicked. Apologetic, Kathy assured me that they would return in one week, telling me the day and exact time when they would be home, and that while they were gone they would call every day. Even though it was a school night, after the wedding Mrs.

Creegan let me stay up late to watch *The Sound of Music* on television, and I felt a little better. The next day, my birthday, I sat in Mr. Rosenthal's science class at school, the bunsen burners and microscopes blurred by tears. My father and Kathy had left me a stereo as a surprise, the largest present I had ever received, with a cheerful, heartfelt note attached to it, saying that they loved me very much and would be home soon. That weekend, I went to Cambridge with my new cousin and her parents, my aunt Gerrie, Kathy's sister, and uncle Denny, and we celebrated my birthday with a homemade chocolate cake. I was embarrassed to cry in front of Gretchen—I didn't know her very well yet and she was two whole years younger than I was—but she turned out to be my stalwart companion during those first few days. Back in New York, the week dragged on endlessly. Each morning upon awakening I felt melancholy, and when Dad and Kathy called each evening, I cried and asked them again when they were coming back. When they did return on the appointed day, as promised, I was flooded with glad relief.

The transition from "Kathy" to "Mom" was nearly seamless. In answer to my question of how I should refer to her, she answered, "You can call me Kathy, or you can call me Mom, but you can't go back and forth." And so I chose Mom easily, although I do recall one day soon after the wedding when she and I were arguing about something, I flounced off to my room in a huff, pointedly shouting just before slamming the door, "All right, *Kathy!*" That was the only time I used her name as a weapon—to emphasize the space between us, where someone else had been before her.

She grew into a strict but fair mother, and I felt safe within her borders. "You have *chores*, just like on *Little House on the Prairie!*" my friend Nikki good-naturedly teased. In fact, sometimes when Mom was laying down the law and Dad overheard and tried to come to my defense, saying that she was being too hard on me, I would patiently explain to him that I appreciated the structure. One stringent rule was an eleven-thirty bedtime, which held through high school. If I stayed up later to study (I never stayed up for any truly reprehensible reason, like talking on the phone or sneaking out), as I heard Mom's footsteps creak on the stairs I quickly turned out the light and jumped into bed. Despite my efforts at playing possum—breathing deeply, one arm limply flung over my eyes—she touched my still-warm metal gooseneck lamp and said sternly, "You just went to bed, didn't you?" To my whimpered excuses of having "*so* much homework," she responded, "Do as much homework as you can by eleven-thirty, and then go to bed. Getting enough sleep is more important." I came to respect this sensible rule, as it prompted me to develop efficient study habits, and left me more alert than those classmates who bragged about "pulling an all-nighter" for a paper. In general, I rarely doubted that my mother's word was gospel. As an adult, I still have to make an effort to disagree with her, and when I do, even if I think I'm right, I'm often anxious.

During the summer that I was eleven and Mom was pregnant with Rachel, my friend Amanda was staying with us for a week out at the beach. One evening, we were having dinner after Max had been put to bed, Mom watching the sun set over the bay while Amanda and I chatted. All at once, my friend asked, "Have you ever wanted to search for your birth parents?"

Thirteen summers later, Mom recalled that she immediately thought, "Oh no, why did she have to bring it up? I don't want Sarah to be sad," but that I promptly responded, "I'd like to find them if it wouldn't cost too much." Then I turned to my mother to ask if I could search. She said that of course it wouldn't cost too much, and that she and my father would help in every way they could, when it was the right time. "I wanted you to wait until you were old enough to handle it," my mother remembered. "Everyone's hormones are in flux in their teen years, they don't need one more thing to pile on top of it. Your birth parents could have rejected you, or they could have been dead, and I wanted to protect you, because you were so vulnerable anyway, always trying to be the perfect child. Perhaps it was also a selfish impulse of not wanting to share you with anybody, but I think it was more a concern about your being ready."

Because of my chronic case of eczema during middle school—using Crisco shortening as moisturizer, wearing layers of sweatshirts in the winter because I was allergic to wool—my mother was constantly examining my flaky, scaly skin. "Come over here in the light for a second. Is that a new rash on your neck?" she would say as I whined in protest, not wanting to draw attention to it, thinking that if I just ignored it, it would clear up on its own. But she stood firm: "Look. If I don't worry about your skin, who's going to? Do you think a little old lady on the street is going to come up and ask about it?"

This became a running joke in the family, the anonymous "little old lady"—who wouldn't blow my nose, listen to my bad dreams, ask me how my math test went—the stranger to whom I didn't have to turn.

With the births of Max and Rachel in quick succession after my parents' wedding, my family was fuller still. Outgrowing the apartment on Lexington Avenue, we five moved into a brownstone near the East River, soon occupying every corner of the house. I lay on my parents' bed with sleeping infant Max, surrounded by pillows so that he wouldn't roll off, putting my ear near his mouth to hear his rapid, feathery breaths, his sweet baby smell luring me into sleep, too. I held Rachel carefully in her soft thin flannel blanket, sitting in the rocking chair in the dusky living room to give her a bottle, marveling at the little pursed mouth sucking, the large eyes staring at me unblinkingly and then slowly glazing over and rolling back into her head. Sometimes I drank juice from the bottle, the fruit taste mingling with that of the rubber nipple, ate the strained Gerber applesauce and carrots. During the summers, my friends and I baby-sat for Max and Rachel and the multitude of other toddlers on the beach—building drip castles with the wet sand, splashing in the shallow waves lapping along the shore, dispensing soggy squares of peanut-butter-and-jelly sandwiches and, afterward, washing chubby sticky fingers in the salt water; then, come late afternoon, we would leave the kids to their mothers and break away, biking no-handed to play rehearsal in the slanting sunlight, crumpled scripts clamped down, pages fluttering, sand deposits clumping in the toes of our sneakers.

I had always been interested in physical resemblances in other families, gravitating toward the photographs when I entered people's houses, and it was intriguing to observe these similarities within my own family for the first time. Rachel grew into an offshoot of Mom, with her clear, cornflower eyes and loping, long-legged gait. Max has our father's brown eyes, wavy hair and darker complexion. Physically, the family is split down the middle, with Mom and Rachel on one side, and Dad and Max, and also me, on the other. When Dad and I are together, I think it is clear that we are father and daughter, but perhaps chiefly because of behavioral similarities—precise speech patterns, animated facial expressions and physical gestures. However, Max and I actually physically resemble each other more than anyone in the family, uncanny as that is.

But as similar to my siblings as I usually felt, our attitudes toward our mother diverged as they grew up. Within the ease and closeness of my relationship with Mom had also existed a persistent desire to please her, and a persistent guilt if I failed to do so. In contrast, I began to notice particularly Rachel's freshness in manner, slowness to help when asked, way of dismissing Mom in the midst of arguments—common enough tendencies among adolescents and teenagers, but tendencies that I hadn't shared. I had challenged my mother—threatening to "hate" her if she didn't let me do what I wanted, running up to my room and writing in my journal *"I hate her!"* so forcefully that my pen ripped through the paper—but I hadn't been casually disrespectful. While I'd had an overall trust in Mom's steadfastness—her unruffled response to my outbursts was inevitably "I don't care if you hate me"—I never achieved a sense of automatic security enough to take her for granted the way my sister seemed to at times.

Despite the decade between us, Max and I went through parallel developmental stages. The "terrible twos" and "terrible twelves" were equally confusing times for my brother and me, each of us caught between pushing boundaries in the name of independence and seeking solace in parental security. In sixth grade, maneuvering around the city on my own for the first time was liberating, chatting on the phone with boys a thrill. One spring Sunday afternoon, after a sleepover at Amanda's house, we went for pizza and a walk in the park with two boys we'd met at a dance. At the end of the day, I split from them to head home. As I walked up Park Avenue, the buildings on my right soaking up the last of the late yellow sun, John Lennon's "Watching the Wheels," running through my head, I was overtaken by a distinct pang of nostalgia. I came to my mother confused, not understanding what I was longing for. She explained, using Max as an analogy.

"When I used to take Max to the playground, he always stayed by my side, holding my hand," she said. "But now he's just starting to test those boundaries, realizing that maybe he wants to let go of my hand sometimes, and I let him. Safety is important, but if he falls and bruises his knee, it's part of the scrapes of life. He runs off to play with a friend, enjoying the freedom he has, but he appreciates the security of knowing that if he looks behind him, I am there, that if he wants to run back to me and take my hand again, he can. The boundaries can be expanded to accommodate him, but they still stand, which is comforting rather than confining. So if you feel lost today, it's probably because you're still adjusting to your own newfound independence. Your father and I are like the guardrails on either side of a bridge: if you get too close to the edge, we won't let you fall in, we'll guide you back to the middle. I've let go of your hand, because you asked me to and I felt that you were ready for that freedom, but my hand is still here if you want to run back and hold it again. It'll always be here when you need it."

Lost

The progress of my relationship with Hannah and Adam continued in a two-steps-forward-one-step-back fashion, as once again, I retreated. Summer turned to fall, and I wasn't ready to visit, as I said I might be. I wanted my birth family to remain abstract for a while longer.

I maintained composure, but barely. The tension bubbled under my cool surface, the slightest incident causing it to erupt without warning, in either anger or despair. One morning, when a computer repairman was unable to assist me over the phone, I slammed down the receiver while he was in stammering mid-sentence, and in a single motion, stood up and hurled my chair across the room. Another day, when a woman working in a token booth was brusque with me, I walked home from the station slowly, as if injured, sobbing the whole way. Waiting for the subway, the train's silent approach would terrify me, two piercing lights in the blackness, but I was fixated on it, tearing my eyes away and stepping back from the platform's edge at the last moment. I frequently stumbled while going down stairs, abruptly forgetting how, my mind lapsing for a few instants.

Chris, a budding photographer and amateur collector, owned several old cameras—Polaroids, thirty-five millimeters—and usually brought one of these along when we explored the city on weekends, poking around in flea markets and used bookstores, walking and talking for hours. A picture from one morning in October depicts me as so utterly alone that I might not have realized Chris was taking it. We are at Bella's, a little coffee shop near his apartment where we regularly ordered challah French toast. There is a plastic bottle of maple syrup in the foreground, and with chin in hand I am gazing searchingly out the window. Even though it is not an extreme close-up, I can discern the inflamed texture of the rash on my face, feel the itchy sting and tightness of it. I have dark circles under eyes that are shrunken, undoubtedly from crying. My look is of quiet desperation, as though I feel imprisoned in my own red bumpy skin, a moment past longing onto defeat, resignation that I won't ever be able to have what I am longing for—security, contentment, relief?

Finally, in November, I wrote back to the Leyders, breezily catching them up on my life, opening up only enough to tell frankly of my conflicting reactions to their photographs. I also selected some of myself at various ages—little pieces of me—to share with them, along with some articles I had written. My criteria for the pictures were that different stages of my life be represented, that my face be clearly visible and that I look attractive. I enclosed my headshot, taken a year earlier, the day after Chris and I first kissed, four months before Hannah's phone call. As I glanced at the picture before sliding it into the envelope, I felt a fleeting pang of jealousy for that glowing, focused person. I also included a profile shot that Chris had taken just before my rash erupted, because it reminded me of a similarly posed one of Hannah at her wedding—the jawline, the hair, the line of the nose. But while she had been smiling blithely at someone out of the frame, I was serious, focused, contemplative—the features were hers, but the expression reminded me more of Adam.

About two weeks later, I received their responses. I shook as I opened the envelope this time. Was I looking for some kind of approval from my birth parents: yes, you are one of us? Or was that exactly what I feared?

Hannah was cautiously enthusiastic:

It was just wonderful to get your letter and pictures and articles. We only wished there were more. The consensus here is that you do look remarkably like us. In all the older pictures you look, to me, very much like Adam, and therefore like Renee, because they look so much alike. Lucy looked at your headshot and said, "Oh my God, she looks exactly like Renee." She thought the three-year-old picture looked like she did; it does, and like I did, too, at that age.

You didn't mention coming to visit in this last letter. Perhaps the exchange of pictures is enough for you to deal with for a while. But we do want you to know that we would love you to visit us anytime— with a friend or relative for support if you like, or alone. We would love you to stay with us, but can make reservations in a nearby motel if that would be more comfortable for you. Whenever you are ready, we are ready to have you in whatever way feels best to you.

After describing their various activities—performances that the girls had participated in, Hannah's holiday pottery sale, a family trip to her parents' house in Florida, plans to cross-country ski at the first snowfall—she wrote, "Come visit us, and we'll show you our world." That one short, simple phrase made me cry a little. She was so kind, and I was so afraid, and my fear of this kind person made me sad. Also, it was true that, as inviting as she was, it was indeed their world, a world that I could only visit. I wasn't automatically a part of it, and yet I was inextricably linked to it. It felt far away from my own world, which made me lonely. Yet I was wary of visiting, scared of what I might find there, or of what I might find in myself if I went there, or that their world would somehow transform my world.

Adam agreed with Hannah's comparisons: "My first reaction was to send you more pictures of the kids similar to the ones of you, to say, 'You see? You see the resemblance?'"

Sarah, seeing your baby pictures made us sad too, of course. You can see in the face of your great-aunt Ruth the joy you brought to your parents and the rest of your family. This is wonderful. We love the glee in your eyes in that photo. So this is part of what we missed, what we gave up. It was so long ago, such a bad time for us. It's hard to explain our states of mind from fall 68—spring 69 just right in a letter, so this remains something we want very much to talk about with you sometime, by phone if you like, but hopefully in person. Please always feel free to ask us any questions that cross your mind.

I'm so very grateful that it seems to have worked out for the best— that you've come to where you are, ready to go on to wherever you want. This will sound presumptuous, but I'm very proud of you. How could I be proud of a stranger who I never helped or influenced in any way? (What right do I have?) I can't say for sure, but you don't feel like a stranger. You feel like our amazing birth daughter who lives in NYC. We love you very much.

Did I think that they were being presumptuous, in telling me why I looked the way I did, in being proud of me, in loving me? Or did I welcome the genetic link that previously I'd only imagined? I wasn't sure. I felt both.

During this period, I became increasingly insecure about my intelligence. After work one cold, clear night, I trekked out to Queens to take a Mensa test without telling anyone, ashamed of my need for such arbitrary external affirmation, and ended up falling short of membership by two I.Q. points. Playing Trivial Pursuit with friends another evening, I read a question that I knew the answer to and exclaimed, "Oh, this is *such* an easy one," figuring that for me to be aware of a fact, it had to be common knowledge. Sometimes I turned obstinate, clinging to an opinion when I stumbled upon it: My *favorite* color was green. I *had* to have the windows open. I *hated* vanilla ice cream. I *hated* when toilet paper was installed so that it came out from underneath (to the point of correcting any ineptly affixed roll I happened upon—in someone else's house, in a restaurant—like someone obsessed).

Other times, I gave in—as I was unable to pinpoint what I was truly interested in, I became uninterested in anything.

Overwhelmed by information, I felt threatened and ignorant as I watched Chris voraciously reading articles or listened to him animatedly discuss his myriad interests in music, film, art. Early in our relationship, I had come up with the loving catchphrase that he "could make friends with a brick." But now, the compliment soured into a jibe as I grew envious of his ease in getting along with others, an ability that I felt slipping from me, and worried that he had to seek out these new people because I wasn't enough.

But, defiantly, at the center of our relationship there existed a lambent core of goodness. Glimmers shone through even our darkest times. I whisked Chris away from the office one afternoon to share a thermos of hot chocolate on a snowy carriage ride around Central Park. Another day I snuck into his apartment when he wasn't there to strew it with daisies. When I felt particularly lonely in my apartment one night, he turned out all the lights and showed me the beauty of the black water towers on the building tops outside my kitchen window, silhouetted against the glowing purple-clouded sky.

A week before Christmas, we celebrated together at my apartment. I made our favorite meal of raspberry chicken with wild rice and asparagus and chocolate cheesecake for dessert, serving it by candlelight on my coffee table, a giant wooden spool that I had happened upon in the street and rolled home and painted. Then we exchanged gifts. He gave me a remarkable painting done by a friend of ours—at first it appeared to be a blank red canvas, but gradually the lighter image of a Buddha emerged, mesmerizing and serene. My present to him was E. E.

Cummings' *Complete Poems*, in which I had written as an inscription an excerpt from one of the book's selections:

> we are so both and oneful
> night cannot be so sky
> sky cannot be so sunful
> i am through you so i

On December 23, Adam wrote again, returning my photographs (they had made copies for themselves), and sending a few more of their family. In his letter, he told me for the first time about their children's reactions to me.

We've shown Renee, Lucy and Sam all your pictures, shared much from your letters all along, and asked several times if they were ready to write to you, but it seems to be happening later rather than sooner. Renee puts on the happy/scared expression of a kid about to jump off the high diving board and says, "I will, but not just yet." Lucy asked, "When I write to Sarah, do I have to show you my letter before I send it?" (we said of course not) and said, "I just wish Sarah had been my sister all along." Sam seems most impressed that you're a grown up, "even older than Renee." We think they are shy and nervous about writing to you.

Through Adam's descriptions, my birth siblings began to take shape in three dimensions. I could picture Renee's smiling nervousness, Lucy's skeptical privacy, Sam's reaction to my age—all with dark eyebrows raised, light eyes wide.

Of the new collection of photographs, the one that stirred me most was Adam's taxi driver's license.

ITHAKA

I drove a cab in NYC very briefly in fall 68. The other day, I found my hack license in the back of a drawer. The look in my eyes really takes me back to my state of mind at the time. I was living alone in the East Village and seeing Hannah, pregnant with you, as often as I could when she was staying at her parents' house and then later at the apartment in the Bronx. I'd been going through a difficult time of testing and searching, often in unexpected places off the beaten track, and I've wondered where you might be at in this process, where you were last January even before Hannah called you and dropped the reality of all of us into the mix. I wonder if you've had difficult shifts or if your life has had relatively smooth transitions.

Lately I look at pictures of the father I never knew, trying to get a feel for who he was. In almost every photo he has a twinkle in his eye and a shit-eating grin. Sometimes I think it would be good to be more like I think he was. I remember one evening that fall in my apartment, not answering, cringing really, as the phone rang every 15 minutes for 2 hours, because I knew it was my father's cousin calling. I'd met him once when I was 7. He was in NYC on business and wanted to visit me, had gotten my phone number from my guardian mother and said he would call at this particular time. I'd always avoided asking my guardians any questions about my "roots" for fear of hurting their feelings, but that wasn't why I couldn't answer. I saw myself as disconnected, alone on some basic level. This did not seem bad. It seemed natural, the way I was meant to be, a special blessing. I'm sure that without knowing it, I was doing my best to defend myself from the pain of dealing with the loss of my mother and father. And in fact, I was in the process of losing you. So seeing this blood relation again would have been excruciatingly too much to deal with. I hope it wasn't too much like this

*that weekend after Hannah had called you, and you were anticipating
one of us calling you back.*

*When I talk about my situation I don't mean to imply it's like
yours. Maybe some things will strike a chord, maybe not. When I look
at your picture I do see myself at your age. When you say in your letters, "I thought I'd see myself looking back at me," or "I don't know
where to put you" or that you don't want us coming to your life, that
you want to "keep the two separate," it feels familiar. It reminds me of
the struggle to protect and nurture my definition of myself. Maybe along
with everything else this is a part of what you've called "the immensity
of the situation." But what do I know? I wish we were talking now, so
I'd have a sense if my saying this stuff is appreciated or resented or boring. I get heavy a lot in these letters.*

95

I didn't drop out of college to have a soul-searching period, I
reassured myself defensively. Until now, I hadn't come close to
collapsing under the strain of my own baggage.

But I studied Adam's cab driver's license from 1968. He was
only twenty-two in the photograph. He was so young, I could-
n't believe that he was already contemplating fatherhood in that
moment. I recognized the wavy brown hair, flat forehead, dark
eyebrows, light eyes, even the nose and mouth. He was a male
version of me. Most significantly, I saw what he meant by the
look in his eyes. The word that came to my mind as I searched
his face was "lost." A turbulent turmoil of anger, fear, confusion, defensiveness, longing. He looked the way I felt.

1994

Looking into my own eyes, I had the shocking sensation
of finding the mere dregs of my usual self, odds
and ends of an evaporated identity which it took my reason
quite an effort to gather again in the glass.

— from *Speak, Memory*
by Vladimir Nabokov

12

Flake of Sun

One Saturday, when I was nine years old, I woke up early. My father and Kathy were still asleep. I went into the kitchen to prepare my breakfast, which I would eat while watching cartoons. In the refrigerator stood two Archie and Jughead jars that we used as glasses when their jelly was done, one filled with milk, the other with orange juice, each covered with a square of Saran Wrap. On the table were arranged boxes of cereal, a bowl, a spoon and a paper napkin, folded in half diagonally. I relished the precision of the ritual. But that morning, in addition to these expected items, the table also held a note from my father. "Dear Sa-Sa," it read. "Kathy told me that when she checked on you last night, you said this in your sleep:

However, in my flake of sun, there is no one."

Sixteen years later, the phrase held new meaning for me. My birth parents' surfacing had ironically pointed out that there was no one, in a sense: I wasn't really a part of my birth family, because even though we were blood-related, I didn't know them; and at the same time, the fact that I wasn't biologically related to the family that I did know was now emphasized. I was caught between two "normal" families—one I was linked to by nature, the other by nurture, but neither by both.

I wandered through this purgatory with Chris as my lodestar. He was home to me. It was so natural to be with him, more natural than being alone, that it was as though he had become an extension of me. My spurts of discovering him anew as a separate entity were surprising—I found myself fascinated by his hands, his voice, his otherness.

We often indulged in lost weekends at his apartment, emerging only to go to the grocery store for supplies—staying in bed late, cooking, reading the paper aloud to each other, renting movies, talking, talking. I preferred spending time together at his place than at mine because I felt freer there, able to escape the trappings of my life. Sometimes we escaped farther, to his parents' house in New Jersey. The first thing I would notice upon arriving on Fridays was how clean the air smelled, of snow and wood and sun, and how quiet the sounds, just the birds and the wind and the low rumble of the odd car passing, the soft voices of the occasional pair of suburban moms speed-walking by, their breath chuffing out of their mouths in minia-ture clouds. The two of us went to dinner and played board games with Chris' parents, spent afternoons walking in the white woods, swung by the multiplex to catch movies and drove the long way home in the still night air, made love secretly late at night in his boyhood room, after which, giggling, I'd creep back into my guest-room bed, trying not to creak the floorboards. Come Sunday, I would dread our return to the city, to reality.

On the anniversary of Hannah's phone call, at the end of January, I dreamed that my family's house was on fire. We were safe up on the top floor, while the fire raged downstairs. But Max was down there. My father and Rachel were remarkably indifferent, willing to wait for someone to come report on the situation and tell us whether Max was all right. I didn't remember Mom being there, but I knew she was safe. Exasperated and panicked, I snapped into action, running down a long, winding, marble staircase, flights and flights. As I ran, Dad called after me, "Good luck, Saraleh," humoring my concern. On the way down, I grabbed an old pair of Rachel's glasses to shield my eyes, quickly calculating that the weak prescription wouldn't distort my vision, and swept a towel off the floor to protect my hair. Then the momentum of the dream slowed as I came upon a statue of *me*—a lifeless, exact replica in tarnished bronze, standing neutrally, arms at her sides, staring ahead. I paused to gape at this inanimate version of myself. Then the dream's pace resumed as I broke my contemplation and rushed through the vestibule on the second floor, sparks falling from the ceiling. Outside, children and parents were sitting on the stoop and milling around on the sidewalk. I searched wildly through the crowd until I found Max, standing alone, and I grabbed and hugged him tightly. He seemed younger than his actual fourteen years, only about eight or so. He was calm, spacey, telling a joke. I noticed he was holding a sheet that read "Adoption Paper," but with a pink stripe across the top. A blond woman who looked like an adult Kimberly Mays—the teenaged girl who was in the news because she had been switched at birth and her biological parents now wanted visitation rights—approached and leaned down to ask Max, "Are you coming?" gesturing to a waiting van. He nodded blankly. Then she looked at me and said in the same condescending tone, "Are you coming?" and I asked angrily, "Where?" but she just stared. I repeated, "*Where?*" and she said, "Oh, are you on this trip?" As Max started to drift away, I impatiently answered, "No, I'm his older sister," trying to sound authoritative. A little girl in front of us motioned for him to come over to her and he did. Then they were gone.

Around this time, I began seeing a psychiatrist, referred to me by a friend of a friend. She was a departure from the stereotypically smooth New York therapists who practiced in interior-decorated Central Park West offices, dressing in neat sweater sets and tailored knee-length skirts and murmuring phrases such as "Hmm" and "I see." I was unnerved by this one's witchlike appearance—stringy black hair, a hooked nose and a raspy, wheezing voice—and by the two yapping little dogs who scurried around her "office," a room in an apartment littered with papers and books. During my consultation, she asked whether I had ever attempted suicide. I hadn't but had thought about it abstractly—didn't everybody? Almost immediately, she began recommending various anti-depressants, which

I refused to take. As a rule, she interrupted our sessions to answer the telephone, and often had to cancel appointments because of chronic back problems. She disappeared mysteriously for a few weeks to take her medical boards, which she had "never gotten around to," despite the various other diplomas displayed crookedly on her walls. I often sensed that she was distracted, not fully listening to me. I finally wrote her a terse letter to "discontinue services" several months later, after having a nightmare that she molested me, putting her hand under my skirt—which she explained away as "physical therapy"—while speaking in tongues and cackling at me for not understanding her.

Back in February, I continued having dreams of alienation from my family. In one, I was returning home at night. I looked in the window of my apartment and saw that everything—loft, bookcases, furniture—was in the process of being dismantled and neatly stacked. When I came in, Rachel, who was bustling around with a clipboard and checking things off a list, merely smiled at me. Max sat on a stool, unresponsive, his chin tucked into his chest, slack-jawed and glassy-eyed, bloated. "What are you doing?" I asked, horrified, but Rachel just tittered. "How did you take the loft apart? Why did you do this? And what is the matter with Max?" I wanted to shake her and make her tell me what was going on, but there was too much furniture around, like an obstacle course. When I tried to yell, my voice came out in a scratchy whisper. I sensed that her actions had to do with wanting me to move back to our parents' house to be with her.

103

In my waking life, my relationship with my family remained essentially unchanged. I still saw them every couple of weeks for dinner, spoke with them on the phone frequently, attended Rachel's soccer games. One Sunday, when I was over at the brownstone for brunch, my mother told me a chilling story. A few days earlier, she had run into the mother of one of her students on the street. The woman, who was in her late forties, Mom's contemporary, had obviously had extensive plastic surgery done, all sharp cheekbones, tight, pulled lips and pinned-open eyes. At one point, she gazed at my mother, whose silver-gray bob was brushed back from her still-smooth face, subtly showing her years. And the woman said, wistfully rather than condescendingly, "I wonder what I would look like now." A self-inflicted loss of identity.

I did worry sometimes that my parents would think me melodramatic if they knew what the Leyders' presence was bringing up for me. And I suffered bouts of insecurity, as when my mother announced a family plan to go to Club Med for spring break. Suddenly teary, I asked why they hadn't thought to invite me along. "Oh, I'm sorry," she responded, surprised. "I figured that you wouldn't want to be stuck with your parents and brother and sister on vacation, that you'd rather go away on your own, with Chris, with friends."

"Maybe so," I answered, "but if you don't ask me, it really makes me feel left out. Could you please always invite me from now on, and let me decide whether I want to go?" And from then on, she always did.

"I like the writing thing," I wrote to the Leyders on February 17. "In addition to letters being easier to digest than phone calls, I like having our correspondence documented, and the rigor of correspondence is making all of us think harder about what we want to say to one another. It's good." I enclosed more photographs of myself at various ages, still conscious of my appearance.

A week later, Chris and I and a group of friends went ice skating at Wollman Rink in Central Park for my birthday. After pulling on the hideous blue and green rented skates, we all touched the slippery surface gingerly and wobbled out, laughing and clutching one another. But soon enough, I found my ice legs and was whipping around the rink, the cheesy music's rhythm pulsating in my swinging limbs, the surrounding trees and city skyline beyond flying past in a blur of lights, the snap of cold air on my teeth making me realize that I was smiling. Occasionally, I felt a pair of groping hands on my waist and spun around to meet Chris, our flushed faces colliding slightly as we kissed in motion.

When I got home, there was a second birthday greeting from the Leyders waiting in my mailbox. This time, the children had made me cards, as well. "We *all* wanted to wish you a happy birthday this year," Hannah wrote. "We love celebrating birthdays, and I think a quarter of a century is an important one." Renee's card had precisely cut purple hearts glued on the front, and inside she had written, "Sarah, Happy Birthday! Perhaps we can meet sometime. With love, Renee." Lucy had drawn tiny flowers on winding vines in varying shades of pur-

ple and wished me a calligraphic "Happy Birthday." Inside
Sam's card, he had written "I LOVE YOU," the "I" a lit candle.

Despite the warmth that I felt from these cards, early the next
morning, in the gray area between sleeping and waking, I heard
my birth parents' voices say clearly in my head: "Should we be
thanked for running away?" And in March, nearly every night, I
had dreams about exclusion. At social events, weekend trips, parties, I was always overlooked and unable to interact with others. If
Chris were there, he would be included, but not me. Or else I was
desperately trying to get information, confused in a seemingly
familiar situation. No one paid attention to me except to scold,
"Where were you when everyone else was informed?" Other
times, I was made to feel like an impostor: in one dream, Chris
took a Polaroid of me, but when the picture came out, it was of
a stranger, some middle-aged man in a tuxedo. One night I
dreamed that I actually went to the Leyders' house to ask if it was
okay if I came to visit, realizing once there that this made no
sense, of course. I wished I had just called, regretting that I had-
n't thought about it enough, wasn't prepared.

Riding the subway home one evening, I sat across from a
woman who looked younger than I was, with her daughter. I
jotted down a little poem about them in my journal:

I see her on the Number One.
A mother so young, still sucking her own thumb.
Looking blankly ahead while child squirms, as if
saying,
"How did this happen to me?"

Daughter looks up to mother as they leave,
Though mother needs guidance as much as she.

Is this what Hannah and I would have been like? I wondered.

On March 31, Adam wrote to tell me that Hannah's father had died.

Last April, when Morris' prostate cancer was first diagnosed as having spread to his spine, we thought about explaining the situation to you to give you the chance to meet him. We decided you didn't need that added pressure or complication to deal with. Besides, he wasn't supposed to die yet. He had a strong heart and it seemed likely his dying would be a long drawn-out affair with ample warning. It didn't turn out that way. Most of his family missed out on adequate goodbyes. You never got to say hello. I'm sorry.

I'm glad you like this letter writing. What you said about the process reminds me of me. But it makes me sad to think of you thinking hard about what you want to say to us when you could dash off quick notes or call and say whatever pops into your head, the way it sounds like it was in your phone conversation with Hannah. There are lifetimes and worlds of things to talk about, but often I don't know where to go. We want to talk about stuff you're interested in. We want to make you feel good. We don't want to say anything to hurt you (like we waited until you asked about the kids to say much about them and didn't send some great pictures of Hannah with babies because we thought that might make you feel bad). We want to make it easier for you to take the next steps (calling, visiting) toward all of us getting to know each other. We

107

worry about saying something that might slow the process down. We want to give you whatever you ask for. You haven't asked for much. Tell us what you want. I wander between careful unthreatening restraint and motor-mouthing gushy openness. That's why there's often some sort of self-conscious qualifying statement at the end of my letters.

You see, Sarah, we just want to know everything about you, anything you are ready to share. Your hopes. Your friends. Your past. What your everyday life is like. Your relationships with your parents and siblings, past and present. Their feelings about us and your feelings about their feelings. We'd like you to send us 100-page letters, or call or visit and talk for hours and hours.

We loved your last letter. Renee, Lucy and Sam read it, too. Thank you for the photos. As usual, we've made copies for ourselves. You asked if the one of you with the cake looked like one of Sam we sent to you, and in a past letter you described "looking for resemblances." This makes me sad, too, Sarah, because it's all here waiting for you. We can compare your baby and toddler pictures to so many we have of Renee, Lucy and Sam, and find great similarities everywhere. We could send you a bunch of baby and kid photos that most match the ones you've sent us. Do you want us to do that? The image I have, though, is of us all hanging out in our living room, sitting on the couch, and we're oohing and aahing at all these old photos, yours and ours, and at each other in amazement, and maybe Sam is getting upset now and then if someone thinks someone doesn't look like him or that he looks like some photo he thinks looks goofy, but that's OK. You know?

I appreciated Adam and Hannah's caution about rubbing in the fact of their other children, but decided that I would be able to handle seeing baby pictures of Renee, Lucy and Sam. Hannah's previous description of her euphoria after giving birth to me, despite the grim circumstances, had already included me as one of her children. She had made me feel like less of a mistake by telling of her unconditional love for me then and now, never voicing a hint of resentment because I stood for something painful.

I also welcomed Adam's self-awareness in admitting his "motor-mouthing gushy openness." But his words—"everything about you," "your feelings about their feelings," "100-page letters," "call or visit and talk for hours and hours"—continued to pressure me. He seemed to think that he was being sensitive by reaching out, but I needed him to be sensitive by leaving me alone. I didn't want his pity but his understanding—that looking for resemblances was all I could handle right now, that I wasn't ready to sit on their couch and ooh and aah. I didn't consider my birth family casually, not yet. This potential relationship was fragile because of its significance, so why would I want to say whatever popped into my head? Adam said he respected my desire for distance, but then he kept harping on how sad he was that I thought so hard about the letters, pushing me to call and visit.

On the other hand, learning of my birth grandfather's death did provoke a first small jolt of urgency about the Leyders. I regretted that now there would be one fewer person to know. I recalled that prior to Hannah and Adam contacting me, when I thought vaguely that I would search for my birth parents someday, at times I was struck with a fear that when I finally decided that I was ready, that it was convenient, it would be too late.

Nevertheless, I didn't write back immediately. Occasionally throughout the correspondence, Chris—to whom I was reading almost all of the letters—would ask if I had written. Sometimes I appreciated his interest and encouragement, but other times I felt nagged: "Maybe you shouldn't be so hard on him," he'd say, trying to convince me to look at the situation from Adam's perspective.

"I don't have to write back to them ever again if I don't feel like it," I'd snap defensively, parroting the words of Millie Burns from Louise Wise. "I don't owe them anything, you know." I chalked up my reluctance to a lack of time, feeling too busy and tired to sit down after work, reread their letters, and write a thoughtful response.

I took walks alone around the city, the buildings and streets assuming a human quality, sensing me and sending messages back. As I crossed the wide avenues in heavy traffic, turning cars engulfed me like knowing waves. Passing a construction site one morning, I thought I heard mingled in with the other noises a high-pitched wail, like an opera singer being tortured by the drill. Going over gratings in the sidewalk at night, the "ding dong" of the closing subway doors, echoing underground, was such a plaintive, far-from-home sound.

While I couldn't imagine ever actually attempting suicide, for fear of physically hurting myself if I failed and emotionally hurting others if I succeeded, I sometimes took comfort in contemplating a passive way of ceasing to exist—crawling into a dark corner, falling asleep and never waking up, evaporating into air. I composed a mock note in my journal in April:

The only reason I don't want to do this is because I don't want to hurt anyone else. I just want to stop existing and have no one miss me. But since that is not possible, I guess I am as self-centered and cowardly as I feared.

And more filled with self-loathing than anyone can realize.

I am deeply sorry.

One night soon after, I dreamed that I had AIDS. I was throwing up, and I had to have an operation to sew my vagina shut. I wondered how I'd been infected, worried I had given it to Chris, wished I wasn't going to die. When I woke up with a start at five in the morning and realized that I was actually safe in my bed, I kept touching my sheets and my face, slow warm tears washing the sleep from my eyes, as I whispered aloud into the soft darkness, "Thank you. Thank you."

On April 14, Hannah wrote about her father's death:

It has been very hard for me. We were very close, very much alike, and I loved him very much. It's hard for me to believe that he's not here anymore. I guess I never thought he would die—ever. He's always been there, and I guess I expected, irrationally, that he always would be. I feel like there was so much left unsaid, because I thought there would always be another opportunity. I think, probably, no one is ever ready for a loss like this, and I'm very grateful for all the time that we did have.

The way that Hannah talked about her father sounded like how I would have talked about mine. Our closeness, our likeness, my love for him, my inability to conceive of him not being there. I had never approached imagining life without him until now, until these alternate parents had presented themselves, concretely positing a "what if?" that was impossible to consider.

Hannah went on to update me on her other children. Lucy had been a great success as Tinkerbell in a school production of "Peter Pan"—"She really is a bright and shining fairy." At twelve, she was just a year younger than Rachel, and they sounded similar, with their sports, interest in drawing, buzzing social schedules. Renee, fifteen, who had switched from an alternative school to the larger, more traditional one, was busy perfecting her hurdles for the track team and working hard for her straight As. "She has her own mind and a strong sense of who she is," I read, recollecting myself. As for seven-year-old Sam, "he would like to stay home in his PJs and read *Garfield* comics all day. He is quite a prankster, and just lost his eighth tooth." School plays, grades, losing teeth—all part of the growing-up process, which I had done without them, with my own family.

"I remember during our first communication over the phone," I read on impassively, "when I asked what sort of a relationship you'd like—just medical history, or letters, or phone calls—and before I could finish, you said that you would love to come up and see all of us."

So I wonder now what your thoughts are about visiting—is it scary, overwhelming, unappealing? I'm not asking to pressure you at all, Sarah. I'm asking just to know what your thoughts are about it. I real-

ize, too, that I got your very first reaction, and then the full meaning of our finding you penetrated deeper and you had many layers of emotion and thought. I'd just like to talk about it sometime.

One summer evening, a friend and I sat on a stoop in the Brooklyn Heights twilight, sharing a beer. Cheryl, who was between jobs, began telling me about a battery of aptitude tests she had taken recently at a place called the Johnson O'Connor Research Foundation. The philosophy behind the tests—which ranged from putting pins into holes as rapidly as possible to listening to tone patterns on headphones—was to gauge one's innate abilities in an effort to find a suitable vocation; being in a career that either called upon skills one didn't have, or didn't tap into the skills one did, could lead to frustration and unhappiness. I was immediately curious about how I would be assessed—perhaps I was feeling unfulfilled simply because I was in the wrong career. When Cheryl told me that the tests cost nearly five hundred dollars, I schemed to pitch an article on career counseling to my editor, offering to take the tests as part of my research. With a sixty-inch story assignment on my plate and a free pass in my hand, I walked into Johnson O'Connor one bright morning, brimming with fantasies of the director pulling me into his office, closing the door, and exclaiming, "Quit your job *today!* You are the next Leonardo Da Vinci! You were meant to be a rock star! There is a gifted topiary gardener inside you, desperate to get out!" After three days of evaluation, however, I was crestfallen to learn that journalism was indeed an ideal vocation for me, as it utilized my heavy flow of ideas, detail orientation and penchant for working collaboratively. The problem, as I had known all along, ran deeper.

At the office, I often caught myself in a stupor, not knowing how much time had gone by as I sat staring at my computer screen, and occasionally escaped into the ladies' room to weep quietly in one of the stalls. I also developed a habit of passing the book editor's desk looking for any self-help galleys that had come in from publishers and swiping them guiltily, like some kind of addict. I usually flipped through each one in bed the first night and then consigned it to the top shelf of my book-case, where they gradually accumulated, unread.

I delayed in responding to the Leyders' spring letters until September. After apologizing for not writing sooner, I expressed belated sympathy to Hannah—"I hope that your father is able to live on in your memories and in you," explaining that I related to the feelings she had toward him.

"I'm not ready to visit," I confessed at the end of my letter. "I can't believe a year-and-a-half has already gone by since that first phone call. But I still need to write letters and take it slowly. Thank you for being patient."

One night in October, while walking to Chris' apartment, I noticed several jigsaw puzzle pieces discarded in the cobble-stone street. How like my thoughts and feelings, both waking and sleeping, I realized—haphazardly strewn. How like the pieces of my life, my identity, which I was trying to assemble in order to make out the picture.

❋ 13 ❋

Re-Searching

I was inspired to take Adam up on his first letter's suggestion that I go through the motions of how I might have searched after coming across this passage in Jean A. Strauss' book *Birthright: The Guide to Search and Reunion for Adoptees, Birth Parents and Adoptive Parents:*

> the *act* of searching is very empowering. Certainly it carries its frustrations and emotional ups and downs. But it can also be cathartic. You are taking charge of your own destiny.

I began to recognize that my genuine wonder about my birth parents and my gradual approach toward them, through my own efforts and ingenuity, had been short-circuited. I decided to do some post facto research of my own.

First I called Sheldon Fried, adoptee, certified social worker and head of an advocacy network. A veteran crusader against adoptee discrimination, Sheldon was adamantly in favor of open records—spurred by his own experience of having been sold on the black market and obtaining his adoption records after a legal battle, only to find them full of lies. Over the phone, he railed freely against the powers-that-be—government organizations and adoption agencies—that kept records closed. But when I asked about ways around these rigid and, in his mind, unjust laws, his speech turned oblique. "There are certain cities in this country, at least half a dozen, where if you request your birth records, a judge will give them to you with few questions asked," he said. He pointed out the unfairness in such an inconsistency—"It can't be justice if the right to know who I am is dependent on where I was born"—but wouldn't specify which cities these were.

In New York, as well as in most other states, Sheldon told me, adoptees do have the right to what is called "non-identifying information" about their birth parents—the mother's age, education, occupation, hobbies, ethnicity, religion, medical history—up until the time of the surrender. Any of this can be withheld, however, at the discretion of the agency or the Department of Health, if it is deemed "identifying." But even such seemingly innocuous facts are often sufficient to complete a search legally, he said, "if you know where to look." When I asked him to elaborate, he again resisted, explaining that because there were so many forces invested in keeping adoption records closed, if these loopholes in public information got out, they would be promptly blocked. But as searchers' secrecy was in the name of guarding their efforts from those who would try to hinder them, not from adoptees or birth parents for whom they were supposedly providing this service, then why couldn't he tell me?

That people like Sheldon took for granted that adoptees wanted to be found seemed presumptuous. I resented that I was once again being told what was best for me. As I saw it, according to this black-and-white perspective, birth parents and adoptees were the good guys, eager for contact but being kept apart by the bad guys, the adoptive parents and the agencies and registries. Considering my own ambivalence on the issue, I was startled by Sheldon's unwavering support of open records and even open adoptions—whereby the birth mother has a role in the child's upbringing, a practice that was slowly being instated, against much resistance.

I did agree with Sheldon that being provided with detailed non-identifying information could enable both birth parents and adoptees to achieve a sense of connection. As he spoke, I realized that the healing worked in opposite directions: for birth parents it was a looking forward, to find out what happened to their children after being relinquished, to be reassured that they were healthy and cared for and developing into their own people; for adoptees it was a looking back, to become acquainted with their roots in order to achieve a fuller understanding of who they were. I also understood the desire to take that connection a step further toward reunion, and thought an intermediary an effective way to ensure that both parties were ready and willing to meet.

But even I, a relatively well-adjusted person who had known I was adopted for most of my life, felt violated by my birth parents' ability to call me without warning. What if I'd had a terrible relationship with my adoptive family? Worse still, what if I hadn't even known that I was adopted? Hannah had had no idea whom she had been calling, what can of worms she could have been opening. I reasoned, maybe unfairly, that perhaps children, but not parents, should have the right to search; birth parents' curiosity and concern, though significant, did not seem as crucial a motivation as adoptees' need to complete the picture of their identities. Like Sheldon, I maintained that it was "my constitutional right to know where I came from." Adoption was the birth parents' decision, not the adoptees', so in a way I thought there still existed a parental obligation: birth parents owed it to their children to inform them of their origins, but adoptees didn't owe their birth parents anything. Or did they?

I could appreciate some benefits of open adoption. Always having a relationship with one's birth mother would eliminate the need to search, and with it, any potential feelings of betrayal toward one's adoptive parents. And being adopted would no longer automatically engender a sense of secrecy and incompleteness, a link to an unknown, to somewhere and someone else. However, I thought that open adoption could also be destructively confusing to a young child. I believed that children should be told as soon as possible that they were adopted— being told at seven had still been early enough for me to interpret the information simply as a fact of life and incorporate it into my sense of identity. But could a child necessarily handle the ambiguity of having two mothers, two sets of parents, two families? If assimilating the existence of another family was this hard for me as an adult, how would it have been as a child or an adolescent? True, I had been raised in a society where the two-parent nuclear family was the norm, whereas in some cultures, communal living and group raising of children was standard. If having such an extended family were the child's reality from day one, maybe there would be no one and nothing to assimilate. I was being too conservative, perhaps, too closed-minded. But I could only base my opinions on what I knew.

"Adoption is an industry," quipped Sheldon, interrupting my reverie of a sprawling country compound teeming with children who called the adults "Mama Jane" and "Daddy Frank." He cynically explained that "with a hundred thousand dollars, you can order a baby of any ethnicity, hair color, whatever." While I was aware of how much more cutthroat the field had turned since 1969—how much scarcer newborns were now—my memory of feeling special when my father said that he and my mother had requested me specifically was momentarily tainted. Flipped over to reveal its seamy underside, adoption appeared not much more humane than ordering a baby through a catalogue.

After I had told him my story, Sheldon suggested that I come to one of his support groups. "The emotional upheaval is the hard part," he said. "There is nothing more painful to heal from than the loss of a mother or a child. So that's what meetings tend to focus on." I had never attended a support group and throughout this experience with my birth parents, despite their recommendations and my palpable "emotional upheaval," I had not once been tempted. Being a combination of private, resolute and repressed successfully squelched any impulses to "share." My self-protective reaction was prompted by a long-standing concern that such "help" would only succeed in causing problems, by fostering self-pity and dependence. But then I became curious. I decided to attend a meeting, shielded in the armor of objective reporter. I was simply doing research, educating myself about the field of adoption.

I ventured into my first support group one Sunday afternoon. The weather was cold in that ominous late autumn way that seems to say with each wintry gust through your inappropriately light early autumn jacket, "This is only the beginning." I felt particularly alone on that gloomy day, but all the while defiant of my loneliness as I strode into a small, cluttered room where people—all women—had begun to congregate on the few couches and folding chairs. Meeting Sheldon in person, I found him to be a soft-spoken, pained-looking man probably in his late forties, with one of those mild, nasal voices that was initially soothing but turned irritating over time. He welcomed me warmly, taking my check for twenty dollars and gesturing to a folding chair. As I sat waiting for the meeting to begin, I looked around at the walls. They were covered with cartoon drawings of animals' faces, each expressing a different emotion, which was written underneath in block letters—"CONTENT," "CONFUSED," "CONCERNED"—lending the room a peculiar, nursery-school ambiance. Once the meeting got underway, I learned how the pictures were used. After a brief "Serenity Prayer," Sheldon gently addressed the eight of us.

"How's everyone doing today, hm? Look around the room at the various emotions," he encouraged, pointing at the drawings. "Would anyone like to begin with a statement, 'I feel . . . '? You have to feel to heal." Over the course of the three-and-a-half-hour-long session, it became clear that the six adoptees present mostly felt "ANGRY" and "FRUSTRATED," while the two birth mothers felt "REGRETFUL" and "SAD."

At one point, Sheldon suggested to the woman sitting on my right that she check in with her "inner child." The idea was that inside each of us existed the child self who had been abandoned by the birth mother. The woman, a large, redheaded adoptee who was evidently a regular, tuned out from the meeting while physically remaining in her seat, eyelids closed flickeringly and mouth frowning in concentration. I glanced over once or twice as the group continued without her, wondering if she would ever resurface. When she did about ten minutes later, she and Sheldon shared a knowing nod.

I seethed inside but said nothing when Sheldon referred to the child who would have stayed with the birth parents as the "authentic self." He went on to explain how adoptees were forced to "pretend" that they were who they were told to be, to "pass" within their adoptive families. How is saying that we've been impostors up till now a way to help us feel more whole? I thought. Why should identifying myself as Sarah Saffian be a lie? That I was she, and glad to be, had never really come into question until Hannah and Adam had entered the picture,

121

introducing the tangible possibility of another self. Sheldon's comments seemed to confirm my greatest fear: that by coming to know my birth parents I would lose my adoptive parents, that Susan Morgan would usurp Sarah Saffian, disqualify the person I had been for the nearly twenty-four years before Hannah's phone call.

Sheldon also explained that adoptees were never allowed to mourn the loss of their mothers, because it was not officially considered a death. I understood his reasoning, that the trauma inherent in being separated from one's birth mother should not be taken lightly, but he spoke about adoptees as so many orphans, completely parentless, left to their own devices. Even though I had lost not only my birth mother but my adoptive mother, as well (an official death), I still hadn't felt abandoned in this extreme way; my father was to thank for this, and my mother Kathy. True, some adoptees always felt disconnected from their families, but so did some biological children. For adolescents to suspect that they had been adopted when they felt their parents just didn't understand them was not uncommon. I, on the other hand, hadn't felt that I was masquerading as a member of a family to which I didn't really belong; rather, I had doubted at times that these other phantom parents who were supposed to have physically created me actually existed. What if a feeling of disconnectedness was simply something that some children—biological and adopted alike—experienced, and others didn't? Why did being adopted have to be a bad thing? Why should giving birth to a child be deemed more significant than raising her?

One woman, who had clearly been a member of Sheldon's support group for a while, grew increasingly upset as the meeting wore on, first choosing such emotions as "HOPELESS," and later progressing to "ENRAGED." About twenty years old, she had the aura of a distressed ballet dancer—all thin limbs, long neck and hair back in a severe bun that pulled at her throbbing temples and furrowed brow. She had never felt at home in her adoptive family, she explained, and recently, she had experienced the archetypal adoptee's nightmare: she had searched for and found her birth mother, who had responded by rejecting her, saying that she wanted nothing to do with her, even changing her phone number to an unlisted one. "'I feel' mad at *you*, Sheldon," she said, dashing away tears with an impatient hand. "I keep coming here, and nothing ever gets better." Sheldon nodded.

Toward the end of the session, one of the birth mothers, the only black woman present, sitting on the couch across the room from me, spoke up for the first time. "Most of the adoptees here keep talking about how 'ANGRY' they are," she said, her voice cracking, "but I'm searching for my daughter, because I've cared about her her entire life. I've worried about her ever since I gave her up, which I did because I thought it was the best thing for her. All I've ever wanted to do was to show her my love."

The young adoptee burst into tears. "What is it, dear?" Sheldon asked in a tone suggesting that he had expected, or even provoked, this outburst, and that it was a kind of breakthrough.

"I feel your love," the young girl choked out to the birth mother, "and it feels so good. But I'm crying because I realize I've never felt love before." She collapsed, her gaunt frame racked with sobs. The birth mother came over to the girl, who turned up her smeared face and stood, and they hugged for a long time, crying, wailing, even. The rest of us watched mutely, some of the regulars beginning to cry, too, in empathy.

My eyes remained dry throughout the spectacle, as I tried to answer Sheldon's earlier question—how do "I feel"? I felt embarrassed. I felt uncomfortable. I felt claustrophobic, in that cramped room with the hissing radiator and crying strangers, longing for cold fresh air and solitude. I felt sorry for the girl and the birth mother, but as removed from their experience as if they were from another planet. I knew in that moment that I would never come back to that place, or see those people, again. Though I had made every effort to remain open-minded during the meeting, rhymed adages like "You have to feel to heal" and concepts such as "Serenity Prayer" and "inner child" rang cultlike in my ears, making the hair on the back of my neck stand on end. I did agree that feeling was necessary for healing; it was a lesson I was trying to teach myself, even as I attempted to pinpoint what exactly I was healing from. But sitting around swapping stories as a social worker murmured vague sounds of sympathy did not seem to be the way, at least not for me. I hoped it was the way for these others, that this extreme expression of emotion was helpful to them, that they weren't merely latching onto Sheldon for lack of birth mother or sense of self.

On the plus side, though, the meeting reminded me how fortunate I was. At the beginning of the session, Sheldon had asked us to go around the room and tell our stories. When my turn came, I offered a thumbnail sketch, to which the adopted girl responded that she felt jealous of me, for fitting in so well with my adoptive family, and, more significantly, for being found by my birth mother. It occurred to me for the first time that as jarring as Hannah's call had been, it had shown that she loved me enough to seek me out. Perhaps she should have made contact through an intermediary, or by letter, but the girl's reaction told me not to take my situation for granted. I came away from the support group shaken and drained, but with a fortified sense of gratefulness.

I decided to cross over to the other side of the closed versus open records debate—to check in again at Louise Wise. I wanted to know what methods might have been used to find me, and whether I could obtain a copy of my file. Now that everything was out in the open, what could be denied me in terms of information? I thought of dropping by the agency unannounced, but reconsidered, thinking it too aggressive, and telephoned instead. As Millie Burns had recently retired, I was transferred to another woman in post-adoption services. Fran Cohen was as sympathetic and friendly as Ms. Burns had been when I relayed my nutshell account.

Ms. Cohen's understanding was that since the numbers on an adoptee's original and altered birth certificates were the same, I would be listed twice in the city Birth Record: once under my birth name (Susan Morgan), and once again under my adoptive name (Sarah Saffian), both with the same number. So all that my birth parents would have had to do, she said, would be to look through the numbers in the Birth Record for a match, a tedious but uncomplicated task.

If birth parents knew approximately when their child was placed with a family, they could also have someone consult the court dockets. "The dockets tend to be sealed, but there are ways," she said. "They know people, or sometimes it can be a mistake, like a dumb clerk who'll open the records. It's amazing what people will find. I won't say they do things unlawfully, but they do." If adoption were an industry, as Sheldon presented it, searching seemed to be shaping up into one as well—a business, whereby people were compensated, sometimes several thousand dollars, for their detective skills. "It's a lot of legwork, some illegal, with relation to getting names." Once the adoptive name was known, however, the search became more straightforward. "Then you can look in telephone directories, call the Department of Motor Vehicles, voter registration," Ms. Cohen explained, "and the more unusual the last name, the better." Considering that two of the three Saffians listed in the Manhattan phone book were my father and me, I was aware how helpful it had been that my last name wasn't Smith.

I thought again of adoption as an industry and suddenly wondered what I had cost Marvin and Nancy back in 1969. "You mean how much your parents paid for you?" Ms. Cohen teased.

"I know, I don't mean to sound callous," I said, playing along, "but I just have no idea and I'm curious what the price of such a transaction would have been."

At first she was hesitant to answer. "Well, the only way, really, to find out that information would be to ask someone who was here back then."

I tried to ease her into it. "You know, just a ballpark figure, because I'm sure it varied." She finally relented and located, after minimal poking around, a record from 1966 that listed a half-fee down payment as $626.50. So three years later, I estimated, I had probably been worth about fifteen hundred dollars. Less than a new car. But then, aside from hospital fees, most people had their children for free.

And if I also had come forward expressing interest in a reunion, would Louise Wise have orchestrated it? "No, we would have referred both of you to the Department of Health, to register for identifying information." This seemed an unnecessary step, if both parties were willing to meet. "But most reunions do not come about through registering, unfortunately," Ms. Cohen harrumphed. I assumed she was implying that people searched by other, sub-legal means, like hiring a searcher, for example, as my birth parents had. "Louise Wise would always be willing to be part of the process, however, if either party ever wants us to intervene." What did she mean by "intervene," exactly? Was this an indirect offer to me, in case my birth parents ever came on too strong and I felt unsafe? As much as I wanted information, I also felt an impulse to protect

Hannah and Adam, and didn't want her calling them up, berating them for what they had done. A chill of anxiety passed through me that I was jeopardizing their safety somehow by talking with Louise Wise. This concern hadn't crossed my mind a year and a half earlier when I had come to speak with Millie Burns.

As Ms. Cohen and I seemed to have such a good rapport, I gently asked whether, considering that my birth parents and I knew one another now, I could have a copy of my file. "No." Why? Whose privacy was left to protect? "It's a long, complicated explanation," she said evasively, "because so much is intertwined with other parties, including your adoptive mother, who is now deceased." When I still didn't understand, she answered, friendly but firm, "Until the law is changed in New York State, it's considered a closed record. It doesn't matter what you or they did." I asked if I could at least obtain non-identifying information, as would have been my right even if I hadn't been in contact with my birth mother. She promised to send it, but I would never receive it.

There was something still gnawing at me. Even after all this time, and with all the matching facts between Hannah and me, I had never confirmed that she was my birth mother. I wasn't suspicious of her, but as we progressively opened up to each other, I occasionally worried that she or someone else had made an innocent mistake. Could the similarities have been mere coincidences? Were the slight inconsistencies more than oversights? Hannah thought she had given birth to me around midnight, for example, but I had actually been born at two-twenty-five in the morning, according to my birth certificate. A minor and easy error to make, but what if she had given birth at midnight, to someone else? I knew I was being overly cautious, but I wanted to be certain, considering that my roots, which had been buried my entire life, were so suddenly unearthed. "Could I verify that my birth mother is who she says she is?" I asked. "You know, for my own peace of mind? I want to make sure that all this isn't too good to be true." Still concerned about getting Hannah and Adam into trouble, I added the last bit to suggest that I was fine with having been found.

"Okay," Ms. Cohen yielded. "Let me pull your file and get right back to you." As I waited for her call, I was surprised by my own nervousness. The phone's shrill ring a few minutes later jolted me. "I have some information about your birth mother on an index card here," she said, waiting. Of course she wasn't going to volunteer the name, I realized—people undoubtedly used this ploy all the time to try to extract information.

"All right," I said, taking a breath. "Is her name Hannah Morgan?"

"Yes!" Ms. Cohen answered, sounding as pleased as I felt.

After Louise Wise, I went to the genealogy room at the New York Public Library. There I encountered the Birth Record that Adam had mentioned, arranged in annual volumes, compiled by the New York City Health Department. I settled in at one of the long, wooden tables with the record for births reported in 1969, which gave a whiff of dust and chocolate when I opened it, as old books do. I looked up my name in the alpha-

129

betical listing, and was shocked to find no entry for "Sarah Saffian." I felt like a ghost sitting there, as if I didn't really exist, as if Sarah Saffian had never been born. I glanced at the people around me, working. Is anyone here like me, I wondered, searching for a record of his or her origins? Or am I alone?

Across the table I noticed a young woman, perhaps in her late teens, sitting with, I assumed, her mother and father. Overhearing the librarian telling them about an adoption registry, I created a scenario for the girl: she was here searching for her birth parents, and her adoptive parents were helping her. How doubly empowering, I thought—not only to take the initiative to search, but to have actively involved adoptive parents. While my parents were supportive and understanding, I still felt that my separate relationships with each of my families made my two identities all the more discrete, that this project of self-discovery was mine alone.

Then I looked up Susan Morgan, and sure enough, the line read:

> [Name] MORGAN, SUSAN ... [Date of Birth] 02 23 69 ... [Mother's Maiden Name] MORGAN ... [Father's Given Name—blank] ... [Boro] Richmond ... [Certificate Number] _____.

I then looked up friends who had been born in New York—Ginna, Nikki, Eliot—and as I recognized their mothers' maiden names, their fathers' given names, I envied the simplicity of their lineage, that there was a record that they—under the only names they had ever known for themselves—had been born. I felt cheated, because there was no record of *my* name, of *me*, in the Birth Record. The only listing was this name that I had never heard until I was nearly twenty-four years old, this strange name identifying someone I barely knew. But that someone was me.

I recalled a childhood conversation I could never participate in, the one that began with the question, "What has your mom told you about the day you were born?" My friends would regale one another with tales of mad dashes to the hospital in taxis, underwater births, umbilical cords wrapped around necks—"I almost *died*, you know." Usually, I was able to listen without being bothered, interested in their backgrounds and feeling exotic because of the mystery of my own. If one of them asked me my story, I would either dodge the question, make up something vague and uneventful or else matter-of-factly declare with an air of superiority, "Well, *I* was adopted, so I have no idea," which was impressive enough to stop the chatter for a few stolen moments.

Pretending that I was doing research for a paper, I asked the librarian about the discrepancy in my Birth Record entry. He explained that the adoptive name was rarely listed, simply because adoption processing customarily took too long for the new name to be ready in time. So my birth parents or the searcher couldn't have located me by comparing birth numbers—looking up the number for "Susan Morgan" and then scanning the whole book for that same number again, to find "Sarah Saffian"—as Fran Cohen had suggested.

131

Turning back to the Birth Record, I noticed that the single Saffian listing that year was for a "J—— Saffian," born on December I, whose mother's maiden name was also Saffian and father's given name was blank, similar to my Susan Morgan listing. I wondered if this J—— had been given up for adoption, too, leaving his birth family, the Saffians, just as I was being adopted into it. I felt a connection to J——, curious if he, now a young man of a different name, had also come searching for himself in the genealogy room but found only Saffian listed in the Birth Record, the name that I so longed to find for myself.

I wanted to venture even further back, to my birthplace. I phoned the Medical Records Department at Staten Island Hospital, and a woman there advised me to send my inquiry in a letter.

Dear Sir or Madam:

I was born at Staten Island Hospital, and would greatly appreciate any and all records and information that you have on the circumstances of my birth. This is the information that I have:

BIRTH NUMBER: _____

MY FULL NAME: Susan Morgan

SEX: Female

DATE OF BIRTH: February 23, 1969

TIME: 2:25 A.M.

MOTHER'S MAIDEN NAME: Hannah Morgan

MOTHER'S BIRTHPLACE: New York, NY

FATHER'S NAME: Adam Leyder

FATHER'S BIRTHPLACE: Los Angeles, CA

If there is anything else that would facilitate your locating and send-ing this information to me, please do not hesitate to call.
Thank you so much in advance for your attention to this matter.

Sincerely,
Susan Morgan

I felt deceptive going undercover like this, especially when I received, a few days later, a letter addressed to "Susan Morgan" in my mailbox, along with my other "Sarah Saffian" mail. But Susan Morgan was also my name, wasn't it? According to the Birth Record at the library, if my name wasn't Susan Morgan, then I'd never been born. I opened the envelope eagerly, only to find a form letter, stating that they had made a thorough search for my records but were "unable to locate [them] at this time," and that they apologized "for any inconvenience this may have caused." Not surprised by the roadblock but still not satisfied, I followed up.

"This is Susan Morgan," I announced over the phone to the woman whose name appeared at the bottom of the letter.

After I reminded her of my situation and request for infor-mation, she explained, "The hospital isn't responsible for birth records after twenty-one years."

"What do you mean, 'not responsible'? What happens to them?"

"They're destroyed," she responded plainly. "First they're stored, then they're microfiched, and then they're all destroyed."

My heart sank. I felt like a part of me—whoever that was—had been obliterated, as well. "So they don't exist anywhere?" I asked again, hopefully. "There's no one else I can call?"

She probably sensed the desperation in my voice, despite my efforts to remain detached and professional. "No, honey," she said, her impersonal, businesslike tone softening. "I'm sorry."

Having been advised by the genealogy librarian that birth certificates are public record and kept at the Bureau of Vital Statistics, I called to see if I could obtain a copy of my original birth certificate. The outgoing voicemail explained that one could order birth certificates over the phone with the necessary vital information and a major credit card; having one located and mailed cost twenty dollars. More and more throughout this search process, I felt as though I were investigating J. Crew or L. L. Bean, rather than the field of adoption—I'd like one set of files, two birth certificates and one baby, size small, please. After waiting on hold for several minutes, I was connected to someone with whom I could place my order:

"Hello, I'd like to request a birth certificate."

"Is it for yourself?"

"Yes."

"Okay, what is your name?"

I hesitated only briefly before responding, "Susan Morgan." Again, I felt like an impostor, even though I wasn't technically lying. After asking for other facts—mother's name, father's

134

name, date and location of birth, all of which I could provide—she put me on hold again to locate me in the system. But
she came back a few moments later, perplexed, saying that she
couldn't find anything on "me."

I decided to come clean. "Well, you see, I was adopted, actually, and Susan Morgan is my birth name, not my adoptive
name. I was looking for my original birth certificate."

"Oh," she exhaled with relief, "when you're adopted, your
original birth certificate is a closed case." I gathered that this
meant that it still existed, but that it was sealed, unavailable.
What secrets were left? "You need to go by your *new* name."
Since I already had a copy of my altered birth certificate, I
thanked the woman for her time, and hung up.

Although I had half-expected a dead end here, the inconsistency of my birth's documentation hit me: in the Birth Record
at the New York Public Library, I existed only as Susan
Morgan; but at the Bureau of Vital Statistics, there was a birth
certificate only for Sarah Saffian. My identity felt more split
than ever. Each of my two names stood for a distinct person.
Susan Morgan had been born on February 23, 1969, at Staten
Island Hospital, was the child of Hannah Morgan and Adam
Leyder, and had two sisters and a brother who lived with her
parents in New Hampshire. Sarah Saffian had been born eight
weeks later at Louise Wise Services, was the child of Marvin
and Nancy Saffian, then Kathy Saffian, and had grown up in
New York with a brother and a sister. It was not the fork that
was bewildering, but the confluence. My identity had been relatively easy to track while it remained linear: when I was Susan

originally, Sarah didn't exist yet; when in foster care, I was neither Susan nor Sarah; and when I became Sarah, Susan went into hibernation. Then on January 29, 1993, nearly twenty-four years later, Susan reemerged, with her own previously unknown history. But I was still Sarah, too, or trying to be. How could I be both?

Origin

I was over at my parents' brownstone one Indian summer evening, sitting out in the garden with my father as he had a smoke. There was still so much that I didn't know about the beginnings of Sarah Saffian, about how I had become the person I was. After a pause, I asked him to tell me in detail the specifics of my adoption, beginning with why he and Nancy, whom we both always referred to as "Mommy"—since that was what I had called her, and also to distinguish her from Mom—could not have children.

"After Mommy and I had consulted and been tested by numerous doctors, sperm specialists, et cetera, this doctor told us that the fault lay with me," Dad began matter-of-factly, flicking ash into a half-shell on the ground. "Over ten years later, when Mom became pregnant with Max, I went back to prove him wrong, and he denied ever telling me that I was infertile. 'That's not something a man forgets being told,' I said to him.

"Louise Wise was the only agency in the city that we knew of where Jewish people could adopt. After filling out the application forms we were interviewed, there were visits to our apartment, we had to submit financial statements, all of that. The big concern was that the parents were monetarily secure and had a room for the child, in addition to being nice people, of course. It wasn't as difficult to adopt as it is now, but it was still highly selective. The agency only accepted about sixteen couples at a time, I think. Then we had to wait for a baby to become available. We weren't notified when you were first born, but when you were ready."

I remembered having asked Fran Cohen at Louise Wise about the lag time. "Eight weeks is a standard period for a newborn to remain in foster care," she had explained over the phone. "We want to make sure that everything is okay with the child before we notify the potential adoptive parents, and in the interim before signing the relinquishment papers, the birth mother still has the opportunity to change her mind. In your case, because you were jaundiced, you had to stay in the hospital for a while longer than normal before you were transferred to foster care. Our infant boarding homes are those of individual families, and thus the care is personalized, not at all of an institutional nature."

Back in the garden, my father continued impassively. "Someone at Louise Wise called us one weekday morning saying that a girl was available and that we could pick her up the next day. I was never curious about who your birth parents were. I couldn't have gotten information on them even if I'd wanted to, but I didn't really care.

"The following morning, Mommy and I went over to Louise Wise to pick you up. We brought you home, plopped you down on the living room couch, and said, what do we do now? All that square, clichéd stuff shown in movies and television programs about young couples with newborns is true." For the first time during his story, my father's eyes lit up and he smiled proudly as he recalled me as a baby. "We were overflowing with happiness that we had a kid at last, and you were such a pretty little thing, with big eyes, smart, cooey, lovey-dovey. But there was the apprehension, of course: How do we change a diaper? What if she falls off the couch?

"We named you after my mother, Sadie, and Mommy's Aunt Sarah. I'd also had an Aunt Sarah, and you were the first girl in the family since her daughter, so it had been a long time. Your middle name, 'Ruth,' came from Mommy's Aunt Ruth. Your southern relatives always called you by both your names, 'Sarah Ruth.' Mommy and I sometimes called you 'Sarah Ruth,' sometimes 'Ruthie,' and then from Ruthie came the nickname 'Rufus,' which you may have seen written on the backs of some old photographs. And, of course, 'Sa-Sa' and 'Saraleh.'

"The adoption wasn't final for about a year and a half. In that time, social workers from the agency visited us at home and interviewed us periodically, so that they could check on your progress, make sure we were being good parents. There were also four or five seminar-type meetings, informal discussions with other couples who had adopted at around the same time. These people were so *nudgy* about whether they were

139

doing the right thing!" he said, irritated. "'Should I tell her she's adopted?' 'Should I pass out cigars, or keep it quiet?'

"In June of 1970, we brought you to the chambers of Justice DeFalco, the surrogate court judge of Manhattan County at that time, for your adoption to be officially approved. He was a nice-looking Italian man, with wavy black hair. You were a real person by then, you walked and talked, wearing a frilly dress and ribbons in your hair. You sat in DeFalco's lap and chattered away, and he was just delighted. Once the court had approved the adoption, it drafted your 'Sarah Saffian' birth certificate."

I recalled an earlier conversation with a friend. "My mom and dad were too young to have me, totally unprepared to be parents," he had told me. He hadn't chosen to be born to unprepared parents just as I hadn't chosen to be given up. No one was able to take charge of his or her destiny in that way. My birth parents had been unprepared, too, but had admitted it, and—with Louise Wise's assistance—had given me to parents who were prepared.

Talking with my father, it occurred to me for the first time how odd it was that driver's licenses and jobs required tests and applications and interviews, but raising another human being, an infinitely greater responsibility, did not. If subjecting biological parents to examination smacked of genetic engineering, then why wasn't scrutinizing adoptive parents, simply because they were unable to conceive, considered unfair? Because the trade-off was that adoptive parents didn't run the risk of having a child with physical or mental disabilities (unless they chose to) or even of the gender they didn't prefer? Both my parents and I had been carefully screened: just as I had been kept in foster care until I could be deemed undamaged goods, my parents had been monitored in order to determine that they were fit parents. On the one hand, I reasoned, why should anyone have to be raised by unfit parents? But on the other hand, who should have the authority to decide who is "fit" and who isn't?

15

Parallels

The bulk of Adam's October 18 letter was devoted to telling his side of our story. It was fourteen single-spaced pages and read like a novella. A former aspiring writer—who kept a novel he had written in the 1970s stashed away in a drawer—Adam crafted characters, scenes, dramatic tension. I read the letter several times, underlining, making notes in the margins, his answers to my previous questions provoking further questions.

"In January of 1968, I dropped out of college for the second time and moved into an apartment in the Bronx," Adam began. He took the long ride by bus and subway to Manhattan to unload trucks or work the night shift at the post office and hung out at the neighborhood bar, gaining experience. "After following all the rules all my life and a lot of academic and athletic achievement, I had become very skeptical of the ivory tower and easy answers and was obviously on some sort of vague solitary quest." He regularly corresponded with his guardians, the Smiths, but seldom saw them. Their son, Mike, had graduated from Carnegie Tech and was married and living in Boston. Hannah was in Durham finishing her senior year. She drove to New York every few weeks to visit Adam, staying sometimes with him, sometimes with her parents in Queens. The young couple had to meet on the sly, because the Morgans didn't like Hannah seeing Adam. He wasn't Jewish, and he was a dropout. "I couldn't rationalize my actions to them," he wrote.

Early in June 68 Robert Kennedy was shot. I saw the news report live in the bar at 2 or 3 in the morning after I got off work. A few days later I rented a tux and went up to New Hampshire to be in a friend's wedding. Everyone had graduated and seemed unquestioningly sure of themselves, setting out on their well-mapped lives. That weekend, due to carelessness on my part, Hannah got pregnant.

During my senior year of college, I fell in love—completely, obsessively, dependently. John was a history major at Yale whom I had met through a friend the previous year, but it wasn't until New Year's Eve, 1991, when he and I crossed paths at a party in New York, that we realized how we felt. The next semester, we spent nearly every weekend together, in either Providence or New Haven, studying side by side in the Rock or in the weenie bins in CCL, taking long drives through New England, staying up talking until the black sky faded into pink. John's mother had also died when he was a child, so perhaps we clung so tightly to each other because we both had lost something.

On Valentine's Day, my housemates made themselves scarce so that John and I could be alone. We spread out a picnic of bread and cheese and fruit and chocolate by candlelight, and transported ourselves from my little room to someplace better. Soon we were making love on the rug, always an experience in discovery. Afterward, we lay there a few moments, me on top of him, smiling together sweaty and shiny-eyed, both twenty-one years old. When we eventually pulled away from each other, he gave a look of alarm as we realized that the condom was still inside me. I laughed nervously and took it out. Soon after, we fell asleep.

"Two weeks after the wedding in New Hampshire, Hannah, not knowing she was pregnant, left for Europe." Adam gave up the Bronx apartment and drove to Los Angeles, then to San Francisco, where he lived for three months in a "crazy woman's" basement. He spent time at a friend's house in Marin County, camped out in Muir Woods and near Stinson Beach, but was generally unhappy. He missed Hannah. That summer, there were riots at the Democratic convention. The war in Vietnam was on. "I mention these few historical events because they were part of the craziness and hopelessness of the times." In September, he drove back east, San Francisco to New York in four days, dying to see Hannah, with vague plans of getting a cheap apartment in the Village, working, writing. He was staying for a few days at a friend's place near Union Square when

Hannah, who had been back from Europe for a week, came in from her parents' house to see him.

When she told me she was pregnant, my first reaction was to take her in my arms and say something like, "OK, let's just hold each other for a minute before we figure this out." She was over 3 months pregnant, so an illegal abortion was not a safe option.

❧❈☙

Two weeks after Valentine's Day, I was in New York for a gynecological checkup. I nonchalantly asked the doctor to run a pregnancy test on my urine sample; my period was about a week late, but as I was often irregular, I wasn't very concerned. The test turned out to be positive, though, and then a blood test officially confirmed that I was pregnant. All at once, I felt completely hollow from head to foot, and as though with each dry swallow I were consuming a bit of myself. This was something that happened to other people, I thought, and yet I was unable to come up with anyone I knew who had experienced it. I walked zombielike to the phone in the waiting room and automatically dialed home. Upon hearing my mother's voice, I collapsed, breaking the news to her in rattling sobs. At first startled and incredulous, she then softened, asking if I wanted her to come pick me up (I thanked her, but said no), telling me that everything would be okay. Back at my parents' house, I called John, who was shocked and scared. Then, mechanically, I phoned the gynecologist's office and scheduled an appointment for an abortion in a few weeks, not taking the time that the doctor had offered to think over the decision.

❦⋘⋙❦

"Over the next couple of weeks, Hannah and I saw each other every few days and talked on the phone a lot, trying to decide what to do, or rather, arguing, because we didn't agree on what to do."

Hannah wanted to put all this behind her. Her post-college life as an independent woman was just beginning. She was not ready to be trapped with me and a baby and no clear prospects. She was scared. She wanted to put the baby up for adoption. What was to happen between then and when the baby was born she was not clear on. She wanted to tell her parents, even though she was dreading it.

146

I felt differently. I had a vision of us living in a white-painted sunny apartment overlooking the Charles River in Boston. I thought it made sense to move someplace away from NYC and her parents and friends who she might want to hide all this from, live together, and see how we felt, and then, hopefully, get married and keep the baby. I wasn't demanding a commitment, just time to think. I also thought it was very important that we were set on a plan before Hannah told her parents, because I was worried about their influence on her decision. When Hannah rejected this, when she said, this is not your problem this is my problem, I was devastated. I was not worthy. I'd made a mess of my life and now hers. I was defeated and absurd. She was right to reject me. I was not entitled to anything. In some vague way I even doubted my paternity. I think without my realizing it, a tiny bit of that doubt remained until I saw your picture.

❧⟨❧⟩❧

Back at Brown, time went by in a haze. I attended classes, wrote papers, confiding in no one. John cut school to come be with me, but as I didn't want to discuss the matter, he brought it up infrequently, only occasionally to ask how I was feeling. But I didn't feel pregnant at all—no queasiness, no cravings, no fatigue. Aside from not getting my period, I had no way of knowing that I was pregnant. Sometimes I suspected that it was a mistake, or that the doctor was playing an evil trick on me. Like Hannah, I had made a decision to get rid of my problem; like Hannah, that was all the awareness I had of what was happening inside me.

❧⟨❧⟩❧

147

"Finally, and I remember the moment clearly," wrote Adam, "something broke in me."

We were sitting in Hannah's parents' car one night, arguing. I got this sudden horrible calm empty feeling, like something had left my body. I said something like, "OK. You've taken this away from me. I'll stand by you, but I don't feel like this baby has anything to do with me." I'd given up all hope. I've thought a lot about that moment since. I think it has a lot to do with the death of my mother. That is, at some point I accepted the inevitability of loss. My guardian, Shirley Smith, said once that when she told me the day after Christmas, 1952, that my mother had died, she started to cry and I started comforting her, like my own emotions shut down, went away or deep inside, leaving only emptiness.

My mother Nancy had also died the day after Christmas, 1975. She was forty-two years old and I was in first grade when liver cancer claimed her. The period when she was in the hospital—only about a month—was a blur of sleepovers at friends' houses. We never had a final goodbye, because my father didn't realize how sick she was, that she wouldn't be coming home. When her health sharply declined in November and the doctor told him that "she might not make it," he was stunned. "You were made aware that she was sick," Dad commented during our conversation in the garden, "but it's hard to tell how much a child understands."

Returning home the morning of December 26 from a sleepover, I came into the apartment alone; my friend's parents must have dropped me off with the doorman. I remembered going into the kitchen with the yellow flowered wallpaper, where my father was standing, his back to the window, facing me. He didn't have to say anything, we just hugged and I knew that my mother was gone. He recalled instead that it was the front hallway of the apartment where he greeted me: "I crouched, held you in my arms, and just told you, in as short and sweet and reassuring a way as possible."

A day or two later, my mother's memorial service was held at a funeral chapel on Fifty-first Street. There were over a hundred people there. The rabbi recited Dylan Thomas's poem, "Do not go gentle into that good night." Reading the poem again in 1994, I wondered, had my mother refused to go gently, had she raged, or had she succumbed with tired relief? "Everyone remarked on how brave you were, how well-behaved. You sat there looking so . . ." As my father trailed off, I recalled us standing side by side at the service, holding hands. I glanced at him and saw that he was crying, no sound or movement, just his head bent slightly downward, eyes closed, a tear streaking his face. I had never seen him cry before, and it made me afraid. At the reception, I do remember everyone saying how brave I was. I didn't cry.

At school, I sat next to the teacher during homeroom while she told the class that my mother had died, and we all discussed it. I felt adult, more like the teacher than my classmates. Taking my cue from her, I sat silently solemn, determined to be the perfect daughter, unconsciously setting out to make up for my father's loss, to comfort him. Perhaps I also feared that he would go away, too, if I wasn't perfect, even though he never gave a sign of leaving, even though the pressure on me came entirely from within.

149

⁂

Hannah told her parents that she was pregnant. "It was awful," Adam went on. "Their reaction wasn't unusual for those times." He moved into "a dump" on East Ninth Street and took the taxi driver's license test. He drove a cab for one day and quit and then worked sporadically, gutting and renovating brownstones in Brooklyn. He and Hannah often had lunch together near her midtown office. She met with the people at Louise Wise. Soon after Richard Nixon was elected president, she moved into the Bronx hideout. Adam stayed at his apartment, hung out with college friends who were in the city, but spent most of his time with Hannah—sleeping late, taking long walks, reading, watching television. "We were hiding from the world. We grew closer than we had ever been."

Once a week Hannah's parents came in the evening to take her out to dinner and to a shrink. I would disappear at these times. If the Morgans suspected Hannah was seeing me they did not acknowledge it. There were apparently a lot of tense silences during their visits.

I was not still trying to turn Hannah to my way of thinking, to seem more worthy of her love and trust so she'd come around to my previous plan. I was going along with what was happening, in a state of continuous pain, trying to be kind to Hannah but also now needing her terribly. My dependency on her that evolved as we lived in this limbo state was another powerful sign of weakness to me. Self-doubt became self-loathing. Sometime in January, a month before you were born, Hannah, all the while worried that I would get angry, told me she felt like she was changing her mind. She thought she wanted to keep the baby. What did I think? This is the hardest part for me to tell and accept. Even though I could see the baby moving in her belly (I agonize now over whether to say "you" or "the baby"), I felt like it was already lost to me. I felt weak, cowardly, and resigned to the fact that all too soon this existence in the Bronx would be over and I would be alone again, and that that was the way it was meant to be. And yet being alone was now the most painful thing of all. I've often thought since that this was a copout, that Hannah had let me off the hook in September and I didn't want to get back on. But I don't really think so. Many times over the years I've wished I was stronger then, as strong as I had been in

September, said, great, let's do it, it will all work out. But I didn't say that. I said something like, I'm sorry, I can't go along with that. I don't even know what I meant. So Hannah, alone with her feelings, guilty that she had hurt me so much with her rejection, guilty in the eyes of her parents and society, enmeshed in the process with Louise Wise, also fell back to an acceptance of our fate, bound to her earlier decision. Toward the end it felt as if you're watching the blood flow out of your body and you're dying and you simply accept it. Like passive suicide.

Hannah went into the home on Staten Island. I missed her very much. I'd visit her and we'd take the bus into the town there and get something to eat, see a movie. It was odd hanging around this strange town in such pitiful circumstances. I went up to Durham for a quick trip. I got a call early the next morning from a woman at the home to tell me Hannah had had the baby three weeks early. I got on the bus to NYC and the ferry out to Staten Island and got to the hospital that evening. I hadn't even been there for Hannah during the birth. She seemed very happy right then, not because all this was coming to an end—for this short time she wasn't thinking of the end. She was happy because she had had you. She wasn't looking past the moment. She took me to the nursery and we looked at you through the glass. You were tiny and beautiful.

❦❦❦

April 13, 1991, was the date of the procedure, a Saturday morning. Upon waking, I was struck with terror, but at that point my fear was strictly physical, not philosophical; I had always been afraid of doctors anyway, habitually fainting when having a simple blood test. I ate no breakfast, as I had been instructed, but pulled on my clothes from the day before and stumbled downstairs to the kitchen, where my mother was waiting. The early morning streets were empty and foggy as we walked in near silence. In the waiting room, I answered some questions and signed a form headed "Consent to Abortion." Soon after, I lay shivering in a paper gown on an examination table, waiting, listening to the strains of The Association's "Windy" being piped in softly over the speakers like a sick joke. The song's carefree lyrics and cheerful melody made me chuckle bitterly as I hummed along in spite of myself, but in a dissonant, minor key:

> Who's trippin' down the streets of the city,
> Smiling at everybody she sees?
> Who's reaching out to capture a moment?
> Everyone knows it's Windy.

Then the doctor and nurse came in to examine me before administering Valium and a local anesthetic. I panicked, crying and wriggling on the table, recoiling when they touched me, simultaneously wide awake in mind and sluggish in body, as in a nightmare. After much patient coaxing, the doctor finally snapped that if I didn't calm down she would have to take me to the hospital, and did I want that? I sobbed no and she slipped my legs into the stirrups. As the Valium took full effect I felt nothing and heard a muffled sound, like a vacuum cleaner in the distance, and then it was over. The entire procedure took fifteen minutes.

I was helped into my clothes and given a couple of prescriptions and a follow-up examination appointment, and then I staggered home with my mother's assistance, trying to resist the pull pavementward. Still in a groggy stupor, I nonetheless felt a discussion brewing and insisted on launching into it, despite her resistance, her suggestion that we speak later, after the drugs had worn off. According to my vague recollection of the conversation, Mom was understanding and concerned, but also let me know how hard this was for her, considering her Catholic upbringing. "I'm being as supportive as I can," she said deliberately. I could tell by her tone of voice that she hoped I had learned my lesson when she sighed, "You made a mistake, and you had to correct it." But the whole, brief experience—from conception to abortion—had been completely unreal.

Exhausted from the morning's events, after a strong hug and an "I love you, no matter what" from Mom, I dragged myself upstairs to my room, where I slept heavily and dreamlessly for several hours. I emerged sometime in the afternoon to eat and spend time with my tolerant father and oblivious brother and sister, went back to bed early and returned to school the next morning. Later that week, I took the train from Providence to New Haven, where John met me at the station. We walked around the Yale campus in the unseasonably chilly mist, talking. Refreshed by a few days' distance from the experience, I said how relieved I was that it was over, that now we could "get on with our lives."

153

❖⟨⟩❖

"Hannah moved back to her parents' house, then got an apartment with a friend and a job in the city," Adam continued. "I moved back to Durham, beaten, to hide. We were not relieved. We did not 'get on with our lives.' We were devastated. Without question, giving you up remains the most traumatic event of Hannah's life, and of mine, since my mother's death. After 1969, we moved into years of suppressed grief, non-commitment to each other, and in my case, somewhat self-destructive behavior." He described an aimless existence of living in a dilapidated farmhouse, hanging out in the local scene, closing the bar some nights. Working on his novel, he wrote to rationalize his lifestyle to himself, with no long-term goals in mind. "I was hiding from the issues surrounding my parents' deaths and giving you up." He wouldn't see his guardians, who were retired in Los Angeles, for seven years.

The emotional impact of what I had gone through sank in slowly. Gradually, as other people who'd had abortions came out of the woodwork, I saw how commonplace an occurrence it actually was. But while it was a difficult experience for any woman to go through, I started to understand that for me, a mistaken pregnancy myself, having an abortion had been a particular tragedy. Because of this, I continued to keep it a secret. My parents and I never spoke about it, and I tried not to mention John in their presence. They had met him once, when he'd come for dinner the week after our New Year's encounter, and they'd liked him in a casual way. In the rare instances when his name did slip out, my father sometimes referred indirectly to what had happened, half-jokingly muttering something about getting out his proverbial shotgun, like in the old days. I told no one else about my experience, not even my closest friends, and couldn't say or write the word "abortion" for many years. Just as giving me up had been Hannah's secret, I regarded my experience as a private, almost sacred thing.

I had participated in a couple of pro-choice demonstrations over the years, despite feeling slightly hypocritical, being an adoptee. In April 1992, I went to Washington, D.C., with a group of friends, including John. Now, as an adoptee who had also had an abortion a year earlier, I felt even more ambivalent. Though John was the only one who was aware of my inner turmoil, he seemed unsympathetic. During the drive down, I sat in front with him, crying quietly into the windowpane as he chatted and played Twenty Questions with our friends in the backseat. At one point during the protest, he hoisted me up on his shoulders. I appreciated the perfect view of the immense sea of people, chanting in unison and marching down Constitution Avenue, as a large looming sculpture of a bloodied hanger led the way toward the Capitol. But I also felt completely isolated.

In retrospect, I was grateful to have had access to a safe, legal and private abortion. Not once did I worry about my health, not once was I preached to or harassed. It was my own personal choice, for a procedure that was swift, hygienic and about which no one else had to know. But at the time, it felt too automatic to be a conscious decision. Though I could have pursued other avenues, as many young women do—dropping out of college, marrying John, raising the child when I was still a child myself, or else having the child and giving it up for adoption—I didn't even consider them at the time. Looking back, the event seemed more like an inevitability than an actual choice.

Abortion was my reality, just as adoption had been Hannah's. In 1968, abortion wasn't legal or even medically safe at three months, and a twenty-one-year-old unmarried college graduate keeping and raising a child herself was discouraged as shameful. Getting a shotgun marriage was another option, but an unattractive one. In a way, Hannah didn't make a choice, either. Across two decades and a generation of difference in political and societal norms, I could relate to Hannah's initial desire to deny what had happened and her eventual sense of loss, through my arguably less lingering experience. The one thing I envied Hannah was that although nearly twenty-four years of our relationship were gone, she had the opportunity to know me from then on. My child was completely lost to me.

However, I've never believed that an aborted embryo is a human being, or deemed that incarnation as a soul's only chance. The way I've always resolved my own personal paradox is to imagine that had I been aborted instead of given up for adoption, my soul would have gone on to be someone, or something—a daisy, a breeze, a drop of water—else. "I" am not inherently this five-foot-five, brown-haired, green-eyed piece of flesh, but what is inside, which just as well could exist in any body or thing.

Eventually getting married and raising a family was wonderful, Adam wrote, "but it made us that much more aware of what we

had lost with you, and more importantly, what we were not giving you."

*We worried and wondered and hoped for the best for you, but never
considered intruding on your upbringing. Hannah always wished there
was a window into your life that she could look through to see what you
were like and that you were all right.*

If there had been a window into my life, this is what Hannah
would have seen in 1978. That year I turned nine and began
fourth grade at Spence, knobby knees peeking out from
beneath my green plaid tunic, long hair pulled back in a cloth
headband. Kathy was living with my father and me, and
Hannah would have seen the two of them calling me into the
living room that autumn evening to ask, "What would you
think if we got married?" While Renee was being born in July, I
was spending my second summer at sleep-away camp. Each
morning I had swimming instruction, the cold lake knocking
the wind from me and stiffening my joints, leaving me afterward with a tingling sensation, as if every cell of my body were
fully awake. The soggy earth sank under my boots, emitting a
clean, nutty odor, as I hiked through the White Mountains,
sucking on fingers still sticky sweet from oranges. While my
birth sister was wrapped in a blanket in Hannah's arms, I was
tan and sinewy from the outdoors, picking raspberries when I
was supposed to be tending goal in soccer, my shorts damp
from the slick, dewy grass. I had my first kiss from Todd that

summer, on the shadowy volleyball court, and wrote letters about it to friends from home in my bubbly pre-adolescent handwriting. My bunkmates and I held seances, playing "light as a feather, stiff as a board," and read in whispers sexy passages from Judy Blume's "grown-up book," *Forever*, under the covers with flashlights, giggling. Our counselors taught us the lyrics to the Grateful Dead's "Casey Jones," which we sang loudly and obliviously around the dinner table in the mess hall: "Driving that train, high on cocaine . . ." On August 16, we commemorated the one-year anniversary of Elvis' death with a moment of silence at the flagpole. That summer, while Hannah and Adam were marveling at the newborn daughter they could keep this time, my father and mother-to-be—the parents to whom I had been given, the parents I knew—came up on visiting weekend, bringing stationery and sweatshirts and Toll House cookies, to swim and play tennis and sing songs around the campfire with me, to marvel at how much I'd grown.

I had been lying on my bed as I read Adam's letter, and at one point I rolled onto my side. Noticing the shape of my stomach in this position, I recalled that as a little girl I had always thought it resembled a ravioli—small mound in the middle, smooth slopes down the sides. Then I thought, there was once an embryo in there, and wondered, what would my abdomen look like fully pregnant one day? Finally, before pulling my T-shirt back down I examined my belly button, imagining the umbilical cord that had once come from it, attaching me to Hannah.

Further Parallels

Adam had seen his guardians—"I call them Mom and Dad"—now and then since the year before he and Hannah married. It had always occurred to him during these trips that Don, his birth mother's brother, lived not far away, in the San Francisco outskirts. But it wasn't until August 1994, when Adam was planning to visit his guardian mother (Peter, his guardian father, had died two years earlier), that he felt ready to take a journey to his origins, as well.

159

I'd been shying away from this for years. Sometimes it gets harder to make contact when you feel guilty you didn't contact someone sooner. I hadn't seen Don since I was six and hadn't communicated with him even by mail from 69 until 77, when I sent his family a wedding announcement. We'd exchanged Christmas cards since then. Don was the last good source of information about my mother if I was ever going to learn more. It dawned on me for the first time that he had named his

only child Laura, after her. Suddenly, I was very excited about seeing
them. I called them. They sounded very happy to hear from me. I would
visit them for a day and a night before heading down to Mom in LA.

The problem was I didn't want to tell Mom where I was going. I
realized that the primary reason I hadn't visited these folks for all these
years was that I was afraid of hurting Mom's feelings. I was in a bind,
a no-win situation, in that I wanted to like Don and his daughter.
They were my blood. But if I did, if I felt too comfortable or liked them
too much, I was betraying my guardians, to whom I owed so much.
Now I thought, how can I expect Sarah to visit us if I don't have the
guts to visit these folks? Who knows how it works? You don't always
decide these things. Suddenly they just feel right, or at least possible.

I had always been wary of talking about Nancy in front of
Mom, for fear that it would hurt her feelings, just as I hesitated
to bring up Hannah and Adam with my father. My parents had
each replaced others, and I didn't want to remind them that
they weren't the original ones. I was concerned that they would
mistake my thinking about these previous parents as some kind
of betrayal, as though in letting them linger I was telling my
mother and father that they weren't sufficient somehow.

Thus, while I had been sharing my letters to and from the
Leyders in depth with Chris, I still discussed them barely at all
with Mom and Dad. Taking our cues from one another, I was
as cautiously open as they seemed to want to be, and they were
as tentatively supportive as I seemed to need. Adam had a
point: we were indeed tiptoeing, all of us. But I was waiting for
the next step in my interaction with my birth parents to "feel

right," not wanting to force anything and thereby jeopardize my relationship with the Leyders, or the Saffians, or both.

Adam called his mother to tell her about his plan to visit Don.

I asked her if she thought it would be OK to call up her sister, who lived in San Francisco, for a place to stay Thursday night. It was a perfect logistical solution, as well as a great way to gracefully involve both my "families" in my journey. That was fine, she said. She'd call and set it up. But why in the world did I want to see Don after all these years?

"Mom, remember Aunt Meg in Ohio? I didn't get out there until her funeral, and I was real sorry I hadn't gone sooner."

"But we did visit her. We were driving across the country. We went out of our way to stop there. Don't you remember that?" I remembered an evening of strained talk among the grown ups, no mention of my father, the place steamy and sweltering, Aunt Meg nursing her dying husband in an adjustable bed in her tiny living room, my brother Mike and me fidgeting until we headed back to the motel.

I rented a car at the SF airport, stayed at my aunt's Thursday night, and headed out early Friday morning. When I crossed the drawbridge into Don's tiny town, I felt that I was in a place truly strange to me and yet profoundly comfortable and familiar like home.

I wondered if I would have this combined sensation if and when I ventured to Hanover. As long ago as our last encounter was, perhaps my eyes or the shape of my face would ring a bell for Hannah and Adam. But because I had no recollection of them, any feelings of familiarity that I might have would be unconscious, instinctual. If Hannah did something that she had done in my first few days—stroked my hair, held my hand—perhaps a memory would come rushing back. Did I want that to happen? Would feeling connected to them be comforting or threatening, familiar or strange? Both?

Don was working in the yard. We hit it off immediately. He took me into the house their father had built next to the levee, primarily from lumber salvaged from the river. Don had so much to tell and show. He talked about my father, what a charming, fun-loving, hard-working, intelligent man he was. He gave me the hunting knife and field glasses my father was wearing when he was killed. "Wiped his blood off them, of course," he said. "They're very good glasses. I been waiting forty-two years to give you this stuff." We exchanged and pored over old photos. There were several of two little girls in long white dresses, high black lace-up boots, big floppy hair bows, holding a baby—my mother, her sister and Don—sitting on the front porch steps.

I left the next day after lunch. "I'm glad you showed up, buddy," Don said.

"I'm glad I showed up too, Don," I said, choking on the last words, tears coming to my eyes only once I was driving off. Crossing the bridge out of town I thought, I can do anything I want now. I felt powerful in a way I never had.

That night in LA when I told Mom about the field glasses (I didn't tell her about Don wiping the blood off) she said, "Well, remember I gave you those beautiful field glasses from the church sale a couple of years ago. That's one pair for Renee and one for Lucy."

1994

"It's funny," I said. "Don thought it was kind of ironic he ended up living in that same house his whole life, after trying to sell it cheap before he went off to war."

"Your mother Laura gave her share to Don." She shook her head. "Half of that place should be yours."

"Mom, the place wasn't worth anything anyway. He couldn't sell it. They were dirt poor. Don's a good man."

"Wasn't Dad a good man? Wasn't he a good father?"

"Of course he was, Mom."

It was very sad to see her threatened. It took me by surprise even though I'd been aware of it all along. I wish I'd drawn her out about it right then, but I didn't. I stopped trying to share my excitement at my new knowledge and kept it to myself, a familiar move. I love her. Someday I'll talk to her about all of it.

For inheritance and sentimental reasons, Shirley and Peter Smith adopted me in 1981 (I have two birth certificates, too, both for Adam Leyder, but each with a different set of parents). They didn't do it at first, because my mother told them she wanted me to keep the Leyder name. Later, they decided to, because being careful people they thought it would make things neater when they died. It became more emotional than we thought. I had mixed feelings about being adopted, having always had my Lone Ranger image. Since then, Mom will jokingly say, "Don't forget you're my son. I've got a piece of paper that says so."

163

I was Kathy's daughter, even though she didn't have a piece of paper that said so. She and my father had discussed the implications if anything should happen to him, and concluded that adoption would be an unnecessary formality. Because of their marriage contract, Mom automatically would have become my legal guardian, and my father's will stipulated that his assets would have gone to his wife and three children. It wouldn't have made an emotional difference, either—we didn't need an official contract, as the bond was already there. It never failed to irk me when people referred to Mom as my "step-mother," because while it may have been technically accurate, it wasn't spiritually so. Now and then the subject of adopting me came up in conversation casually, even jokingly—"Oh, yeah, we have to do that," one of us would say, but it always slipped our minds. But reading Adam's letter, I thought I might like Mom to adopt me, too, "for sentimental reasons." How different being adopted as an adult, after having established a relation-ship over so many years, would be from the first time.

164

"Sunday night, after saying good night to Mom, I thought, night before last I was sleeping in my mother's childhood room, in the house her father built," Adam continued.

It was like at that moment I was being nourished by these day-old memories, yet with this resignation that I might never see Don again. Like he was wonderful but lost already. Then I thought, what I'd like is to live there for a while, to hang out with him. I found myself wanting to ask him to teach me to hunt. It hit me that they didn't say, "Where have you been?" but, "How long it's been!" No blame. And then they said, "Thank you for visiting us, Adam." In a confused way it started feeling like Don was my lost father and his daughter Laura was my sister. Even though I knew this was kind of wacky it was a tantalizing and precious feeling. I loved them. It was real. It was peace I didn't know existed. I'd been denying myself all these years. I didn't know what I was missing. I wasn't betraying anyone. I deserved this feeling. I wanted to hold onto it, not let it slip away.

Would I achieve a sense of peace when I met the Leyders, and would it be as tempered by defensiveness—"I wasn't betraying anyone. I deserved this feeling"—as Adam's seemed to be? I supposed that would depend on my adoptive parents' reaction to the reunion: if they acted threatened and detached, I would feel guilty; if they were supportive and interested, I would feel whole.

Before I left for California, I was telling this guy at work who has a ten-year-old adopted son how my greatest concern with the trip was that I was hurting my mother's feelings by showing interest in these blood relatives after all these years. He said, "Someday my son's gonna want to meet his birth father, and that's the way it is," shrugging like it was a necessary evil. What I want to say to him now is, when that time comes, you bring it up. Encourage him to find his birth parents. Make him feel that it's something you want him to do. Because if he doesn't feel that, he may wait a long time to do it or never do it, out of homage to you. If you do this for him it will bring you even closer because you are not threatened. He can be open with you about his feelings.

I felt mixed about Adam's hypothetical advice. If this man were too emphatic about his son searching for his birth parents, then the son could possibly react by thinking, if I have you for my father, why do I need someone else? Are you trying to give me away, too, give me back? Whenever I brought up the subject with my father—from that first conversation after I had discovered his 1969 datebook, to mentions of wanting to search for my birth parents someday, to telling him about Hannah's phone call, and since then—he was always willing to talk. True, it was plain that it wasn't his favorite subject, which put me in an awkward position between wanting information and not wanting to hurt him. But I thought that had he been too encouraging, too eager for me to seek out these other parents, I might have felt rejected by him. Just as my guilt was a sign of loyalty to him, his reticence was a sign of loyalty to me. He would be supportive, from a distance, of my investigating the Leyders, but in his eyes they would never be my parents. I recalled a certain tape recording of me at age five—at one point my father sounds as if he is hugging me as he gushes, "Oh, my very own Sarah."

But then I remembered watching the girl sitting across from me in the genealogy room at the library, imagining that her adoptive parents were helping her search for her birth parents, and feeling comparatively solitary in my own efforts.

"How I wish Mom had encouraged me to visit Don," Adam concluded.

The other night I looked through all my old stuff for some newspaper clippings from 1946 about my father's death. I searched for several hours and couldn't find them. I had tears of frustration because I had so little of him, and now it seemed even this piece might be gone.

The leaves are turning. We love you very much. Don't forget.

Mistakes

In November, I found myself going through the motions of my life as though it were already a memory, no longer concrete. My job, my friends, Chris—I remembered working there, I remembered hanging out with them, I remembered loving him. Sitting in a crowded subway car one day, the vinegary smell of bodies pressed too close together giving me a headache, I recalled a compliment someone had overheard and passed along to me once. After I had graduated from high school, a younger student meeting with the college adviser at Spence said that she wanted to go to Brown, as I had. "Sarah Saffian," the adviser responded archly, "doesn't waste a bus ride." Nostalgic for my former self, I noted that now I preferred not to read or write or make lists or plan as I rode the bus or subway, but just to sit.

One Sunday night, I plummeted to my nadir. I was at Chris' apartment, torn between not wanting to leave him and not wanting him to see me fall apart yet again. So I sequestered myself in the spare room, door closed, lit only by the street-lamps from outside. Sitting on the gray-carpeted floor, I thought about hurting myself and tried, banging my head against the wall, pulling my hair, scratching until I bled. Chris had often worried aloud that my nervous habit of picking scabs was oddly masochistic. After several bouts of knocking on the door went unanswered, he came in, gently defying my stony solitude. Feeling his arms around me made me sob, full-throated, tumbling, as Chris seemed to be the only one who appreciated this jaggedness in me. Eventually we went to bed, where, though calmed, I still cried—tears running into my ears as I lay motionless, looking up to where I imagined the ceiling to be in the darkness—long after he had fallen asleep. In the morning, waking before him, I sat up and looked out at the sunny day past his fire escape, embarrassed, bemused, as though the person the night before had been someone else.

At the end of the month, I drummed up the strength to respond to Adam's October letter. He answered me three weeks later. As the second year of our correspondence drew to a close, the letters became increasingly immediate—a single exchange taking on a conversational, call-and-response quality.

Dear Hannah and Adam,   *November 25, 1994*
    Adam, your letter was overwhelming and wonderful and difficult all in one. It made me cry, laugh, approach understanding. You must realize that your entering my life so suddenly left much unexplained.

*To warn you, some of my reactions are rough-going. And please
don't answer anything that you feel uncomfortable talking about, if it is
too personal.*

*You said that you learned "it is good for adoptees to have their birth
parents find them." Shouldn't what is "good" for an adoptee be up to
her? Shouldn't it be up to the adoptee to find her birth parents if she so
chooses? How can you generalize? You also wrote, "Hannah and I
decided that the first thing to do was to call S. Saffian and see if it was
you . . . Hannah got up her courage and called you that morning. It
was one of the happiest days of our lives . . . Of course it's been sad
since then that things have moved slowly . . ." It's hard for me to get
over feeling angry about being found and about the way you chose to
contact me. Why did you think calling would be the best thing? If you
had to contact me, then why not at least do it by letter?*

169

"We did not think calling was the best thing," Adam responded
on December 19. "We would have preferred to write, but we
didn't know where to write to," being uncertain whether a letter
sent to my father's address would reach me, or whether the "S.
Saffian" they had seen listed in the Manhattan phone book was
me. By calling, they reasoned, they could be sure.

*We thought of asking whoever answered if Sarah Saffian lived there then
hanging up, or posing as a free-vacation-giveaway-type person and then
later writing to you. That seemed too weird. We thought of going down
there and staking out the street to see if someone who looked like it might be
you came out of your building and if they did then writing you. That
really seemed too weird. Since then, we've heard about another method of*

contact, the use of a third party. *We could have asked someone sensitive, intelligent, trustworthy, to call "S. Saffian" and if you answered, to give you Hannah's name, address and phone number. If we had known about or thought of this approach at the time, we would have considered it.*

"*I* didn't have a chance to get up *my* courage that morning," I went on in my letter.

Hannah had been planning and preparing for this phone call. She probably took a deep breath before lifting the receiver, probably felt a knot in her stomach with each ring, a leap when a voice answered on the other end. For me, it was just a phone call, like any other, and I answered it casually and unsuspectingly. You had made the decision to make the call, but I hadn't made the decision to receive it. It was one of the happiest days of your lives, because for you, it served as the completion of a search, the healing of a twenty-four-year-old ache. For me, it was just the opposite: it presented an opening, like a wound.

"Was this a new wound, or the opening of a wound already there?" Adam asked. "Was this opening the beginning of the healing process for that wound?"

For an adoptee, the birth parents are not around to offer the love to cancel the fact of their "mistake." The adoptive parents give love and nurturing, but they didn't make the mistake. So I can see that for an adoptee, the pain could linger. Maybe this is a pain that can be eased some by expressions of love, though belated, from the birth parents. However, I do hear you when you say that you wanted to pick your own time to begin the healing. Some wounds may never fully close, and there may be hidden wounds yet to be reopened, for us as well as you.

I continued. "It was not one of the happiest days of my life, but one of the most difficult."

After the phone call, I rushed off to work, only to sit dumbstruck at my desk and then leave to unload my burden on my father. Because that's what it was, and still is: a newfound burden, imposed suddenly. The only way I could approach trusting you was to step back from the initial rush and slow things down to a pace that was digestible for me. You owe me your patience. I never resented you for giving me up, because I understand that there are reasons for that, and I can appreciate how difficult such a choice can be. I also have had a very fortunate life and a loving family that I am extremely close to and feel very much a part of, and wouldn't want it any different. What I do resent is that you took away my right to find you when I was ready, and the way you did it.

"I question the focus of your anger," Adam challenged.

I can think of other things for you to be angry about. You say you understand our actions in 68–69. A therapist once told Hannah that there was no good decision to make then, but that giving you up was an act of love. Maybe so. But it feels more like it was for us an act of desperation, confusion, selfishness, fear and helplessness. I had hard times coming to an understanding of Hannah's desire to get on with her life in the fall of 68, or my angst-ridden weakness in early 69 when she was wanting to keep you, or seeing you in the hospital and then walking away. How could we then end up together, have other children, and keep them after not keeping you? These things are understandable. They are also painful.

We are relieved and glad that you have a loving family that you feel very much a part of. The fact that you repeat this affirmation in almost every one of your letters like a mantra makes me worry that you see a developing relationship with us as potentially threatening to your family. But we have read and heard firsthand that an adoptee who has a half-decent relationship with their adoptive parents experiences a strengthening of that relationship after reuniting with the birth parent(s). Mysteries are removed.

"Why didn't you wait until my parents and I had registered," I asked, "either with Louise Wise or with one of the adoption networks?"

If I hadn't registered, perhaps it meant that I wasn't ready to meet you yet. In your yearning to find me, did you ever consider how I felt? How I might react to being found, to being called on the phone out of the blue? Or did you just think of your own feelings and needs, considering me only in this fantasy you had of a mutually joyous reunion?

"In 1968–69, except for Hannah's hoping you would have the good home she felt we were unable to provide, we were motivated by our own feelings, not yours," Adam wrote.

The major factor in our searching for and in our communications with you has always been how you felt, your well-being. Fantasies? I've had lots of them, one being the mutually joyous reunion which I sketched in an earlier letter and which obviously offended you. If we were to meet, with-

out question my greatest joy would be knowing that you were finding out where you came from, empowering yourself with that knowledge. Searching was difficult for Hannah. As well as worrying about what we would find if we did find you, she was very aware of the possibility of having to face the resentment and shame of being the intrusive birth mother. She often felt the most wonderful thing imaginable would be for the phone to ring and have it be you, not only finally to learn all about you and that you were OK, but also to know she was forgiven, so she wouldn't have to search and risk intrusion and blame.

Hannah, like you, is cautious, fearful for everyone of the painful emotions that are surfacing in dealing with this. I'm trying to respect your and her directives, but because I'm so sure, due to my own experiences, that it is good to deal as soon as possible with emotional pain and good to learn about your origins, I display greater urgency. I'm aware of the mistakes I made in my own life by delaying these things, and I don't want you to do the same. That's where I'm coming from. Of course this doesn't give me any right whatsoever to impose that urgency on you. We recently came across some new psychological buzzwords. In relationships, there are "distancers" and/or "advancers," and if there aren't any advancers, things don't develop. I translate that to mean, "Someone's got to risk making a schmuck out of themselves and it might as well be me."

173

Adam, why did you feel "powerful" after meeting your birth mother's brother? I feel just the opposite—out of control. Could it be because you orchestrated the reunion with Don, rather than being caught unawares, as I was by your phone calls?

Maybe I felt powerful because I had dealt with and survived something I had dreaded doing for years. Primarily it was that I felt rooted to two live people and a place, and had learned a lot about my natural parents. If and when you "orchestrate" a reunion with us, which is in your control, not ours, I am sure you will come away empowered. I'm familiar with feeling out of control. We are out of control when people who are supposed to love us abandon us by giving us up for adoption or by dying on us.

Something else still weighed on me. Throughout our correspondence, the "We love you" ending to their letters had persisted in making me uncomfortable, though I had never before been able to express it.

174

How can you truly love me if you barely know me and have never met me? Just because you gave birth to me? I can't feel love toward you, not yet, because although you gave birth to me, you are strangers. I don't know who you are, neither in relation to me, nor independent of me. I don't know where you fit into my life. I think that you are using love as a framework for other emotions: relief, closure. Perhaps you love the idea of me.

Sarah, are parents, natural or adoptive, loving the "idea" of their newborn or eight-week-old baby when they hold her for the first time? Can they love her even though they don't "know" her? I think they can, and have the right to. When you give a baby up, however, maybe in someone else's eyes you also give up the right to love. I think part of "unconditional" love is that you don't have to "know" much about the person you're loving. After you and I ended our conversation on February 1, 1993, I was overcome with new joy and the real love and sorrow I'd tried to squash down since 1969. I'm profoundly glad that

I feel what I feel. All of it. Nonetheless, when you tell someone you love them, the idea is to have them feel good, not creepy. I won't say it anymore unless you say it's all right.

In closing, I softened my tone—not to sugarcoat or apologize, but to let them know that negative feelings were not the only ones I had.

I hope my letter isn't harsh or jarring. I don't mean to attack. I have been mulling over these thoughts and feelings the past two years and have only partially expressed them in previous letters. Your last letter brought a lot of this out. I have to be honest, even with my anger. I hope you see this letter, painful though parts of it may be to read, as illustrating that being candid about my mistrust is itself an act of trust.

I do hope that you had a warm and joyous Thanksgiving and that you are all well.

Sarah.

Ask anything, Sarah. Say anything. Think of yourself.

Adam.

When we began writing, I had predicted that the touchier relationship would be with Hannah, the birth mother, the more direct link, the one who ultimately had made the decision to surrender me. But Adam and I were the ones letting the polite guards down and stepping into the ring with each other. The barbs that

175

we exchanged struck me somewhat as angry lovers' words. Perhaps our gender difference was a factor in provoking this sparring.

A more likely reason, though, was our comparable backgrounds, as children simultaneously hardened and made vulnerable in the face of tragedy, and the different ways we chose to deal with having that role imposed on us. Hannah, despite her emerging similarities to me, was a clearly distinct person, while Adam was coming to me not only as birth father but as fellow adoptee, as well. I began to realize that this was why my response to him was more loaded, because our connection was uncomfortably close. When he described himself as openhearted, I envied that openness. When he looked lost in his cab driver's license photo, I saw my own feelings laid bare. He was revealing a side of myself that I didn't want to acknowledge, something raw, as I wrote, like an open wound. I had put a bandage on it and left it alone, but he was forcing me to rip the bandage off, examine the wound, and expose it to the sun and air and salt water, where it would first sting, then heal.

"I was very saddened to hear that you had an abortion and at such a young age," Hannah's letter began.

It is such a difficult thing to experience, and I understand why it was particularly hard for you. You're lucky that you could turn to your parents—I'm not sure I would have in your situation. You echoed many of my own thoughts and feelings. I too am pro-choice (not pro-abortion) and have attended pro-choice rallies. Women must have the right to choose what they will and will not do with their bodies and they will find abortions

*whether they are legal or not. And of course, the ones who will suffer the
most at the hands of incompetents, rather than being whisked off to Puerto
Rico by well-to-do parents, will be poor women. But I certainly do not
think of abortion as a means to empowerment. My God, what a thought!
It is a grave and horribly sad decision to make.*

She went on to explain that about three years before searching for me, she had started attending a monthly birth mothers'
support group in Hanover. "I was looking for some 'company.' I
so much wanted to have a place to go where I could talk freely
about all the emotions and thoughts I'd had for all these years
with women who would truly understand," she wrote. "A lot of
us, including me, felt, as you do, that we had no right to search.
I hoped, as I had your whole life, that one day the doorbell or
the phone would ring and it would be you." This comment,
along with Adam's that if I had contacted Hannah she would
have known that "she was forgiven," made me wish that I had
acted sooner and done the searching, not so much to protect
myself from their intrusion as to grant her this wish. I realized
for the first time that a birth mother could experience as much
anxiety as an adoptee while searching, if not more. I saw that
being found could be reassuring, to either party.

After several months, Hannah wrote, the Hanover support
group organized a "triad meeting," including adoptees, adoptive
parents and birth parents, primarily mothers. She wanted to go,
but was scared. "I was sure that every adoptee in the room
would hate me, as would every adoptive parent. There would be
accusing fingers pointed at me for what I had done—what kind

177

of person can give up a child, then marry the guy, have more kids and go on with her life? I guess I don't know what kind of person can do that. It would also be the first time I was out in public as a birth mother." She did attend, with Adam, who was one of the few birth fathers present. They were both happily surprised by the compassionate understanding among members of the group and by the underlying theme of the meeting, which was that it was good for adoptees to be found. "Adam and I left that meeting feeling for the first time that we *had* to search for you, for your sake. We thought that it would be helpful for you to know that we wanted to find you."

Although I didn't like the idea of the phone call, it seemed like the only definitive way to know if we had found you. I didn't think clearly the morning I called you—I came home after taking the kids to school and just walked directly to the phone and called. I had thought about it and thought about it until my head was spinning, and that morning I decided to stop thinking and make the call. I don't think I actually expected to get you—truthfully, I'm not sure what I expected. But I felt so honored to have spoken to you. Telling you who I was was like jumping off the high dive—just close your eyes, Hannah, and do it!

After Christmas Eve dinner at my parents' house, I lay on the couch in the library, digesting along with my meal these latest letters—mulling over the heightening pitch of this written conversation with my birth parents, contemplating what it meant to make a mistake and to be one.

1995

And the king said, Divide the living child in two,
and give half to the one, and half to the other.
Then spake the woman whose the living child
was unto the king,
for her bowels yearned upon her son, and she said,
O my lord, give her the living child,
and in no wise slay it . . .
Then the king answered and said, Give her the living child,
and in no wise slay it: she is the mother thereof.

—from I Kings 3
The Holy Bible, King James Version

18

Chimera

The Story of Solomon in the Old Testament tells of two harlots who came before the King, each claiming the baby living in their house to be her own. As a test, Solomon ordered that the child be cut in two with a sword, and that each woman be given half. The woman who protested unwittingly proved to Solomon that she was the true mother—the one who would selflessly do whatever was best for her child, even if it meant giving him up.

The ancient tale came to mind in 1995, as I absorbed the many cases in the news of birth parents and adoptive parents fighting for custody of children who were two, four, even seven years old. Articles and television specials abounded with stories of children like Baby Richard and Jill Bond, usually slanted in the adoptive parents' favor. The struggles between sets of parents seemed to devolve into battles of wills rather than acts of love. The children's best interests were rarely taken into account by the courts, either, which tended to base decisions on the arbitrary and potentially damaging assumption that a child is always better off with his or her biological parents—no matter who he or she was raised by from birth until the point of contention, how long that period of time was and how attached the child had become. What about the importance of the link to the "psychological parent," the one the child calls mother or father? Seeing the movie *Losing Isaiah,* about a boy caught between his black birth mother and white adoptive mother, and reading Jan Waldron's birth mother memoir, *Giving Away Simone,* I was struck by the sense of loss inherent in the titles. *Losing* Isaiah. *Giving Away* Simone. Understandable, but what about the liberating, opportunity-providing, caring experience that an adoptive family could offer a child—freeing Isaiah from living with a crack-addicted mother, or Simone from being raised by the frightened, unprepared seventeen-year-old girl who had given birth to her? And for the adoptive parents: having Isaiah, having Simone, having a child to love?

Because of my developing relationship with my own birth parents, I managed to see the grayness of the issue. I recalled Hannah's description of the way she and the other birth mothers had been treated in the hospital—"disdainful . . . like we were the scum of the earth, tramps"—and how unfair and illogical this sounded, considering that at that point I was still her child, not the hospital's, the court's, or my adoptive parents', yet. Watching the news or reading the paper, however, I was less sympathetic toward these other birth parents, grateful that my own situation, though confusing, was not dangerous like Richard's or Jill's. Hannah had never come for me, had never fought over me, despite her changing mind and senti-ments of regret. Waiting had been a selfless act for her and Adam, I realized—noticing my birthday go by unacknowledged each year, wondering how I was, who I was. I was gradually coming to appreciate a mother's impulse to know her child as an understandable, almost unavoidable, need.

I received a phone call at work one January afternoon:

"Sarah Saffian, I saw your byline in the *Daily News*. My name is Regina Saffian, and I'm calling to see if we're related." She had a slightly Jewish, New York accent, and said that her family was from Russia. She asked my father's and mother's names, and I told her, but she didn't know them. "Well, my name is Regina and my sister's name is Bea. Do these ring any bells?" They didn't. I was on deadline and had another call, so I asked her as politely as possible if she would mind calling back, but she never did.

Though I had rushed Regina off the phone, initially both-ered by her inquiry, I thought about it on and off for weeks afterward. Like "J—— Saffian" in the Birth Record at the library, her call served as a reminder that aside from all the dig-ging I was doing into my Leyder-Morgan roots, the family that was the closer one to me remained a partial mystery, as well. "Saffian" was an unusual enough name that Regina and I could have been related, somewhere, several generations back. In the building where I had spent my childhood, we'd had a down-stairs neighbor whose last name was "Safian," spelled with one "f" but pronounced the same. Out of a small handful of

Saffians and Safians living in New York, for two to find themselves a mere two floors apart had been a remarkable coincidence.

Every so often a new theory arose about the name Saffian. It
was not necessarily Jewish or Polish, even though that was Da Da
Fred's background. We knew that there existed a type of Russian
leather called *saffian leather*—made from goat or sheep skins
tanned with sumac and brightly dyed—which suggested that perhaps our forebears had been Russian leathersmiths, shoemakers.
But the word and type of leather were also sometimes attributed
to Turkey and Persia, and other times to Germany. Once, someone suggested that the name could be Sephardic, of Spanish-
Jewish or Portuguese-Jewish derivation. My father favored this
explanation for a while—even though his family hailed from
Ashkenazi Eastern Europe—probably because he likes romance-
language countries, and when he is traveling, often pretends that
he is a native. At times in my life, I, too, have luxuriated in the
freedom of the unknown—during college I went around saying
that I was an "honorary Armenian" because of the "ian" ending,
in order to link myself to my actually Armenian friend Vanni.
But the unknown also provokes a sense of untetheredness. I
began wishing that Regina would call back and even checked
information in all five boroughs, but there was no listing for her.

Another day, I took my watch to a little repair shop a couple
of blocks from the office. The store was owned by a kindly,
elderly, Jewish man, all thick glasses and knotted hands, who
stood stooped behind the counter, tinkering, chattering. At one
point, he looked up at me and asked with a smile, "Where did

you get those dimples, eh?" I just laughed softly, taking in the compliment, but not answering his question.

I was used to this sort of observation, had been confronted with it all my life, and usually responded in this way, demurely brushing it off. My father sometimes even played up our physical resemblances, ungrounded though they were. "She has broad shoulders, like her father," he would point out. Sometimes an announcement like this wasn't even for another's benefit, but just for our own: "Unfortunately, you have inherited the Saffian stomach," he would groan if I complained after a spicy meal or a stressful day. I had always been comforted by these comments, and didn't consider them a charade, knowing no other benefactor for my physique or delicate constitution. Since being contacted by my birth parents, though, the tie to my father hadn't slackened, but it had become less automatic. While I now knew that he couldn't have given me his actual shoulders, he could have given me his posture, his carriage, his gait, the way clothes hung on his frame, which mine happened to resemble. And these traits, whether inherited or acquired, were equally important.

But the old jeweler, not knowing my situation, repeated his question. "Where did you get your dimples, your mother or your father?"

"I don't know," I finally answered, truthfully.

I had a similar encounter a few weeks later, when meeting my father for lunch. As his company had recently moved, I had never been to these offices before. When Dad introduced me as his eldest daughter to the new receptionist, she was astonished. "You *are?* You don't look *anything* alike!" At first I thought she was simply making a joke, as she saucily followed up her exclamation with, "I mean, you're so good-looking, and he's . . ." We all chuckled, but then she persisted. "So, you must look more like your mother, then, hm?" I didn't know how to answer. I quickly catalogued my parents: If comparing me to Mom, I resembled Dad more. If comparing me to Nancy, I resembled her more. And if comparing me to Hannah, I not only resembled her more, but the physical comparison to my father became irrelevant, or at least shifted to a separate category. *Which* mother, I wanted to ask the receptionist?

I paused, and Dad swept in to respond, "She's just like me," encompassing personality as well as appearance. And in many ways he was right.

186

As I walked back to my office, lost in thought, a man called out to me in a condescendingly merry tone, "Smile!"—presuming that I had no reason to be contemplative, and that his single command could lift my spirits. Gum on the bottom of your shoe? Smile! Missed your bus? Smile! Got a call out of nowhere from your birth mother and lost your sense of self? Come on, smile, carefree girl! I scowled instead.

The next evening, after seeing a friend in a play, a group of us went out to a late supper. During a conversation about high school, I told an anecdote about Max. "How old is he?" one friend asked, to which I answered, "He's fifteen. He's in ninth grade at Riverdale."

Noting the large age difference, a woman in the group whom I'd never met before wondered, "Is he your half brother, or your whole brother?"

I pondered her question, as stumped by it as I had been by the receptionist's the day before. Max wasn't my "half brother," because we didn't actually share any blood. Yet we shared a father, as Dad was my whole father officially, and so Max wasn't my stepbrother, either. To answer completely would have required a great deal of background information. But then I considered the issue more simply, thinking that Max was my brother in every way, wholly, just as Mom was my mother and Rachel was my sister, wholly. My parents and siblings were my whole family, in the ways that mattered. And so I answered the woman—who had no idea what had gone through my mind during the seconds-long pause—as honestly and succinctly as possible: "Ah, it's complicated. But he's whole, in my heart."

❖ 19 ❖

Birthday

The night before my birthday, I was hurtling in a taxi down the F.D.R. Drive at eleven-thirty, coming home from my parents' house. All at once, the literal significance of a *birth day* hit me like an eighteen-wheeler. It was not just an occasion for a party and cake and jokes about getting older, but the anniversary of one's birth, a profound event. My thoughts turned to Hannah and Adam and all they had written and told me about my first few days, the joy in having me, the agony in giving me up. I thought of Hannah twenty-six years ago at that moment, three hours before giving birth to me. At Staten Island Hospital? In labor? Already put out?

It dawned on me that the influences from my various mothers were not mutually exclusive, that the realness of each woman's motherhood didn't diminish the realness of the others'. From Kathy, who was my mother by circumstance, I gained my sense of right and wrong, my organization, my discipline. From what I remembered of Nancy, my mother by adoption, and what my father and relatives and friends told me, I could see her emotional, intellectual, feminine nature in myself. And now that Hannah, my mother by birth, had reentered my life, I was exploring what I had inherited from her, discovering that perhaps there was more than merely bone structure and eye color between us.

Just as each of these three women had distinctly affected and continued to affect me, each had her own day. Mother's Day was reserved for Kathy, in that she was Mom, the person whom I immediately thought of as mother, my current and steadfast one. It was on December 26, the anniversary of her death, when I contemplated Nancy and all she had been, as a person in general, and as my mother in particular. And now I saw that my birthday, February 23, was Hannah's own personal mother's day, because at my birth, she was the only mother I'd had. She had spoken to me while she was pregnant with me. She'd had second thoughts about giving me up toward the end of her pregnancy. She had held me after I was born and felt pride when she looked at me through the nursery window. She had made the sacrifice of surrendering me so that I could have a stable family. She had thought of me in the years afterward, wondering how I was. She had sought me out to let me know she cared about me. And since contacting me, she had been consistently sensitive to my needs. Even though she had only been my mother actively for those few first days, she had mothered me from a distance all along. I began to cry quietly right there in the shadowy backseat of the cab, saying a little prayer to Hannah, thanking her.

20

Sea Changes

One afternoon in March, looking through the letters to and from Hannah and Adam over the past two years, I noticed a couple of things: nearly all of mine to them opened with an apology for not writing sooner, and I had only sent them seven letters in total. I hadn't written since November. Beginning a new letter, I examined on the page why I tended to take so long to respond, and was surprised by my frank self-exploration.

> *My attitude toward writing to you is similar to the attitude I had toward finding my birth parents, before you contacted me: whenever anyone asked if I'd thought about looking for them, I'd say, yes, I'd like to someday. I was sure that I would eventually want to find the people to whom I was genetically linked, but it was never urgent, mainly because there was no void that required filling—I was happy in the family and life that I already had. The concept of my birth*

parents was always a passing curiosity, a nebulous future encounter, never a distinct plan or a burning need to know.

Thinking about it now, though, maybe I didn't have that drive to find my birth parents and often don't have that drive to write to you in part because I don't want to admit that these things—being adopted, and also my mother dying, to which I have reacted similarly—have happened to me. It's a complete sense of apathy. I'm so unwilling to be affected by these events, that if I do choose to open up (and that in itself is a big step), I almost always feel removed, impassive.

I reflected that while I had been a sensitive and at times fragile child, I had managed to stave off full-blown insecurity about myself until college, a common time for self-esteem issues to crop up for anyone. Until then, there had been the usual mad dashes from the talons of the clique of popular girls. I had my share of afternoons coming home crying, either because Robin had lifted up my skirt on the playground (fittingly enough, she has since gone on to become a gynecologist), or Susy had accused me of having milk breath, or Amanda had teased me for trying to make a sleepover date with a girl who, in her opinion, was out of my league. But other than withstanding these run-of-the-mill social pressures that perhaps turn somewhat crueler at an all-girls' school, I rarely lost confidence in my own abilities. I knew that I had interests and goals, and I pursued them.

One day during the end of junior year of high school, as I was beginning the college application process, my adviser, who had somehow heard about my background, asked if she could include it in her recommendation to show how I had triumphed over adversity. I balked, nauseous at the idea, and told her absolutely not. It didn't cross my mind to base my college essays on these events, either, as I opted instead to write about acting and my brother. I didn't consider myself a "survivor," wearing my experiences on my sleeve like badges; I simply ignored them altogether.

Upon arriving at Brown, for the first time I couldn't seem to make academics my priority. I had come from a structured household atmosphere where I had trooped up to my third-floor room each evening to study for hours uninterrupted, where my mother had cut in on my phone conversations to tell me to get back to my homework, where I had proudly read essays to my attentive parents and had never been afraid to bring home the infrequent bad grade. Away at school, I was confronted with a freedom I had never known before, and I didn't know what to do with myself within it. Rather than embracing it willingly, I was getting swept up by the watery intangibility in spite of myself.

Though I still worked hard for my accomplishments, they were tinged with a new feeling of fraudulence, like I was getting away with something, pulling the wool over my judges' eyes. Observing other people—some older, some my peers—I found them more fully formed than I was. I wondered when I, too, would realize my potential, become the person I was destined to be, as I waited for my life to begin in earnest. By graduation, I had made my way back to land, but my body shivered and ached, my skin remained waterlogged and wrinkled, I tasted the salt on my tongue and felt the slimy seaweed in my hair for years afterward.

Hannah's 1993 phone call was the turning point, when the insecurity, the unresolved experiences, the unknowns still inside me began truly to emerge, and I was forced to deal with them fully, finally. "This is all related," I continued in my letter. "Our developing relationship, what you went through in giving me up and in searching for me, what I am going through in being found and in coming to terms with what has happened to me in my life."

I'm amazed by how much time has gone by since that first phone call, how long it is taking for my feelings to change and develop and grow— after two years I'm still hesitant, cautious and sometimes not willing to deal with it all. But even through the course of writing this letter I feel more trusting and closer to you. I'm starting to realize that I can't make the bogeymen under the bed go away by pretending they don't exist, because they still keep me awake at night. I don't have to indulge them, because then they'll never leave, but I can invite them out, get to know them, realize they're not so scary after all, and when we're done talking I can send them on their way.

"I identify with what you said about repression, Sarah, because I sometimes react to things with that kind of apathy," Hannah responded in early April.

I could have written that part of your letter myself, because it so closely describes me. I hate being the object of pity. I like to appear "okay." I have a lot of trouble opening up. I do not cry or show emotion in front of people. Sometimes I want to, even, but I just can't. I am so good at this repression that I, too, can feel nothing, as if I'm up high somewhere

193

and looking on as an observer. That is how I got through giving you up. I'm sure that experience magnified my tendency to shut down. I would like very much to feel connected to all that is deep down inside me about you. For a long time I was very afraid to look at that, and it is still scary to me, but now I am sure that it's a good and healing thing to do. The defenses are helpful, sometimes, in getting me through difficult times in my life, but I really do believe, at some point, the feelings need to be dealt with in order to feel real and whole.

Hannah was describing the person it had become increasingly difficult for me to be—someone in control, with her feelings in check. I seemed to be emerging as an emotional blend of my two birth parents. "All the things that have happened to me in my life, especially having you and giving you up, have formed the person I am and I like that person (most of the time)," she wrote. "It somehow makes me special, different, individual in some way." I strove for that place of contentment, for these elements to help define me, to clarify rather than obscure who I was.

About Lucy's recent *bat mitzvah*, Hannah wrote, "It all went beautifully and was an incredible experience, mixed with the intense sadness of my father's absence." Would I have had a *bat mitzvah*, and not exchanged Hebrew school for ballet class, had they kept me? I suddenly suspected that my recent impulse to take a Hebrew reading course had been prompted by getting to know the Leyders. And I thought again about Morris Morgan, my birth grandfather—that I would never meet him now, that time was limited.

I also mused on life's thresholds, landmarks in growing up— *bat mitzvahs*, graduations. Lucy's grandfather hadn't been there for

194

one of hers, and Hannah and Adam hadn't been there for any of mine. And for the first time in reference to my birth family, another threshold crossed my mind: marriage. By the time I got married, would I want them at my wedding? Would I feel obligated to invite them? While I assumed that they would want to come, I wondered how they would feel once there. And how would my parents and Max and Rachel feel? I could see Mom and Hannah simply as two people in the world, both strong women of the same age, finding common ground; but I could barely imagine Dad and Adam—fifteen years apart and emotional polar opposites—holding a conversation, unable as I was to separate them from the circumstance that linked them. How would *I* feel having both my families together?

In my previous letter, I had described one of my last memories of my mother Nancy. She was in the bathtub, and I remembered commenting that her skin had turned yellow and that she assured me, "Mommy is all right." Adam wrote that this image recalled his own mother, "propped up in bed in her darkened bedroom, drenched in sweat, weakly whispering to me."

But I have very few memories of her. My guardian Shirley once told me it was probably because my mother, being a "proud woman," didn't want me to see her looking bad. Perhaps it was also because of the tendency in those days to overprotect children from anything painful, cultivating denial, really. During her last months, I was for the most part kept away from her.

I had often felt unmoored in mourning my mother Nancy. I didn't ever visit her in the hospital, because children weren't allowed in hospitals in those days. After she died, when I asked my father what we would do now, he replied, "You're going to go back to school, and I'm going to go back to work." Her still-healthy organs were donated to patients in the hospital who needed them—I was always proud that my mother helped save other people's lives. The rest of her was cremated, and my father had her remains disposed of quickly and without cere-mony. There was no grave where she was buried, no hillside or seashore where her ashes were scattered, no specific place where I could go to be close to her. Even the funeral chapel where her memorial service was held no longer existed. My parents had wanted my life to be disrupted as little as possible by her ill-ness, and then my father wanted it to be disrupted as little as possible by her death. But the loss of a mother is inherently disruptive, whether that disruption takes place immediately or is put off until later, coming out in indirect ways in the mean-time. The mourning has to happen sometime and somehow.

"There was also the matter of figuring out where I would be placed after my mother died," Adam continued. "She had remarried, but her husband, my stepfather, showed no great affection for me. She considered her brother Don. There was another couple with a son, friends of hers in San Jose, whom I stayed with for a few weeks before she died, confused and not knowing what was going on. And there were the Smiths." Being adopted soon after birth rather than at age six, I'd never had to experience consciously the feeling of being completely orphaned, of being raised by people other than my parents. As far back as I could remember, my father had always been my parent, had been the first and only father I knew and had remained a constant through the loss of Nancy and the introduction of Kathy. There had never been any question that he would be there to take care of me. "When my mother died, I think I felt a sense of relief," wrote Adam.

The worst had happened, but the confusion was over. I think I felt guilty at this relief, like I was betraying her. I know in some way I felt responsible. One of the few memories I have of that time is finding a misplaced medicine case right after some adults had rushed my mother to the hospital, feeling distraught that I hadn't located it sooner for them and somehow saved the day. Jesus Christ, Sarah, my eyes are filling up with tears as I write this now.

Adam's outpouring of emotion moved me to the point of making me uncomfortable, self-conscious for both of us. He had put off reacting to what had happened to him as a child, as I had. He, too, had striven to achieve, "trying to please, but never asking myself what was truly important to me." As I was coming to know myself through coming to know him, I still guarded my experiences, not sure if I wanted to share them. But even in this hermetic impulse, Adam matched me. We were together in our very aloneness.

I remember walking around as a kid with my secret tragedies, and then as an adult, with the secret tragedy of you. It's always seemed to me a painful irony that I could feel alone, solitary, detached (and, in fact, strong for that), and yet at the same time feel the need to be perfect

197

in the eyes of some unnamed judge. This seems like the worst of both worlds: if I'm solitary, I'd just as soon dance to my own drummer, answer to no one; if I'm trying to be perfect or to please, I'd like to feel deeply connected to humanity.

I, too, felt both misanthropic and needy. I craved escape, at times guarding my solitude greedily, resenting any intrusion, not seeing why people had to interact at all. Lately, I would turn claustrophobic if people walked directly in front of me down the street, restricting my movement, or behind me, tailing me, as if they were attached to me by an invisible string and I were trying to shake them off. One afternoon, in a near-empty subway car, an elderly woman entered and chose to sit right next to me. Flabbergasted, I turned to look at her blankly and then moved across to the unoccupied facing bank of seats. There I rested elbows on knees, face in hands, shocked and ashamed by my own rudeness. Other times, I ached just as deeply for security, thinking existence without communication meaningless.

"As I talk about parallels in our lives, it's not to suggest that there is some cosmic significance to them (even if I might think that)," Adam continued. "It's to say that I think I can understand some of the things you are going through, and to help explain why I've felt such urgency in wanting you to be able to deal with all this. I'm not surprised at the pain you described. I regret it. I'm glad you're able to tell us about it."

I had asked the Leyders for their interpretations of "However, in my flake of sun, there is no one." Adam analyzed the phrase in his typically thorough, painstaking manner.

"However" implies that your situation is different from one(s) previously considered. You are different from someone, or everyone, else.

A "flake" is a tiny thing. How could you, or anyone, occupy a flake? Does it imply that you see your world, or yourself, as diminished? Or does everyone have their own flakes, tiny worlds? It's an intriguing word, with all sorts of connotations (flake of snow = bright and cold; flake of gold = precious, gold like the sun).

"Sun" implies a bright and warm place.

"Is" means right then at the time of the dream, presumably you seeing yourself at 9, not long after your mother died, not long after you found out you were adopted.

"No one" could mean you see yourself as alone, that there is no one with you in your world. This could be a sad and lonely image, but it could also be one of strength and self-sufficiency. "No one" could also imply that you don't even see yourself in your tiny warm world—that you have no image of yourself, that you don't know who you are.

199

I appreciated Adam's close reading, struck by the insight in his detailed analysis. But it overwhelmed me, too. After reading the letter over a few times I put it aside, exhausted by his effort.

The very next day, I was startled to find another letter in my mailbox, a half-page follow-up note from both of them.

Dear Sarah,   *April 6, 1995*

After we dropped the last envelope in the mail, we realized we hadn't said something very important and very simple: we're sorry for the pain we have caused you by giving you up for adoption.

You hadn't told us of your loneliness, insecurity and depression and your resentment toward those feelings until your last letter. Your feelings, of course, come as no surprise. Our grief and guilt for your pain is mixed in with relief and gratitude at your being able to express it. In the past, it seemed inappropriate to apologize for pain which you had not yet acknowledged. Now is the time. We accept your pain and anger and welcome your openness. And of course another selfish motivation in helping you in whatever way we can to heal the wounds we caused is to make ourselves feel better, to heal our own wounds of remorse, as well as loss.

It's hard not to sign this "with love."

Hannah and Adam.

200

I finally understood why an out-of-the-blue phone call from my birth mother had been so disruptive to my life and was causing me so much pain. Yes, I resented that my sense of family and self was thrown into flux by the intrusion. That had been the initial impact, like a stone thrown into a placid lake. But the ever-widening circles were the feelings I had never fully acknowledged that the phone call had tapped: namely, feelings about being abandoned by the woman who had given birth to me, and then being abandoned a second time by the woman who had adopted me. Before I knew who my birth parents were, I had never been angry at them for relinquishing me—rather, on the rare occasions when they had occurred to me, I had felt grateful. But I was realizing that my love for my family did not preclude the pain of being surrendered; I could still feel abandoned, even if the parents who adopted me were as good, or better, than my birth parents might have been. Perhaps Adam was right—that I should have been thanking them for calling me, enabling me to deal with the initial anger of having been given up.

21

Twins

I began noticing a pair of identical twins at the gym. They looked to be in their early thirties and had that "coltish" attractiveness for which Julia Roberts became famous: long-limbed, with brown eyes and manes of brown hair. They came regularly early in the morning, as I did, and worked out together, usually doing the StairMaster side by side in matching black leggings. I ran into one of them at a deli once and chatted with her, but the next day at the gym I was afraid to say hello, not knowing which one I had spoken to. From a distance, then, I revered their mystique. Remaining inconspicuous was a challenge, though, as I could hardly keep my eyes off of them.

The first twins I had ever encountered were Adele and Alicia, the bullying granddaughters of my nanny Mrs. Edsill. Ever since, twins had fascinated and terrified me, evoking a combination of envy and pity. I envied them because of their obvious physical connectedness, something that I had always only observed in others or experienced by coincidence. With their unmistakable relation to each other and often intimate relationship, twins had a bond that was hard to compete with. But this was also exactly why I pitied them, because their connection was too close. I saw no one who looked like me, and each twin saw someone who looked exactly like her—and yet, I realized that although our circumstances were opposite, we were confronted with a similar dilemma about identity. With an adoptee, the lack of blood relation could lead to a sense of detachment; with twins, I supposed, the inescapable blood relation could overshadow their individuality.

Ginna, my best friend during grade school, and her sister Mary Dixie, a year our junior, always dressed alike and had a relationship of twinlike closeness. One day, our class was allowed to wear play clothes because we were going on a field trip, but Mary Dixie's class, which was remaining at school, had to wear uniforms as usual. Respectful of the quandary that such a discrepancy would present to their mother, I wasn't surprised when Ginna appeared for the outing in her uniform. I strove to belong to this sameness. In the lunch line each afternoon, Ginna and I insisted on having identical meals, sometimes even arguing about what we would order rather than daring to differ. And unbeknownst to her until years later, I contrived an intricate system for dressing like her, and therefore, like her sister, as well. The green plaid tunic was required Monday through Thursday, but we could choose what to wear with it; and Friday was free dress day. I kept a chart in my school shirt drawer at home, on construction paper and written in my neatest script: whatever Ginna wore Monday (style of white blouse, color of tights or socks, type of sweater and hair ribbon), I wore Tuesday and so on throughout the week; whatever she wore Thursday I wore the following Monday; and whatever she wore Friday, I wore the following Friday, as well as I could approximate, supplementing my wardrobe with exact items—a pair of red corduroy overalls, a velour Izod pullover—whenever I could convince my father. When Melissa, Dad's girlfriend whom I didn't like, took me to Indian Walk to buy school shoes, lace-up Oxfords just like Ginna's, even the difference in color—hers red, mine blue— troubled me.

However as an adult, I had often been confronted with that question, "Has any one ever told you that you look exactly like . . . ?" Juliette Binoche. Matt Dillon. A fellow reporter in the *Daily News* office. Someone's best friend in high school. A friend of a friend at a wedding shower ("You two could be *sisters!*"). A harmless and common enough occurrence, but it always irritated me pointedly. As an adoptee, I considered resemblances carefully, unlike those people who sloppily insisted that I looked "exactly" like someone merely because I wore my hair the same way, for instance. Being compared to someone else made me feel invaded, and sometimes I resisted vehemently, thinking a person impertinent for telling me what I looked like, imposing an identity on me.

At other times, I yearned for the delectability of truly belonging. In 1995, Uncle Hal—my father's older brother— and Aunt Gertrude had their fiftieth wedding anniversary. Mom, Dad, Max, Rachel and I went to the celebration in

Pennsylvania, a huge family affair. Among other relatives present were my cousin Scott, in his early forties, his wife, Amanda, and their two young sons, Myles and Gavin. The afternoon turned into a whirlwind of conversations about resemblances. My father had always said that Scott looked just like he had as a young man. Max also looked just like Dad. Myles looked just like Scott. Max and I looked just alike. I wanted so badly for it to be true, for my physical similarity to the others to be based on genetics, too, not merely on chance. I had always prided myself on being a Saffian, and even that day I was an enthusiastic member of the clan. But now that I knew who my biological relations were, the gathering left me feeling like I had one foot out the door.

Over dinner one night, a fellow adoptee told me the story of a woman named Linda, who was frequently mistaken for someone called Georgette. Linda had always known she was adopted, but it wasn't until she was fifty years old and had done some detective work that she discovered she had an identical twin sister who had been adopted by another family. Just the mention of twins separated at birth riveted me. I had read about numerous studies of twins who had been raised under drastically different conditions—urban and rural, rich and poor, loved and shunned—but still turned out to have uncannily similar personalities, problems, even mannerisms and quirky habits.

Linda's potential reunion with her long-lost twin presented a double dose of both connection and identity loss. Connection, because for Linda, instead of merely recognizing a jawline here, an eyebrow there, seeing her birth sister truly would be like looking in the mirror. But her situation could also intensify feelings of identity loss, in going from one extreme to another, from no physical link to an identical physical link. Sensational as the story was already, it had a tragic ending: Linda searched for and found Georgette, only to discover that her twin had died six months earlier. I imagined that for any adoptee, but for a twin especially, unearthing a dead birth relative would be like having a part of oneself die, too. If the Leyders had died before we had come into contact, Susan Morgan would have died along with them.

In the articles that I read about twin studies, two facts in particular struck me: First, it had been determined recently that many more pregnancies began as two than doctors had previously thought (only a fraction of these were carried to term as twin infants; more often the weaker twin was flushed out at some point long before birth). Second, left-handedness was more common among twins than singletons. All at once, I concocted a fantasy that I had originally been a twin in the womb. I knew that it was unlikely, that my left-handedness was probably no more than an inherited trait, considering that Hannah, Lucy and Sam were all southpaws, too. Research showed that the tendency toward twins was partially genetic, and neither the Morgans nor the Leyders had a history of twins running in the family. Also, a woman's chances of conceiving twins increased with age, and Hannah had been only twenty-one when she became pregnant with me. Still, I was moved when I read that singletons who had once been twins in the womb experienced the same feelings of loss throughout their lives, even when unaware of having been twins, as twins who were knowingly separated from each other or whose other halves had died. The sense of isolation that an erstwhile twin felt sounded similar to that of an adoptee—in both cases, a primary bond had been severed.

My fixation on twins was borne out of my ongoing struggle between gaining the structure of knowledge and maintaining the fluidity of mystery. Was I putting off meeting the Leyders because I was resisting making the link to my birth family official? Because I wanted to maintain the autonomy of my adoptee-hood a bit longer? Because I feared that rather than the bond helping me to know myself better, it would prove so close that I wouldn't be able to distinguish myself from it?

22

Finding Faith

Though Chris continued to offer insights and encouragement—to write to Hannah and Adam, to think and talk about how I felt, to work toward feeling ready to meet them—I began shopping around for a therapist. The hunt was challenging, in that I had to rely on gut instinct but didn't want to launch into a relationship with someone—as I had with the psychiatrist a year earlier—only to realize after several months that it wasn't working out.

I was happily surprised by my unwavering knack for screening someone after a mere forty-five minute consultation. I had even efficiently boiled down my answer to the perpetual question, "Why are you here?" into a two-tiered sound bite: 1. the significant things that had happened to me in my life, which I rattled off in a list (adoption, mother's death, abortion, birth parents calling out of the blue), and 2. how I was feeling now (depressed, insecure, identity-less). One therapist wore garish green eye makeup and mentioned more than once that she had to finish on time because she was going to the opera that evening. Another had a thin and slightly whiny voice, which didn't bother me much at that first meeting, but which I could tell would become grating. Yet another's modus operandi was to be the dreaded passive, sympathetic ear: "Well, of *course* you would feel that way after *that* happened."

There was one last person on my list—Faith. From our first conversation, over the phone one evening in May, I could tell that we clicked. She was matter-of-fact, solution-oriented, offered understanding without pity. "Sure, it's important to explore your past to try to decipher the reasons for why you feel the way you do. But our first goal is to figure out how you can feel better in the present." She reminded me a bit of my mother Kathy, which was unexpected considering that Mom hailed from the stiff-upper-lip, haven't-got-time-for-the-pain school of thought. I took this as a sign that Faith was the therapist I had been looking for, even though I hadn't known exactly whom I was looking for until I spoke with her.

A week after our phone call, I went to my first appointment, one evening after work. Faith's building had that same lonely smell of all old New York City apartment buildings in the late spring—slightly musty, like books neglected in a damp, dusty corner, slightly of something cooking, like broth simmering on an old woman's stove. Faith's door was ajar, as she had said it would be, and opened into a small anteroom with the standard chair, rack crammed with out-of-date magazines and wooden pegs for coats—bare today, because of the warm weather. The

209

walls were painted the color a grandmother might refer to as "dusty rose." It was quiet, building and traffic sounds muted. I sat and waited, staring at the molding on the wall in front of me. Then I heard a door open, and out stepped Faith. She was tall and slim, like Mom, and had strawlike blond hair, keen eyes behind glasses, a kind, tired smile, a calm, sensible air. She greeted me and led me into her office, another small room, with two armchairs facing each other, a desk, bookshelves.

During this first session, I told Faith everything I could think of that was possibly relevant, prompted by her probing questions. As we spoke, I hastened to find explanations and draw conclusions, characteristically taking notes all the while:

1. Finding out that I was adopted when I was seven and receiving Hannah's call when I was twenty-three were both occurrences that could potentially shake my sense of identity, because they changed my idea of reality.

2. Surprises are a basis for insecurity. The way to gain security is to search out the pieces of what is unknown—my mother Nancy, my birth parents. I have to understand them better before I can put the pain of losing them behind me.

3. At what place do things affect me emotionally? A six-year-old place of Nancy's death? A seven-year-old place of finding out I was adopted? I lost my mother twice.

Faith paused, I continued to scribble. When I noticed that she had stopped speaking, I looked up. Our eyes met, and she smiled and resumed.

4. Everything I feel in the present is matched to things that happened to me around ages six and seven. Reactions now can be different: feeling emotions that I didn't let myself feel then, belatedly mourning.

5. My functioning outer facade served to protect me as a child and has had the positive effect of helping me accomplish much. But it ultimately hinders my ability to deal fully with these unresolved feelings.

Many months later, I would sit in Faith's office empty-handed, talking and listening. At one point, she commented, "Do you realize that you haven't written a single word this entire session?" I hadn't realized, but now that she mentioned it, I felt liberated. She then explained that while jotting something down now and again was normal, my former habit of assiduous note-taking had been a sign to her of my need for control in my life in general. "It helped me to figure out what you were all about," she said. "Control was a huge issue for you."

Indeed, after our first meeting, I left Faith's office with a sense of purpose. Doing something active about my problems lent them boundaries—they didn't have to bleed into every aspect of my life. And I was relieved to be paying a trained professional to help me, rather than constantly burdening Chris. I plunged into therapy with determination, planning what I wanted to discuss in advance of our appointments, listening carefully, doing anything I could to assist Faith in helping me help myself.

It turned out that I had signed on with Faith not a moment too soon, because with the balmy breezes of June came a new blow, a new abandonment: after much deliberation and a visit to Los Angeles, Chris, my primary support and confidant, decided that he was going to move to California in the fall to enroll in film school. I knew that he had applied to some programs outside New York, but I had never seriously imagined that he would actually go to one. After talking about his impending departure over a weekend, I finally broke down. "It's not fair," I sobbed, simultaneously resenting him for leaving me and blaming myself for his decision. After this outburst, though, I settled into a numbness, the idea of his absence unreal.

Resurrection

"Oh, Sarah," Hannah's June 15 letter began. "The only way out is through." Mostly, it was reassuring to learn that she had reacted similarly to me to experiences in her own life. But out of the corner of my eye, I cynically glimpsed the irony that the person who arguably had caused my problems was now parceling out advice on how to solve them. Or perhaps it wasn't ironic, I reasoned, in that she was trying to help heal the pain for which she considered herself responsible.

Prompted by questions in my May letter regarding her ambivalence about giving me up, Hannah's story emerged, like layers of a palimpsest, gaining depth, dimension and shape in its retelling.

I think it was hiding out in the Bronx apartment that I fell in love with Adam and the pregnancy and the baby. But then I started feeling like I couldn't imagine going through with the plan. I tentatively brought it up with Adam, who said he couldn't go back to the way he had felt in the beginning, after I had taken it away from him. I was afraid to push, thinking, what right do I have, after the way I acted initially? I never told my parents I was having second thoughts, and I don't remember my conversations with my therapist. I was scared to say anything after the mess I'd made. Everyone was expecting me to go through with it. It seemed like it was out of my hands.

Adam went back to New Hampshire three weeks after you were born, before I'd signed the relinquishment papers. I resented him for leaving, feeling that he was the only support, the only ally I had. But he needed to get away from the city and all the pain. We saw each other every few weeks, but we were both seeing other people, too, and not talking about it. I think I was trying to find that nice Jewish professional that my parents wanted for me. And how could I end up with Adam after what I'd done? But I couldn't let him go, either.

I was surrounded by people who knew nothing about what had happened to me. When I went to visit Adam it was worse, because I met two women in Durham who had become pregnant and kept their babies, one who had gotten married and one who was raising him herself. Everyone talked about how strong they were, and no one knew about me, and I thought Adam was tired of hearing me talk about it. But I was extremely jealous of them and thought that I had made a terrible mistake. At other times over the years, I have felt confident that I did the right thing.

I had also asked for more details on their reaction to Renee's birth, wondering, "Did you contrast it with how you had felt when I was born?"

Of course the doctor had to know I'd been pregnant before. It was such a relief to tell someone the truth—fun, really. But lots of other people asked, and I would say it was my first. Friends had all kinds of advice and sometimes that irritated me. I wanted to share the whole story with everyone, and was saddened and frustrated that I couldn't. As much as I reveled in the pregnancy, there I was, lying and hiding again.

But when Renee was born, I felt I had been given a second chance. It was almost too much to believe that a baby was born, a girl, and I got to take her home. Maybe everyone feels that way, but it seemed so much more of a miracle for me. I remember going to the grocery store with her those first few months and looking down at her, and I couldn't believe she was really mine. Adam and I were overprotective. We had a hard time leaving her, except with each other. Maybe as many times as I can count on one hand we left her with friends or with my parents when we visited them. We did not worry about her physical safety, but about her psychological, emotional well-being. I realize right this second that I worried about her thinking I had abandoned her. Oh my God—that's what it was about.

In his letter, Adam wrote that when Renee was born he "felt an unfamiliar connection to the human race. I had a blood relation. It took me out of myself. I remember driving home alone the first night from the hospital at three A.M. very slowly and carefully, almost fearfully, because there was someone I had to be alive for other than myself."

215

A week later, Chris and I would go to dinner with a friend of his whom he wanted me to meet. Cory, a thirtysomething from North Carolina, had also been adopted. We sat at a secluded corner table in the back room of a new little place on Elizabeth Street. After fueling ourselves with small talk, wine and bread dipped in olive oil, Cory and I began to swap stories as Chris listened, occasionally asking us questions.

Cory's beginnings had been more homestyle than my agency-mediated transfer. "The doctor who delivered me was also the one who arranged the adoption, and he lived next door to my family when I was growing up," he said evenly, his naturally bulging eyes and hollow-cheeked face betraying no emotion. "He knows all about my birth parents, but he won't answer any of my questions, thinking it best to leave well enough alone." The last time Cory had been in North Carolina, he had done some poking around on his own and uncovered the last name of either his birth mother or birth father. But he had not yet drummed up the courage to track them down. "Part of me is afraid of what I'll find, that it'll be anti-climactic or traumatizing," he explained. "Part of me doesn't want to end the mystery." Cory said that his older brother was the biological child of his adoptive parents. "He and I have never gotten along, but I don't know if that's the reason." I realized how fortunate and perhaps unique it was that there wasn't antagonism between my siblings and me. If I had ever felt different or excluded, envious of Max and Rachel's close relationship, it had been more because I was so much older than because I'd been adopted.

What was particularly interesting was that Cory was gay, and said he had always assumed that he would never have children. But the previous year, a single woman friend of his who wanted to have a child had asked Cory to inseminate her. She had become pregnant, but ended up having a miscarriage. The woman, understandably shaken and in her forties, was now ambivalent. But Cory was eager to try again. What had begun as a favor to a friend had prompted a significant shift in his own perspective: for the first time, like Adam with Renee, he seriously considered the notion of knowing a blood relative. His eagerness to father a child despite his trepidation about finding his birth parents made perfect sense to me: in giving life, he could gain a sense of connection while maintaining a sense of self-determination, because rather than being about uncovering the past, the act would be about creating the future.

The conversation made me consider my own increasing desire to have children. I had grown up around them—baby-sitting, teaching, older-sistering—and had always known that I wanted to have my own—to conceive, to be pregnant for nine months, to give birth, to see myself in them. As Chris and Cory moved on to chat about other subjects, I gazed through the French doors at the restaurant's garden and imagined that when I eventually had a child myself, I would feel what Hannah had felt with Renee—that happy disbelief.

217

Reading Hannah and Adam's letters, I was saddened at first that my birth had caused them so much sorrow and Renee's had brought them so much joy. But then I remembered that just as they had been especially grateful when Renee was born, having given away their first child, my father and mother Nancy, who had been unable to conceive, had been especially grateful when I came along.

"I don't think it's at all unusual for tragedies to cause breakups," continued Hannah. "In our case, though, it brought us closer." Adam agreed. "The closeness we felt from having shared this tragedy connected us." Maybe they wouldn't have gotten married and had three other children if it hadn't been for me. Adam may have ended up as just one of the guys Hannah had dated back in her college days, nothing more. Indirectly, I had been a source of joy as well as sadness for my birth parents, or at least a catalyst for their eventual joy.

Hannah wrote that she and Adam, the only birth parents in their area who had ended up married with other children, had recently participated in a panel discussion organized by her support group. "I imagined you in the audience and found myself wondering what you would think of us." Indeed, I would have liked to be there—but as a fly on the wall, observer only. As Hannah had yearned for a window into my life while I was growing up, I, too, wished I could glimpse them occasionally, but without having to reveal myself.

Everyone at the panel discussion—mostly adoptive parents—had been kind and sympathetic, choosing their words carefully so as not to offend. She and Adam hadn't prepared a speech, but had worked on the questions beforehand, deciding who would answer which ones. "It was gratifying to help people gain understanding and lose fear," wrote Adam. "It felt good to give something back." They learned from the adoptive parents present that when they had adopted their children in the 1960s, they had been told by the agencies that if they did their job well, their children would never need to know about their birth parents. "So, in fact, they would feel like they were failing if their children did ask," Hannah added. I wondered whether Louise Wise had told this to my father and mother Nancy, and whether my father ever felt that he had failed when I brought up the subject of my origins. I didn't think so, because it was plain to both of us what a good father he was, but perhaps he couldn't see as clearly as I could that my curiosity about my birth parents and my love for him did not have to be at odds. A contrasting story was told by an adoptive mother, who had so strongly encouraged her children to search for their birth parents that they started to feel that perhaps she didn't want them. As I had suspected, the threat worked in both directions.

219

"It is logical that our finding you would be confusing and painful, and it is such hard work, but to get to the point that we have gotten to seems so good," Hannah concluded. "You will not be abandoned again by us, Sarah. We are here to stay." How much more comforting this "We are here to stay" was than the "We are . . . not going to go away" of Hannah's very first letter, which I had read as menacing. The wording of the two phrases was virtually the same, as was the sentiment behind them. After two and a half years of corresponding, contemplating, exploring, I was the one who had changed.

"Sarah, finding you, talking to you, seeing your pictures, writing to you and reading your letters, has been astonishing, like a rebirth, or really a resurrection," Adam wrote at the end of his letter. "You were and are so terribly important. You were gone, and gone so long."

Who was being reborn, resurrected? Was I, were they, were we all?

❖ 24 ❖

Transition

One weekend afternoon at the end of July, I came across the piece of notepaper on which I had jotted information during my phone call with Hannah. The words had not registered when I wrote them down; even as I looked at my own handwriting, I could barely remember holding pen in hand. I read snippets about people who had been skeletons then—"Hannah Morgan, Adam Leyder," "Hanover," "U OF NH," "21 yrs.," "5 lbs.," "Renee, Lucy, Samuel," "Susan Morgan"—and marveled at how they had fleshed out since.

Another word on the piece of paper was "Moonstruck," the store in New York that sold Hannah's pottery. I was surprised that going there to see her work hadn't occurred to me before, and decided to walk over to Sixth Avenue right then. Coming upon the store, though, I was quickly disappointed, as I saw no one and nothing inside, save a few empty shelves and debris on the floor, and a sign from the owner in the window that read:

"After twenty-six years of business, we finally had to close up shop. Best of luck to all the dedicated, creative minds who contributed the fruits of their labor, and thank you to all the loyal customers. Ted Moon." My focus of concern continued to shift from the Saffians disappearing if I proceeded, to the Leyders disappearing if I didn't—where I had previously seen the bridge disintegrating behind me with each step across that I took, I now saw it crumbling in front of me, and if I didn't walk faster, I would never make it to the other side.

Chris left on Labor Day. I went to his parents' house in New Jersey to help him pack that weekend, and accompanied him to Kennedy Airport very early Monday morning. I escorted him to the security check-in, the farthest I was permitted to go. After we hugged and kissed—me weepily, him apologetically—I watched him walk through the metal detector and collect his carry-on bags from the conveyor belt. With a "Here goes!" shrug of his shoulders, a nervous smile and a wave, he was gone.

When I came back into the city from the airport, I got my hair cut and cleaned my apartment, and over the following weeks, I began to talk seriously with Faith about my increasing readiness to meet my birth parents. I had always automatically envisioned that Chris would go with me to Hanover. The sudden introduction of Hannah and Adam had come to define my interaction with Chris; the two relationships had developed simultaneously, symbiotically. How could I make the trip without him?

But one hot afternoon, with the air conditioner whirring and the window curtain billowing in Faith's little office, it occurred to me that I could, and should, go to Hanover alone. Chris was going to film school—that was his adventure. Meeting my birth parents would be my adventure. I could come back and tell him all about it, but it was my own journey. Once I had digested this new idea, I couldn't see it happening any other way. I would go to Hanover alone.

❦⬱⬰❦

Sitting next to a woman on the bus after work one Friday in September, I imagined her speaking to me, and me answering her in an accent. When I was a teenager and even into my early twenties, for fun sometimes while shopping or doing errands I would assume a foreign accent—British, Spanish, Italian. In that moment I could make up who I was. It was fitting that I was attracted to acting and journalism, professions in which I could lose myself: in the former, I could recreate myself with each role; in the latter, I could hide behind the position of observer, focusing on someone else. I enjoyed putting on and taking off identities like so much clothing. With childlike glee, I hoped that this woman next to me would ask a question—what time was it, where was the next stop—looking forward to playing my old game. But then I realized that I couldn't play, because a man sitting in front of us had already heard me talking with a friend in my normal voice before getting on the bus. All at once, I felt confined, resenting the fact that I couldn't be whomever I wished.

That autumn evening I was on my way to see a psychic in the West Village. Chris had gone to him once, right before graduation, a different sort of watershed. I considered myself an open-minded cynic—that is, I was skeptical and couldn't be taken in by any old charlatan with a crystal ball and a pack of tarot cards, but I was also willing to believe in clairvoyance, if it was presented convincingly. And Drake was nothing if not convincing. A flamboyant gay man stationed in an upstairs room in an overly decorated duplex apartment, he charged forty-five dollars for an appointment, which one had to schedule weeks in advance by calling a certain phone number between certain hours on a certain day of the week. I had been anticipating our meeting for a month, not counting on any definitive answers, but just seeking some other-worldly guidance in this period of transition.

I sat across the table from Drake, and his black eyes bored into my green ones, as though he were scrutinizing my very soul. When he asked my mother's name and I answered Kathy, he looked baffled. "*Kathy?*" he whined, annoyed. I nodded, wondering where this would lead. On a little pad of paper, he had written the name "Hannah." I gasped, then recovered and explained. He guessed that Adam was an architect and Hannah was a teacher. It was true that Hannah taught pottery classes, but Mom was a teacher, too—perhaps the image of "mother" was coming to Drake as a combination of the two of them. He told me that I would meet the Leyders, and that I would have an ongoing relationship with them, not just a single reunion. He also knew about my mother Nancy, saying that she was destined to have a profound effect on my life. Aware that I had already had one pregnancy, he predicted that I would have three more. Like Hannah, I thought.

A few nights later, I asked my father to dinner. I carefully selected a corner table at a neighborhood bistro, and sat gulping my ice water and smoothing the white linen napkin on my lap as I waited for him to arrive. Nervousness was a feeling I rarely associated with my father—he was the one who put me at ease, who understood me. Chip off the old block. Peas in a pod. But when it came to the Leyders, I felt a protective shell surround him. Sitting there, it dawned on me that perhaps my concern for his feelings was a factor in my reluctance toward a reunion. I had never thought so before, having my own reasons to be hesitant. But maybe I partially absorbed his feelings myself.

The instant Dad arrived, with an easy smile and a wave, the corner of a red silk handkerchief flaming from his blazer's breast pocket, my anxiety subsided. He leaned over to brush my cheek with a kiss, sat down, sipped his ice water thirstily. We chatted on various topics as we ate—work, the family, fall plans. Then I began to speak, haltingly at first, about Hannah's and Adam's phone calls and what they had stirred up in me. My father knew that I had been having a hard time and was seeing a therapist about it, but he wasn't aware of the depth of my despair—Chris alone had come close to seeing it completely—and even now, I glossed over my two-plus years of depression, showing him only glimpses. Never a believer in therapy, at least for himself, he reasoned aloud, "Sure, we've gone through some rough patches, but we've come out of them okay and are basically happy people. So why rock the boat?"

"If you're happy, true, why create problems?" I agreed. "But I've been basically unhappy, actually, and the only way I can move on is by facing these things. Because they're not going to go away by my ignoring them."

Arranging breadcrumbs on the tablecloth into little triangular piles with a flat index finger, I segued into my developing relationship with the Leyders. "Corresponding has been the perfect way to get to know them gradually," I said, "and to reveal myself at my own pace." I asked how he really felt about their resurfacing, whether he was threatened by it.

"No," he answered, head tilted and eyebrows raised casually, stirring his martini. "I completely respect your pursuit of them, but I'm also perfectly happy not to be involved in it." I told him of my thoughts about visiting them, and asked how he felt about that. "I think you're right, that it would be cathartic for you, that it would help you to deal with all you've been going through lately." I explained why I felt more comfortable going to them, rather than having them come here, and that now with Chris gone, I realized going alone felt right, after all.

Then my father said something that startled me: "I'll go up to Hanover with you, if you'd like me to." I was aware that it was probably the last thing he would want to do, even as I was also aware that he would indeed accompany me, if I asked. In my mind, I stood by my conviction that taking the journey alone was the only way, that I would not be acting only out of deference for my father's feelings in letting him stay home. But the fact that he offered, even though I had no intention of taking him up on it, gave me the confidence I needed to go.

25

Balance

I wanted Hannah and Adam to write back before I introduced the idea of a reunion. When I hadn't heard from them in a couple of months, I sent a short note, as a reminder:

Dear Hannah and Adam   *September 14, 1995*
 I haven't heard from you in a while, so I just wanted to check in. I figured you were probably away during August, and then busy with getting back to school and all (Happy Autumn). But is everything okay? Please write back when you can. Hope all is well.

       Sarah.

Hannah answered promptly, but, disappointingly, only in short note form, as well. "I am planning to sit down and respond thoughtfully to all that you wrote, but in the meantime I wanted to get this note off to you quickly and let you know all is well and we're thinking of you." She apologized for the delay, explaining that the summer had been busy. Most significantly, Benjamin, the son of Hannah's brother Stewart and his wife Stacey, had been born. The idea of another relative to meet, of my first birth cousin, afforded a sense of expansiveness. My restlessness escalated.

A week later, I received an envelope from Hanover, but my excitement was checked when I opened it to find a letter from Adam only. Despite the length and various topics of the letter—answering questions I had asked back in July, updating me on their day-to-day lives, asking about mine—what came across most strongly was his continued urgency. But rather than his eagerness having an encouraging effect—considering that I, too, was now eager to move the relationship along, finally—it only succeeded in making me feel pressured all over again. Though he apologized from the outset if he was coming on too strong, his persistence called upon me nonetheless, as if sentence after sentence were a discordant descant, piercing out over the blended melody of the rest:

> . . . *I'm a bit frustrated, because I'd so much like to be talking with you.*
>
> . . . *It's so sad that there are things holding you back from knowing us more, calling us, arranging a reunion. We are here.*
>
> . . . *You long for the connectedness of seeing yourself in someone, yet you delay seeing us.*
>
> . . . *There seems to be so much waiting going on.*

. . . You wrote once that "Having a child out there in the world who was a stranger would eat away at me." Yes, it would. It did for us all those years, and to the extent that distance remains between us, it still does.

. . . We will do anything to facilitate a reunion, to make it easier or possible for you. We just want it to happen, and as soon as possible.

. . . As Hannah was writing her last card to you, she said, "God, I wish I could just call Sarah up." I said, "I wish she could just call us up."

I felt like screaming, "I *am* ready!" But just as back in January 1993, when Adam had beaten me to the punch, calling me before I'd had the chance to decide to call him, now he wasn't letting me come to them with the proposal of a reunion. The most I could offer was for my fortress to surrender at last to his constant sieges. I was frustrated with my reaction, finding it regressive. And as ever, I worried that my volatile responses would have a negative impact on our relationship, that I was sabotaging the very thing that I had been trying to be so careful about all along.

One of the questions I had asked was the name and number of the searcher who had found me, hoping to "add some more pieces to the puzzle." Adam answered, explaining that in January 1993, he had made a follow-up call to a man at one of the adoption networks he and Hannah had joined. The man had given him the number of a woman, who in turn had given him the number of a searcher in New York. Adam had called the searcher and told him all that he and Hannah knew about me. A mere ten days later, the man had called back with information from my adoptive birth certificate, including my mother Nancy's and my father's names, and from my driver's license, which had my father's current address.

We too were "curious about how he obtained the information" on you, but he was reticent to tell us. Shortly after we dealt with him, we heard that because several people in another state doing the same sort of research had gotten into trouble and were caught in the middle of the legal/political battle over changing the adoption laws, he had stopped providing this service.

Because you asked, I called him. I identified myself and explained the situation. He remembered me and was very nice. He asked me please not to give you his name. He said he did not want to discuss with me, you or anyone what his methods were. He described them as "underground," and said they had to be protected.

It made me sad when you said, "It would be really helpful for me to talk with him and add some more pieces to the puzzle." After we first found you, we used to assemble "pieces of the puzzle," or hang onto precious scraps of information——things like your listing in the New York City Birth Book, your altered birth certificate, the Brown yearbook, your News *articles, even the MCI bill listing our phone conversations——but because we had no alternative. Since then, your letters and pictures have been wonderful, of course. At this point for us these things must suffice, because we honor your request not to talk to you or see you. But you don't have any such restrictions. No offense, but this man, this searcher, is not a piece of the puzzle. We are the pieces of*

the puzzle. To think you need to talk with him seems like makework,
like avoiding the issue. Data on you and anyone exists out there at
places like the hospital, the Health Department, the library, the
Department of Motor Vehicles, and somehow, through humans or com-
puters, he was able to access the information. Who cares how? He did it,
and we've found each other, and that's what's important.

I was shocked and angered that Adam was apparently hurt by
my request, and that he could summarily deny me this curiosity
about how I was located—particularly considering his own
meticulous attention to detail and his own hesitancy in meeting
his biological relatives. My identity was not simply a matter of
"Sarah Saffian" or "Susan Morgan," but was wrapped up in a
complex paper trail: were who-I-thought-I-was and who-I-was-
documented-as-being the same person? Couldn't Adam understand that if I felt out of control by being found, gaining insight
on how that had been accomplished might be useful to me?

To his credit, Adam was, as before, remarkably realistic
about our potential encounter, not idealizing it into something
unattainable: "I don't have any delusions that all of us meeting
and knowing one another will make everything perfect, for any
of us." I knew that adoptees commonly built up their birth parents in their imaginations, only to be let down by the reality of
them; but as I hadn't had a distinct picture of who mine might
be, Hannah and Adam weren't facing the challenge of compet-
ing against some preexisting model. As I developed a sense of
them through their letters, I felt grateful that they were who
they were, in spite of these tensions and personality clashes—

fundamentally, we seemed to understand one another, to speak the same language.

Referring back to the few times when I had written that Renee sounded similar to me in temperament, Adam made the interesting point that she and I had both been raised as first children. I wondered how she felt now, knowing that she had an older sister of sorts, for the first time. Did I preempt her first-born status? Or did she welcome the introduction into her life of someone she might one day look up to?

In my last letter, I had told about dinner with Chris and his adoptee friend. Adam's response to Cory's reluctance to track down his birth parents was unsurprising: "It's sad he's thirty-four and still waiting." Then he allowed: "But it will take courage. So much is unknown, and there are things to fear: rejection, dead or messed-up birth parents. Anticipating these fears on your part was a big reason why we searched for you." How much gentler and more reasonable this sounded than what Adam had said in his very first letter: "We took away your search." But as with my evolving reactions to Hannah's statements, it was not the sentiments that had softened, but my reception of them.

"I've been in Manhattan probably half a dozen times since January 1993," Adam wrote, musing on the close calls we'd had over the years.

The couple of times I walked from Port Authority to a friend's office across from St. Patrick's Cathedral, I headed uptown from 42nd St. before I got too far east to stay as far away as possible from the Daily

News *building. I'm always terrified of running into you on the street
even as my eyes search every face as I walk. We were all down there in
April and we took the subway between Hannah's brother's apartment
and Battery Park to go out to the Statue of Liberty. At every stop when
the doors opened, my heart started pounding, envisioning you stepping
onto the train. It would be wonderful to see you, but it would be terrible to take away your control of the reunion and to have you feel that
your space was being invaded. A couple of times when I was going
down to Manhattan, I thought of writing you to say like, on August
15 I'll be on the steps of the Public Library from 12–12:30 if you
want to say hello or look or send a friend or whatever, to make it easier
to make contact.*

As usual, Adam's description of his emotions—"terrified,"
"heart . . . pounding"—struck me as extreme, until it occurred
to me that had I some other reason to be in Hanover—report-
ing a story, visiting a friend—I would have the Leyders on my
mind the entire time and search every face I passed, too. While
I was relieved that we hadn't actually run into each other during
their forays to New York City, I let myself imagine what entering their subway car would have been like, that day on their way
to see the Statue of Liberty.

The doors open and I step on, alone, headed downtown
to meet my parents (*"Hey, Dad, guess who I ran into on the
subway . . . !"*). I grasp the cool metal bar overhead in time to
steady myself for the train's lurch forward, check my hair in the
scratched window's reflection, absently scan the other faces. At
the other end of the car, sitting in a row, I notice the five of

233

them—Hannah and Adam at either end, Sam in the middle. At first I take them in indifferently, as an attractive, close-knit family. Hannah and Renee are discussing something, the daughter making her point in clipped tones. Lucy and Sam are taking turns at a handheld video game, Sam occasionally letting out giggles in spurts. From time to time Adam asks Hannah a question or tells Sam not to squirm so much in his seat, but mainly he stares ahead, shrouded in a cloud of thought. Just at the moment when their identities register, Hannah and Adam look up and my extended gaze pulls their attention toward me. I walk over to them.

Then the fantasy stopped. I couldn't see what happened next.

The most crucial point in Adam's letter was when he confessed for the first time that his desire for a reunion was for his own sake as well as for mine, with four simple words: "I need much healing." I appreciated his honest vulnerability when he admitted to "projecting my own tendencies onto you, worrying that you'll do things that I did which I regret. Like waiting to get on with things. Like thinking, 'when x, y and z happen, then my life will really begin.' And years can go by with that state of mind, life flying by." Acknowledging his own intentions and needs actually seemed more generous than his previous tactic of presuming what was best for me. His description of himself as an "advancer" had been ironic, because each of his steps forward had unfailingly impelled me to retreat instead. In this moment, I realized what I had resented most was that Adam hadn't trusted me to deal with the situation in my own way and at my own pace and to come to them in my own time, that he believed if he didn't "advance" the situation I would slip through their fingers again.

"We have this big maple tree in our backyard," Adam concluded—an invitation, a foreshadowing. "I look at the tree and think, gee I hope Sarah comes up soon before the leaves fall so the place will look nice. Then I remember that I've stood in the backyard thinking this same thought each of the past three years."

Two weeks into November, just as the air was turning colder and the darkness was coming earlier in the evenings, I received Hannah's letter. I grabbed it from the mailbox, but made myself wait until I was up in my apartment—bag on floor, coat draped over back of chair, seated—to open it at last.

Their life had continued in the interim. Sam was now in fourth grade and had begun Hebrew school, inspired by Lucy's *bat mitzvah*. She was in the midst of her first semester at the larger, more traditional school in town, doing a lot of socializing, and had finished her fall season of soccer. Renee was concluding her cross-country season, sometimes running first for the team, and had just sent her early decision application to Williams. I felt a new sisterly impulse to wish her luck, cheer her on, feeling both older enough to offer guidance and close enough in age to commiserate. I was also amazed by how time had flown, just as I had been when Max, whose diapers I had changed, gradually grew taller than I was, or Rachel, whom I had bottle-fed in the rocking chair, started asking to borrow my clothes. When Hannah first called me, Renee had been fourteen, Lucy ten and Sam six. Names with ages attached to them, written on a piece of notepaper.

"I identify deeply with your strong feelings about having your own children," Hannah wrote. "I remember feeling desperate to have time pass and be having a baby I could keep, because then I could hold my head up high and have people tell me how happy they were for me and feel pride in my big belly and be able to have pure, simple feelings of happiness and contentment." We both yearned for a motherhood that we hadn't been able to have the first time around, and I also yearned for a sense of physical connectedness. "I have always felt sorry for men, specifically Adam, because they can't experience the pregnancy, the labor, the birth, the nursing, firsthand," she went on. "It is all truly a miracle."

Hannah told me about a woman she had met once who was both a birth mother and an adoptive mother. Rather than her dual role helping her in providing two perspectives, she instead experienced the worst of both: while she desperately wanted to know the child she had relinquished, she also lived in constant fear that the birth mothers of her adopted children would show up to take them away. I wondered how being an adoptee would affect the way I mothered if I ever adopted children: Would I be vicariously curious about their birth parents, pushing them, as Adam had pushed me, to reconnect? Or would I guard my children jealously, wanting to shower them with nurturing all the more, to reassure myself as well as them that I was their parent?

The ending of Hannah's letter felt like a strong, warm hand on my shoulder.

Sarah, I don't know how to express my happiness and appreciation (strange word, but it somehow fits) that you feel you are growing and making progress and that it feels positive. When I read your letters, I feel we grow a little closer with each one, and when I write my letters to you, I feel more raw feeling for that time long ago than I did then or have since. I have this overwhelming sense of gratitude that you are who you are and that we can communicate with you. It's an amazing feeling, and I didn't ever expect to be able to get here.

A modern dance exercise came to mind: two people stand shoulder to shoulder holding hands, and then lean out away from each other. If either dancer pulls too hard or lets themselves be pulled too easily, they both fall down. It is an exercise in achieving balance.

Contact

Dear Hannah and Adam,   *November 24, 1995*

A belated Happy Thanksgiving to you and Renee, Lucy and Sam! I was so glad to hear from you at last. I notice how my reaction to receiving your letters has changed. When we first started corresponding, I appreciated having the breathing space to put aside a letter from you if I didn't feel like reading it right away. But now, I approached my mailbox each passing day with anticipation, hoping to find a letter, and was disappointed when I didn't. I even began to get a bit concerned, which is why I sent that card. But this new feeling of concern was nice. Wondering about you, what you were up to, whether everything was all right.

I initially opted for letter writing as our mode of communication because I felt afraid and overwhelmed. Often I am most comfortable expressing myself through writing, and the fact that we had a record of the development of our relationship, to look back on and refer to and learn from, gave me a sense of control. But reading your letters and writing to you has turned into much more——an exercise in introspection and exploration, at times confusing and frustrating, at other times heartwarming and completing. Through our correspondence, I have been growing emotionally in ways I never had before. I haven't reached my destination yet, and maybe never will (and maybe that's secondary to the journey itself). From your thoughtful, articulate letters, it seems that you both have been growing and learning during this process as well.

And now, without feeling startled or rushed, but with an excited stirring in my stomach even as I write this——I am ready to meet you in person. I know you've been ready all along, but I've had to catch up——I didn't know that our relationship would begin (again) in January 1993. I've needed this long, and as I've expressed in the past, I appreciate your patience so much.

We're now already in the holiday season, a hectic time, but I wanted to read both your letters and assess my feelings carefully before I took this plunge. Perhaps after the New Year would be the best time for me to visit. I suppose I would come on a weekend. We can figure out logistics, when is most convenient for you.

Write back to tell me your thoughts and feelings on all this, and then I'll call you and we can talk about it. We haven't spoken in almost three years——I'm trying to remember what your voices sound like as I look at your most recent photographs, to conjure a sense of you. I greatly look forward to taking the next step, to sharing with you face-to-face.

Putting this down on paper makes it so much more real than just musing on it, and I'm a little frightened. But I think it's the right time, and not too soon or too late.

Sarah.

ITHAKA

Dear Sarah,   November 30, 1995

    We got your letter today. It brought tears to our eyes. We told the
kids, and they're excited and maybe kind of scared about meeting you.
Well, we are, too. We'll be away from December 26 until January 2.
Any weekend before or after that would be fine. Buses and planes come
to Hanover, or very close. We have room and would love to have you
stay with us, but we can certainly reserve a room nearby. We want to
do what makes you the most comfortable. We eagerly await your call to
talk about logistics and so many other things, and just to hear your voice
again.

                Take care,
                Hannah and Adam.

27

December

It was eleven-thirty on Sunday, December 10. I was sitting in my living room, the quiet, late-morning winter sun filtering in through the windows, about to call Hannah and Adam. I had decided ahead of time that I would call now, thinking that on a weekend they'd both be home and that the rates would be cheaper. But in the instant before calling, I hesitated, my whole body shaking. I held that old piece of notepaper with their number scribbled on it in a trembling hand. Several times, I picked up the receiver and put it down, exhaling briskly. After all my emotional strategizing, I did not expect this reaction. Of course it was reasonable, considering that I was about to call my birth parents. But I had been corresponding with them for three years. I had spoken to them before. Surely the blow should be softened by this already-existing relationship.

Then it hit me—this time, I knew that I was going to speak with them. This time, the phone call would not take me by sur-

prise. I wondered if this was how Hannah had felt before calling me. Now I get to prepare, I thought, and you have to
answer the phone not knowing who it is going to be. But the
sentiment was more empathetic than vengeful, in that I now
recognized how hard making the call was—in some ways
harder, perhaps, than receiving it unawares. I understood that
the person who did the searching was the one risking rejection,
the one already saying "yes" by virtue of reaching out, bracing
herself for the possibility of being told "no" by the person
who was found. I saw how both roles were equally vulnerable,
for different reasons.

It felt good to feel. I had worried at times that I was driven
to write Hannah and Adam to further the process along, but
that I wasn't truly taking the relationship in. Now, in this
moment, I was certain that it was affecting me, that what I felt
directly related to what I was about to do. I felt scared, sad,
curious, excited, knots in my stomach. And in this moment, on
the verge of connecting with my birth parents, I felt utterly
alone.

A cheerful young girl's voice answered. "This is Lucy." Lucy, my
second birth sister. The soccer player and artist of intricately
illustrated birthday cards. The muscular-armed girl canoeing in
the photograph. This was Lucy. We automatically exchanged
how-are-yous and giggled haltingly until she asked if I wanted
to speak with her mom. While waiting, I paced around my little
living room, repeatedly pushing my glasses up the bridge of my
nose as I strained to hear background voices. After a few min-

utes, a woman's voice, slightly hoarse like mine, came on the line to ask in a startled tone, "Hello?"

"Hello, Hannah? It's Sarah Saffian." I was flooded with relief. Following my morning of anxiety, and our years of silent communication, I was presenting myself to my birth mother at last. But at the same time, my name tasted strange as I uttered it, rang oddly as it hung in the air. I now knew that I was also Susan Morgan, the baby to whom she had given birth, the daughter whom she had always imagined out there somewhere. I was not the same person who had answered Hannah three years earlier with a simple "This is Sarah." I was someone else, someone in transit, aware of how far I was from wholeness all the more even as I approached it.

Straight off I confessed how nervous I'd been before calling, asking whether this was how Hannah had felt before calling me, which she admitted she had. Then she pulled back to apologize, or perhaps simply to reflect on how difficult receiving such a call must have been for me. "Afterward, thinking about laying that on you, 'Sarah, I think I'm your birth mother,' without you being prepared, was tough. It's an emotional roller coaster, a journey." There was a mutual understanding in speaking with her, as though she were reading my mind or could feel my feelings along with me. I had always considered coming to know my origins as a journey, but I now realized that this was a journey for her, as well. I was as much a part of her as she was a part of me. She was discovering herself, too.

She and Adam had been discussing the contrasting ways they responded to my letters. "He immediately wants to snap into

243

action, and I withdraw. He says I go into a shell, to process for a while."

I concurred as prudently as possible. "Yeah, sometimes his letters are more forceful," I said, trying not to lose my breath, a physical manifestation of nervousness that I'd never noticed before. "He keeps dropping things—when can we visit, it's taking so long, boy, would we really like to meet you—again and again." As Hannah chuckled, I recalled Adam jokingly confessing once that she had teased him for Federal Expressing a letter to me, and I felt less uneasy. "Your letters were more the way mine were," I continued. "This is how I feel, and we'll see what happens."

"I think part of it for him is having lost his parents when he was so young," reasoned Hannah. "People disappear."

This logical explanation for Adam pointed out my own contrasting caution, despite our similar backgrounds. "I've felt good about the gradual progression," I said, sensing that proceeding slowly had suited her, as well. "No matter what we did, even if we wrote letters for ten years, when we finally met it would be overwhelming. But I think we'll be somewhat more prepared than if we'd met immediately." I smiled then, noting my unintended segue into the purpose of my call. "We sort of know each other already, after the letters and photographs. Meeting in person is the next logical step."

"So," Hannah paused. Then sounding as if she were also smiling shyly, she asked, "Do you think you're really going to come?"

I was startled by the immediacy of the word in my mouth. "Yeah!" We both burst out laughing.

244

We worked out logistics. I considered the seemingly minor details crucial to my well-being. I wanted to visit them rather than have them visit me, because I still wanted to regulate how much of my life I shared with them. This was partly why I wanted to go by myself—if Mom or Dad or Chris came with me, I would feel overexposed. It was also a personal odyssey, and going on it alone would allow me the freedom to experience it fully, and not feel dependent on Chris or worried about my parents or in any way emotionally cramped by someone else. I wanted to fly rather than take the bus because I didn't want to be in transit for hours, unable to read or sleep, thoughts and feelings churning as I sat out the monotonous ride. I was glad to hear that the airport was only a ten-minute drive from Hanover, not wanting to inconvenience them—even though I knew they would come all the way to New York to see me if I said the word, I didn't want to take undue advantage of their willingness. We decided that both Hannah and Adam would pick me up, but that I would meet the children at their house later—being immediately confronted by all five of them, by this entire biological family, seemed too overwhelming. And I didn't want to sleep at their house—sharing a bathroom, padding around in my pajamas, never having time alone to reflect could be claustrophobic. I presented this thought delicately, but Hannah completely understood: "I can put myself in your position, feeling more comfortable having a place to go and close the door and know that no one's going to knock and ask, is everything okay?" And after discussing the pros and cons of Holiday Inn versus bed and breakfast, I chose the former, because it had telephones in the rooms, in case I wanted to call anyone, to reconnect with my world.

Meeting before the holidays felt rushed, but with my new-found urgency, I suggested either of the first two weekends after New Year's. Hannah said both were convenient for them, as they would have already returned from visiting her mother in Florida by then. "So you'll all be tan and I won't," I joked. I appreciated the levity we were able to have, remembering that even in our first conversation—our only other one, but after all the letters, it seemed as though there had been more—we had bantered, when I had facetiously blamed her for my not being taller. But my urgency was tempered by a residual hesitancy. There was no reason not to go on the earlier weekend, but I still wasn't ready to commit to it. I didn't know why or what exactly I needed to prepare.

Either way, though, we still had a couple of weeks until our reunion. "So, would it be okay if I picked up the phone and called you?" Hannah asked. "Or are you not ready for that yet?" I was torn between wanting to maintain control and tiring of being the etiquette police. I worried that I was a tease, dragging this out, even if it was my prerogative. As she assured me that neither of them took my slowness as a rejection, I could hear the peacemaker tendencies she had described in an early letter. I reluctantly agreed that they could call me now, not because I felt ready for them to, but because I felt guilty for constantly saying no.

Adam was staying with a friend in New Jersey for the week-end. "I feel badly that he wasn't here when I called you the first time, and that he's not here now," Hannah said. I promised to call that evening when he returned home, and that I would be in touch once I had determined which weekend I would come.

We had an open-ended goodbye, mine breathless—could she tell how nervous I was?—and hung up. As I had three years earlier, I carefully returned the receiver to its cradle and studied it as though I had never seen or used a telephone before, amazed that a little, black, plastic contraption could so significantly transform my life. But as opposed to the shock and confusion that followed our first conversation, after this one I felt exhilarated.

That evening, though, I grew anxious as I dialed their number again. There was so much to say that Adam and I couldn't seem to say anything at all initially—asking each other "How are you?" in circles and laughing nervously, the tension between us palpable. Then I took a deep breath and plunged in, as was my and Hannah's shared tendency. "I'm going to come visit, if that's all right!"

Adam's chuckle sounded forced. "You keep saying, 'if that's all right!' What do you think?" I immediately felt deflated, interpreting his harmless comment as pointing out, yet again, how much I'd been leading him on all this time, not giving him what he wanted. I said nothing. "I've felt cautious, too, about finding my roots, not wanting to hurt my guardian parents' feelings," he continued, drawing back. "I picked up that you don't want to hurt your father's feelings, your mother's, your brother's, your sister's. If we spend our lives worrying about other people, and I think you do more than most . . . "

247

"Maybe I do," I interrupted, still defensive, "and maybe that's understandable, considering the circumstances."

But just as Hannah had seemed to read my mind at times during our conversation, Adam must have sensed how I felt. "I've been eager for a reunion this whole time, but I've understood that the main thing was you being ready," he said with a reserve that surprised me. "In the letters, when you started asking questions and getting angry, it got easier, because I could answer you. You're so honest, so open. You're really telling us a lot about yourself."

I was glad that my transition into trust hadn't gone unnoticed or unappreciated, because it had taken a lot of effort to get to there. As he went on, I was revived further by his admission of his own over-zealousness. "When we started writing, I didn't know if I was coming on too strong. I was laying a lot of my own emotional experiences on you, like telling about that trip I took out to California last summer to see my birth mother's brother. I don't know if that was presumptuous, or interesting, or what." He laughed, embarrassed.

"No, it was helpful," I answered truthfully. "I'm getting to know myself better by getting to know you and Hannah. Gradually through our correspondence, I've come to see the positive, that there's something of a completion in developing a relationship with you. I've started to understand that people who leave can return, which is encouraging." I was startled to find myself suddenly getting choked up. The surge of emotion was not unpleasant, but not wanting to give in to it, I cleared my throat and shakily pushed on. "When I meet you, maybe I'll have a sense of connection."

Thankfully, Adam didn't seem to notice my strong reaction, as he went on to joke, "I don't know about you, but when you wrote that you were coming up, I started getting self-conscious." I relaxed. "Maybe the girls are right that I'm getting weirder looking!" I recalled how carefully I had selected the first pictures of myself to send, over two years earlier. It occurred to me now that meeting in person would afford less control than a still photograph.

He asked about the rest of my life, the majority of my days that didn't have to do with him and Hannah—it was hard to believe that such a large portion didn't, considering how much of my energy, thought and emotion went into the Leyders. We discussed various recent *Daily News* articles of mine that he had read. I told him about a dance story that I had written for the *Village Voice,* and about performing an essay recently on living in India during junior year of college. As I rattled off my list of projects, it was hard to pinpoint with whom I was talking. It felt a bit like telling a parent, because I wasn't worried about having to be modest, to play down my excitement or pride about my accomplishments, as I might have to a friend. But the conversation was incongruous, because he felt like a parent whom I didn't know very well, a father who had been away for a long time. Well, I thought, that was exactly who he was. The various goings-on in my life weren't important in themselves— even though he was interested in anything I had to tell him, as any good parent would be, and especially one who was starved for information—as much as the act of telling him about them.

"I know this has gone slowly, but it took that long to make sense of all those bottled up emotions spilling out," I said deliberately. "When I got off the phone with Hannah this morning, though, I was looking forward to seeing you so much, and that felt so good, to be unequivocally glad. Scared too, of course, but more excited in a positive way than frightened."

Adam's elation was subdued with significance. "Good. That's great."

Winding up the conversation, Adam, like Hannah, broached the subject of telephone protocol. "You can call us anytime, night or day. I'd like to call you and talk a whole lot, but then am I being too intrusive?" he asked, letting out a small, shy laugh. "And then if I don't call, is that a form of rejection?"

"I really appreciate your patience," I reiterated, "but sometimes I feel badly that I'm the one who's calling the shots. Because I know you've been ready for a reunion since that first weekend. I understand your feelings, too."

He laughed once more, justifiably, I thought, considering all the eggshell-walking I was doing. Tiptoeing still, even after all this time. "Sarah, don't be concerned about hurting our feelings, or being overly polite with us, okay?" He was reading my mind again.

"Okay," I answered, with a chuckle that I hoped said, how can you expect me not to be?

"We'll worry about you," he went on. "I think that's how it should be." Why, because he was my "father"? No, I already had a father, and I worried about hurting his feelings, too. Because he had abandoned me and so he now owed me his worry? I didn't feel that way, but did he?

"All right, I'll talk to you soon, then," I said before hanging up. We still hadn't explicitly sorted out the phone-calling arrangement, but perhaps he could tell how I felt without my having to come out and say it.

For as long as I could remember, I had a tendency to take on everything at once. "Killing multiple birds with one stone" was my catchphrase during high school. Efficient, and, I thought, less lastingly painful. At the end of 1995, in addition to preparing for this impending reunion with my birth parents, which merited all my emotional time and energy, I was also contemplating leaving my job and planning to move out of the apartment where I'd lived for these three years. New home, new career, new parents—all at once.

Furthermore, December 26 was the twentieth anniversary of my mother Nancy's death. I decided that I wanted my commemoration to be considered, ceremonial, somehow. I gathered several photographs of her and of us together and took them with me on a long walk, trying to recall her as specifically as possible, repeatedly running over the few memories in my head. I happened upon St. Patrick's Cathedral and found myself going inside. In the midst of the holiday crowds, I let my serene mood cloak me in privacy as I lit a candle, silently speaking to her, fixating on the flame. After standing there for a while, I went back out into the brisk cold, and felt a weight had been lifted.

Without a mother, a person has no source of being. I had once assumed that Nancy was my only mother. But after she died, I discovered that she hadn't been my source, after all. Then Kathy had wholeheartedly embraced the role of mother from the moment she assumed it. But she wasn't the reason I existed, simply because I remembered existing before knowing her. There was also Marvin, who, for a period of time, had been a mother as well as a father to me. Did it really matter that he couldn't have created me, either? In some ways, he had. All three of these parents had.

And yet, because Hannah was my original mother, I hoped that meeting her and getting to know my birth family would lead me to feel real, solid—even though their emergence was what had foregrounded this sense of fluidity. The people whom I was traveling to Hanover to meet were new to me, but at the same time we shared an inevitable and profound bond. I didn't want to go to my birth parents as a blob of clay for them to mold, a tabula rasa for them to make their mark on. I wanted to be honest, to be myself, the self who had been forming for nearly twenty-seven years without them, with these other parents. Only I was no longer sure who that self was.

1996

Odysseus awoke. He lay on his native soil,
and knew it not, since he had been long absent.

—from "Book XIII, How Odysseus Came to Ithaka," *The Odyssey* by Homer

28

Origin

I'm in the womb, a mere embryo, and it's warm and orange, with
sloshing sounds and vibrating. In these first three months it's
peaceful, but lonely. Although I sense my birth mother physically,
I don't have any emotional connection to her, because she doesn't
even know I'm here. She's in motion, traveling around Europe
with me inside her, and I can feel and hear her there. Chatting
with friends, eating rich foods and drinking wine, sightseeing,
walking, walking. I feel dragged along, like a piece of lint on the
back of a sweater that lingers, unnoticed. It's a carefree but
detached feeling.

It is only when we return to New York that I feel any response
from Hannah. But rather than being welcomed, I now suspect
that she is aware of me, but ignoring me, denying me, not wanting to believe in my existence. So there is still the loneliness, but
more acute than before, because I feel deliberately left alone. The
womb that had moved so easily and naturally with her rhythm is

now seizing up, and I feel crowded within it. My translucent tad-
pole fingers are up by my face as I bend my arms and legs until
they are folded in half, to take up as little room as possible. I feel
guilty, sensing Hannah's unease in the tightness of the womb, the
coldness of the fluid, and knowing it is because of me.

When we move to the hideout, the tension gradually sub-
sides and the sounds outside become muted, gentler. I hear
Adam frequently along with Hannah, but rarely any other people, and even my birth parents' voices come through only as
murmurs. This is a period of retreat: my birth mother seems
placid, resting, and I picture the apartment to be a sunny little
place, quiet, removed. Occasionally, I feel Adam's or Hannah's
hands resting on her abdomen, a firm but tender pressure.
Through the veiny red womb walls I can see the darker hand-
prints as though they are of paint on canvas, or of water on
stone, or making an impression in sand. I lean my face against
the hands, and close my fish eyes, and hum to my birth parents.

One evening, I feel the serenity of a snowstorm. The night city
is blanketed white, muffling sound, no cars or people out except
for us. I imagine sheets of snow falling steadily but landing
lightly, silently. I can feel the love growing between Hannah and
Adam as they walk. She is taking deep, full breaths, and the
amniotic fluid undulates in time with her motion. Over these
months, the womb has expanded and grown warm again, as I feel
embraced by her. I move around slowly, participating in the walk,
fully present, recognized and accepted by my birth parents.

When we go to the unwed mothers' home and then, a week
later, to the hospital, the womb turns tight again, but still

warm. This time, I feel like my birth mother's ally, that her tension is directed outward. I sense that I am still the reason for her distress, but that she no longer resents me, rather, that she wants to protect me. Just as before I felt that she was wishing me away, now I feel that she's trying to draw me ever closer to her, so passionately that her embrace is painful. I am afraid now, because she is afraid. She feels helpless and I feel helpless, too, for myself, and also for her—I want to aid her somehow.

As scared as I am of the situation around us, I don't feel safe where I am anymore. I decide to come out, even though I'm not quite ready. The womb is becoming smaller all the time, and I feel as though I am being squeezed out by Hannah's anxiety. I rotate so that I am upside down, dizzy and disoriented, and begin pushing out. As I leave it, the womb shrinks behind me, like a deflating balloon, clinging to my stomach, my legs. The canal is pitch dark, not glowing like the womb was, and very narrow. As my head emerges, I am struck by the chill of the outside for the first time. I finally slide out, slimy and terribly cold. I am washed and wrapped in a blanket swiftly, perfunctorily, by someone in white whom I don't know, and taken away. Later, I am taken to my birth mother. I know that it is she, recognizing her warmth, her smell, her soft voice. She holds me, and it is familiar, yet different, because I am outside of her now. This situation seems fleeting—her love, while unconditional, is mingled with despair, turning furtive, unconfident.

Then one day I am not taken to Hannah. I look around for her, but everyone is a stranger. The hospital nursery is antiseptic, chilly, the crisp white sheet in my glass crib rough on my

257

new, raw skin. I see other parents of other babies, peering through the window at their children, pointing, smiling and holding them, cooing, doting. I am cared for by the people in white, but I don't feel any love from them—the love that I felt from my birth mother, eventually while inside her, and briefly after being born. But now she is gone, and I am motherless, nameless. Alone.

29

The Infinity Within

Sunday, January 7

I'm at the brownstone, ordering a pizza with my brother and sister while our parents are out. I don't really have to "baby-sit" anymore, Max and Rachel being sixteen and fourteen, but as Mom and Dad are in Connecticut visiting friends and won't be home until very late, they felt more comfortable having me over. I also thought that tonight would provide an opportunity to talk with Max and Rachel about my birth parents, finally. I can't believe that it's been three years since Hannah's phone call, that so much has gone on with me during this time, in my head, in my heart. But next weekend's reunion serves as a good deadline. I can't meet the Leyders without telling my siblings about them first.

Because I have been talking with my mother and father about my birth parents all along, telling them of my definitive decision to go to Hanover was more gradual. Since I first mentioned to my father that I was starting to feel ready for a reunion, over dinner in September, he has been, characteristically, supportive from a distance: "If meeting them is what you want, then I am behind you." Over the past few weeks, I have talked mostly with Mom about calling Hannah and Adam, setting the actual weekend, making specific plans.

"You know, Sarah, if you're feeling at all uncertain about this, I'd be happy to drive up to Hanover with you," she offered in one conversation, as she had before.

"I appreciate that a lot, Mom." As with Dad, I was reassured that my mother supported the reunion to the point of being willing to come along. "But I want to go alone, partly because though I feel ready to visit the Leyders, I don't feel ready to share you guys with them yet."

"Well, I'm not that interested in meeting them, either," she said frankly. "I just want to be there for you, if you need someone familiar to talk with on the way there and back. I could just sit in the car the whole time, waiting, or drop you off and pick you up later. I wouldn't even have to come inside." I suspected that this plan would also work to her benefit, in being able to monitor the visit somehow, to ensure that nothing happened to me. Was she admitting that she felt threatened by them?

"Thanks so much, Mom. But I'm pretty sure that I want to go by myself also because it's something that I just think I should do alone." She said that she understood, and her tone revealed that she admired my independence, a quality that she has spent her time as my mother trying to instill in me. But I'm not going alone merely to test myself, to present myself with a challenge, to see how much I can endure on my own. Going alone feels clean to me.

Max, Rachel and I sit here at the kitchen table over our slices and salads and sodas, chatting about work, school, friends. The only way out is through, I tell myself, my new motto appropriated from Hannah. "You guys, I have something to tell you," I begin, and am met with the customary rolling of jaded eyes and smirking to each other—here we go, Sarah's being intense again. "No, really," I laugh, trying to maintain a sense of both levity and significance, "this is important." And I launch into the story of the Leyders, starting with the phone call, working my way through the correspondence to the present.

My brother's and sister's responses are similar to when I told them that I was adopted and that my adoptive mother had died, around the dinner table that summer in Spain when they were seven and six. But this time, I am encouraged by their reactions, which hold a newfound maturity. "Lucy is only a year younger than I am?" Rachel asks, inviting the comparison. "And she plays soccer, too?" I think, as I have before, that she is private about her feelings, preferring to appear cool to others, squirreling away data to digest while she is alone. Or maybe she actually isn't threatened or confused by the information, but rather is simply curious about these new people.

Max is straightforward, calm. "I gotta say, I'm sort of annoyed that you're only telling us now. I mean, you've been

writing letters for three years. When she called you"—I notice
that Max refers to Hannah and Adam only as "she" and "he"
when he talks about them, not by their names—"we were old
enough to be told. We could have handled it." I agree and apologize if he feels excluded. But I explain that my secrecy was due
not to an underestimation of their ability to handle it, but to
my own jumble of thoughts and feelings, which I wanted to
sort out first. He accepts my defense with a tilted-head nod
and raised eyebrows, a gesture that reminds me of Dad. I am
grateful that he can be open enough to express his irritation,
that he didn't simply say, "So? That's no big deal," and go up to
his room to call a friend, do his homework, brood without
sharing his frustration. I tell him how much his candor means
to me. It occurs to me how similar his sense of disruption—
both nine years ago, and now—must be to my own. We both
responded to the information indirectly, by reacting instead to
the unexpected way it was conveyed—casual family dinners for
him, an early morning phone call for me. I understand how
scary it is to find that your idea of reality was uprooted and
replanted while you were looking the other way. They both
wish me luck on my journey, and I vow to tell them about it in
detail and to answer their questions as fully as I can when I
return.

After Max and Rachel head upstairs, I go to what my family
has always referred to as "the Spanish Chest," a piece of furniture
in the living room that holds many of our photographs, stored in
their photo store envelopes and randomly stacked. Along the bottom shelf are actual albums, vestiges of a spurt of organizational

energy on my mother's part. There is my parents' white and gold wedding album, and then Max, Rachel and I each have one, in red, green and brown leather. Mine begins at age ten, when Mom and Dad got married (innumerable albums featuring younger shots of me are stored upstairs), and Max's and Rachel's begin at birth. I get caught up in these early photos, of Dad—haggard, unshaven and beaming after nights coaching Mom through labor—with each of my siblings as newborns at New York Hospital. I am struck by the look of pure pride on his face as he holds up Max, his "son and heir" as he always refers to him, after believing that he couldn't have children.

In looking at these photographs a week before meeting my birth parents, I can't help feeling that Max and Rachel have something with our father that I never can—they are his biological children, he and Mom *created* them together. I can only imagine how that must feel for any father, but particularly him. Hannah and Adam having Renee was equally significant, but in reverse. I could see it as a boon that I get to have one set of parents who rejoiced in my birth, at least for my first few days, another who rejoiced in my arrival two months later and a third mother who met me at age eight and rejoiced in her decision to parent me. But in this moment, I feel a bit robbed instead, that the parents who experienced my birth and the parents who raised me were not the same. And I feel deficient, too, that in each case I fell short—not able to be kept, not the birth child—because in neither case could I be both.

I sift through the piles to find a few good pictures of my family and of me when I was younger to take to Hanover. I

263

come across one of my father and me from a long-ago summer. Both tan, we are sitting on a ledge outside somewhere, probably in West Hampton. There is a wistful expression on my face, and my hand is lightly resting on Dad's leg. He is looking down at me through sunglasses, cigarette dangling from his lips, saying something with a slightly stern twist to his mouth. I recall seeing the picture before, but for the first time I check the date on the back: September 1975. Three months before my mother Nancy died. And all at once I burst into tears, really sobbing. I feel sorry for the me in the picture, for what is about to happen to her. I decide not to take this photograph to the Leyders.

One of the pictures I do select is of Dad in Italy a few years ago, wearing a straw fedora, smiling and flourishing theatrically for the camera, which completely captures his essence. I can hear Adam's words in my head, saying that he feels self-conscious, that he worries I will think he is goofy-looking, that he wishes the leaves were still on the tree in the backyard. We are eager to make good impressions on one another. They want to show me that I had favorable beginnings, and I want to show them that I turned out okay.

Friday, January 12

As "The Blizzard of '96" pummels the northeast, the enormity of what I am doing hits me full force today. Sitting at work, writing a couple of articles at once, I feel lonely and panicked, worried that I haven't sufficiently prepared, emotionally. I know that I have characteristically kept busy, purposely avoiding the significance of the situation, fearing more than anything having the space to face it truly. But now, the day before my departure, I also feel claustrophobic, surrounded, wishing that I could clear the decks, push aside work and all the people who don't know what's going on and ask me naively, "So, what are you doing this weekend?"

On top of everything else, I told my friends Nikki and Trajal that I would have lunch with them today, to plan another friend's surprise birthday party. I'm desperate to reschedule, but decide instead to meet them and not come back to work. I'm too distracted, dashing off paragraphs in quick bursts and then staring into space or looking manically around my desk for some small task to keep me occupied. The amorphous activity of writing is not enough to hold my attention. I retreat into the pink, tiled ladies' room, which is thankfully empty, enclose myself in my favorite stall, and sob for a few stolen minutes. Then I blow my nose, splash cold water on my face and emerge to tell my editor that I've filed my stories for the Saturday and Sunday papers but that I'm going home because I don't feel well. I laugh to myself when it occurs to me that my relationship with my birth parents so far—from day of initial phone call to eve of reunion—is being bookended by excuses to leave work early.

I slog through the gray slush, sinking my boots deep into icy puddles collecting at street corners, making my way to a diner in Chelsea. Nikki and Trajal are already here, and my sensation upon glimpsing them through the window chatting animatedly is similar to when the urge to vomit is rising in me but I have to resist it until I get out of the car—except that this nausea is emotional rather than physical. I feel like I'm going to explode, because all I want to talk about is the Leyders—or not talk about them, but be left alone to think about them—and now I'm going to have to get through a whole meal with people who know nothing of the journey I'm embarking on. Normally the "field trip organizer" type of person, the one with the impetus to iron out and organize, this time I let the two of them do the planning as I nod my head, mumbling my agreement when they suggest ideas. Sure, I'll call those people, I'll get that, I'll be there then. Just tell me what to do and I'll do it, I think, but please don't expect me to take the reins. It hits me that when I eventually attend this party, I will have already met my birth parents.

After lunch, my two friends wish me a "nice weekend," and I slosh home, where I find that my telephone has gone dead. No dial tone, nothing. Taken aback, I go downstairs to call the phone company from the pay phone outside my building, only to be cut off. My frustration mounting, I walk farther and farther away, trying every phone that I pass, with the same result at each: I get through to hear the recorded "NYNEX" greeting said in a smooth female voice, but after making my Touch-Tone selection to speak with a customer service representative, I am put on hold and then disconnected. I'm several blocks away at the post office when I finally reach a surly woman who informs me that the problem with my phone is probably due to the pelting freezing rain opening up a cable, but that it is too late to send a repair person today. I attempt in vain to chip away at her stoniness, arguing that I need my telephone, that it's barely three in the afternoon, and what kind of shitty service am I paying for anyway—all the while aware that my volume is rising, that others in the post office are turning around to look at me and that whenever I see people getting hysterical in public I always think them pitiful and silly. The NYNEX woman actually hangs up on me.

I take a breath and call Chris in California with my calling card. He isn't there, but the instant that I hear his sweet, familiar voice on the answering machine I break down into exasperated sobs, no longer caring how I appear to passersby—they're just mailing packages, but I'm about to meet my birth parents!—the tension that has been building throughout the day bursting at last, rendering me a dejected, quivering heap. I leave a message from this rock-bottom place, wailing about my lack of telephone, partially regretful as I think that Chris will be alarmed when he hears it. I hang up desolate. But I resolve to call him again later tonight, giving myself something concrete to look forward to, something in the near future, the pre-reunion future, to latch onto.

I trudge home again and expectantly pick up the phone, but with no luck. So I start to pack: the photographs of me at various ages, my family, Chris and a few close friends, to allow the Leyders a limited peek into my life; my camera and a couple of rolls of film, to document this new family, and myself with them; my journal, to write down thoughts and feelings throughout the journey; and a night-blooming jasmine that I bought for them, thinking it an appropriate gift, growing and changing like our relationship.

After making myself dinner, I sit down to watch the news, impatient, as I have been every night this week, for the weather

267

forecast. Another storm watch is in effect for the weekend. I notice my increased anxiety upon hearing this, my complete lack of hopefulness for conditions that would necessarily postpone my trip. As nervous as I am about the reunion, I am more nervous about it not being able to happen. I have been readying myself for this particular weekend enough to be severely disappointed if I am not able to go tomorrow—not entirely because I am so eager to meet them, but because I worry that if I am forced to put off my visit, I will have to go back and brace myself all over again. I'm not looking for ways to delay anymore. Just as when I used to close my books finally, minutes before taking an exam, thinking, well, if I don't know it now, I never will, after all the letters, photographs, phone calls, careful planning, I am as ready to meet my birth parents as I'll ever be.

Late in the evening, I venture out to a nearby phone booth to try Chris and am thrilled to find him at home. I apologize for the anguished message I left earlier, since, as I expected, it concerned him considerably. I know that when I am like that he feels helpless being so far away, wishing he could do more than murmur sounds of support. I explain how much better I feel now, organized, ready. Next I call my parents to tell them about my broken phone and to give and receive some send-off encouragement: I want to reassure them as much as myself that I am their daughter and am coming home Sunday. At one point, my father asks, "So, what's the phone number and address in Hanover?" chuckling as he adds, "I want to write it all down in case they try to kidnap you." I chuckle along with him, worrying, as always, that his joking is a defensive gesture, while at the same time comforted by his possessiveness. My parents wish me luck, and I tell them that I will try to call while I am there. We make a plan for me to come over Monday, to have dinner and spend the night. I find it difficult to imagine time-after-reunion, but I still look forward to the evening as a soothing respite, a reunion all its own: returning to my old family after meeting my new one.

I leave my street-corner post and head home, where I am unreachable. I've said goodbye to those familiar to me. I won't talk to them again until after I've met my birth parents. Once in my apartment, I putter around, putting the last necessary items into my knapsack and selecting clothes for tomorrow, with both my appearance and the weather in mind. But it's not like outfitting for a job interview or a date, where the goal is clear; I'm not sure what I want the outcome to be. I settle on brown jeans and a gray turtleneck sweater, appropriately casual, appropriately warm, clothing that is comfortable, familiar. A memory flashes through my mind as I perform this laying-out-of-clothing ceremony. In second or third grade, I had a ritual of coming home from school and neatly spreading on my bed my favorite play clothes—plaid pants and a turtleneck with a matching plaid kitten on it. Before changing out of my uniform, I would leave the room and return a few minutes later, pleased to find my clothes waiting for me.

I turn to the letters exchanged most recently, back in November, when I wrote that I was ready to visit. Reading over our entire correspondence before meeting suddenly strikes me as necessary, and I only wish that the idea had occurred to me earlier. I want to refresh my memory, to be aware of the whole chronology of our relationship, the gradual steps leading from first phone call to eventual reunion. And so I read, until four-thirty in the morning. At one point I pause to weigh the pros and cons, also deeming it important to be well-rested for such a crucial encounter. But I decide to press on, figuring that I'll have enough nervous energy to stave off any lingering fatigue.

I am surprised to discover how much sooner I thought I'd be ready for a reunion. Already in my very first letter, dated February 17, 1993, I mentioned the possibility: "I am pretty sure that I would someday like to visit all of you . . . But I have no idea when I will be ready. It could be in a month, it could be in ten years, it could be (though I doubt this) never." Later that year, in my August 8 letter, our reunion sounded forthcoming: "I'm . . . thinking about when I will visit. I might like to come up in the fall, whenever it is convenient for you and whenever we all are ready." And in her letter of April 14, 1994, Hannah recalled that in our initial phone conversation, "when I asked what sort of a relationship you'd like . . . you said that you would love to come up and see all of us." Sitting at my desk three years after expressing those sentiments, my eyes smarting from the reading and the late hour, I am only now on the verge of meeting them.

Saturday, January 13

I awake with a clear mind, and to thankfully clear skies, sunny and cloudless. My stomach does a little leap as I realize anew what I am about to do, but I am sure that I am ready. I go about my morning routine methodically, double-checking that I have everything I'll need for the weekend, ticking off items on my mental list just as I did before Hannah's first phone call, just as I do every morning to ground myself, especially mornings of days when I am facing something challenging.

I take the subway to the bus, the bus to the airport. Sitting in Gate Fifteen at LaGuardia, waiting for my noon flight, barely two hours away from being reunited with my birth parents, I allow myself to pause and reflect. I am numbed by the logistical effort to get to this point, over both the long and the short term—phone calls, letters, conversations with Chris, Faith, my family, myself, impending snowstorms, dead phone lines. This meeting couldn't have happened any sooner. Now I am here, with a backpack on my shoulders, a shopping bag in my lap and my heart in my mouth.

As we board the small plane, I glance at the few other people traveling this January Saturday morning. Who are they all going to see? Do I betray any of the significance of my own voyage, or do I appear to be just a young co-ed visiting a friend at Dartmouth? When the plane accelerates along the runway, I close my eyes and say a little prayer, something simple, a hope that the weekend will go well. That first instant—when I can feel the wheels lift off the ground, when the plane is newly airborne—takes my breath away. Throughout the hour-long flight as I sit and stare ahead, my mind alternates between racing and blankness. My emotions vacillate from calm to happy excitement to nervousness and even to dread—wishing that I could turn around and go home, or that the reunion were already over, or that I were on my way to see someone else. With fifteen

271

minutes to go, I scoot back to the bathroom for one last check. Do I look okay? I'm glad that my skin has cleared up, knowing that I wouldn't have scheduled this reunion if I still had my rash. What will I look like as an adult to people who haven't seen me since I was a few days old? What will I look like to people who gave birth to me, but to whom I am a stranger? I think, this is the last time that I will see myself before meeting my birth parents. Will I appear altered somehow when I next look in a mirror?

When the announcement comes over the loudspeaker, "Welcome to West Lebanon, New Hampshire," and the plane touches down with a rumbling bumpiness, I am no longer in my body. I go through the motions of retrieving my belongings from the overhead compartment and thanking the flight attendant and pilot, who wish us all "a pleasant stay." I am the first one off the plane, walking down the narrow metal stairs and crossing the tarmac to the small terminal. I gulp a large breath of cold air like water and enter the building.

The gate is empty. Then I glimpse Hannah and Adam a bit back in the lobby, standing beside a pillar. It's as though the photographs they've sent over the years are now in motion. Adam is tall and lanky, somewhat stooped in posture, somewhat dreamy in gesture; Hannah is more than a foot shorter, sturdy. They are dressed casually, worn-in jeans, slouchy sweaters, sensible down jackets and boots. They see me, too, from across the gate, and smile, not moving forward but letting me come. I give a small wave, and as I walk toward them a feeling wells up inside me, a nameless, formless emotion becoming stronger, making itself known to me. An odd combination of isolation and connection. In a way, I have never felt more alone than in this unique moment of meeting parents. But I also have a sense of coming home, and my first gut impression is not of surprise, but of recognition—they and I are indeed related.

When I am close enough, I say "hi" quietly, laughing a little at how flimsy and nonchalant the word sounds. I go to hug Hannah, and Adam comes and hugs us both, and we three huddle together and cry a little. Not sobbing, just that hiccup of a cry. In the midst of this intense embrace, the observer in me remains apart—feeling awkward and impatient for this intimate, charged episode to be over, but at the same time wishing that I still had the freedom to imagine it. This is it, I think, this is the moment we've all been waiting for. Are we living up to the big buildup? Am I?

273

Soon enough, we slowly pull away, wipe our eyes, peer into one another's faces, laugh softly and self-consciously. The spell is broken. We make our way to the parking lot, seeing as we can't spend the rest of our lives, or even the rest of the day, in the airport. So we occupy ourselves with the activity of walking to the car, beginning our visit, putting one foot in front of the other.

Hannah and I dive into mundane conversation as a means of alleviating the tension—she asks about my flight, I ask about the weather. "When I get nervous, I bake, and when Renee gets nervous she cleans," Hannah jokes, "and so our house is spotless, and brimming with cookies, cakes and breads." When she asks what's in the brown paper shopping bag that she is now carrying, I answer that I've brought them a jasmine plant—saying the phrase "*growing* and *changing*" in an exaggerated, theatrical accent in order to mock myself for the symbolism, which now seems heavy-handed. Adam, on the other hand, is practically silent. At times he laughs uneasily and apologizes, saying, "I'm just trying to take it all in" or "I'm pretty overwhelmed here."

I have the sense that I'm not meeting strangers, really. It's as if we know one another already. Both the way they look, move and speak and their personalities are unsurprising to me. Through our correspondence, I have been deep in their dark private places, and they in mine; I have seen photographs and talked with them on the phone. Who they are has come to me gradually. Meeting in person is a falling into place of pieces. After assembling the puzzle, connecting the borders, filling in the middle, I now see the picture complete.

Am I also as they expected me to be, or do I surprise them? "I was a little surprised when I saw your photos, because I pictured you with lighter coloring when I heard your voice that first time on the phone," Hannah answers. "This is funny, though, because when the other kids were born, I had expected them to be darker, like you had been when you were born. But in getting to know you again, I expected *you* to look like *them!*" As we walk, Hannah continues, examining me. "You do look like all of us, but you're yet another physical type, a distinct person. I remember when Renee was born, I was amazed by how little she looked like me. She looked like herself!" Both connected and individual.

In the car, I sit in front with Adam as he drives, and Hannah sits in back. She suggests that we stop at a coffee shop, to give

Renee time to finish cleaning before we head home. "We arranged for the kids to be out with friends when we got back from the airport, so that you wouldn't be bombarded by everyone at once." We enter a typical suburban coffee shop, its generic quality a striking contrast to the uniqueness of our situation. It is almost absurd, the three of us stopping here. The unsuspecting waitress greets the middle-aged couple and their twentysomething daughter with a smile and a pleasantry, and seats them at a corner table. Realizing that I'm suddenly hungry, I order a cup of soup and crackers. Hannah has a scrambled egg and decaf, Adam just coffee. "Are you sure you don't want anything else, just soup?" Hannah asks, Jewish-motherly. I'm secretly embarrassed by the solace her attention brings me.

We jump from the superficial to the significant without pausing for a breath. Hannah and Adam talk about when they first told the kids that I existed and that they were going to search for me. The girls' initial reaction was to turn to each other and say, "We've got to find her!" and Sam groaned, "You mean I have *three* older sisters?" Later, Lucy asked tearfully, "Do you love her more than us?" I realize that just as I have come to comprehend that Hannah and Adam's presence doesn't negate my parents', Max is trying to accept that my visiting my birth family this weekend doesn't make me any less his true sister, and Hannah and Adam's children are working toward a similar understanding: that my existence doesn't disqualify their own.

As I sit here, asking and answering questions, I eat my soup, adding more and more salt. This triggers an image of my father from when I was little, giving me a nosh to tide me over as he

275

cooked dinner—olives, pinches of uncooked hamburger meat sprinkled liberally with large crystals of kosher salt, *tunk-hein*, slices of rye bread dipped in juices from the brisket simmering on the stove. I can see his tapered fingers handing down these treats to me as I stand not even as tall as the cutting board where he works, and wonder if this is how I "inherited" his taste for savory foods. I miss my father, feeling more connected to him by this mere cup of salty soup than I do to the people who gave birth to me, who sit with me now, nearly twenty-seven years later, on the cracked leather seat of a coffee-shop booth outside Hanover.

We discuss tendencies toward cavities, crooked teeth, myopia, left-handedness. I seem to have hit the jackpot, while their other children haven't had braces or glasses. Even Hannah and Adam have only recently started wearing reading glasses, to correct the slight farsightedness that commonly strikes people in their forties and fifties. Again, I think of my father, who is severely nearsighted, as am I. We both also have unusually sensitive feet. In my memory I can see Dad's, poking out from under the covers at my eye level. He always said that our shared quality of second toes being longer than first ones was a sign of superior intelligence. I lightly tickle his high arches as he wails in exaggerated, but not entirely mock, agony, jerking his feet away. Could I possibly have "acquired" such physical traits as these?

After we finish eating, we drive to the Leyders' two-story house. It is modest, cozy. Hannah and Adam give me the tour, skipping Sam's and Lucy's rooms, because they said they wanted to show me themselves. Both parents work at home: Hannah teaching small pottery classes a couple of times a week in her basement studio and making pieces to sell; Adam drafting house designs from his little office off the living room. They point out how their contrasting workspaces reflect their different personalities: Adam's is neat to the point of being spartan, whereas Hannah's has pots and clay scattered everywhere and a clay-spattered tape player that she listens to while working—rock and roll for energy when she throws, molding the clay on the wheel, classical for concentration when she glazes. She says that while she is more nostalgic and romantic than Adam, he keeps track of memorabilia more assiduously. Indeed, he has several files on me alone: one manila folder holds letters, one is for photographs and one for miscellaneous items, right down to copies of their January and February 1993 phone bills with our initial calls highlighted.

277

There are pictures all around the house, mainly of the children, and I am among them. There is the profile shot of me, displayed on the mantelpiece. Adam shows me four black and white photographs framed together, hanging in his and Hannah's bedroom—one of each of their children, including me—which he gave to her as a present. It feels okay, maybe a bit strange, seeing the four of us together. We end up back in the living room, me seated between them on the couch, and Hannah says that we should probably wait to look at the photographs I brought until Renee, Lucy and Sam return, but suggests looking at theirs. "They think our albums are so boring anyway, they wouldn't be missing anything." I nod hungrily.

Hannah pulls out the one from her post-graduation trip to Europe, when she was pregnant with me but didn't know it yet. There she is in Greece, posing comically on a ruin. There she is on a rowboat in England, smiling in sunglasses. One photograph taken at the end of the trip shows the group of women seated around a table at a restaurant in Italy. "By this time I was becoming nervous," Hannah says, pointing at her younger self, "because one by one everyone was getting their periods, but I wasn't." I study her face in the picture, but her sweet smile doesn't give her away.

I am struck again by the mundaneness of our situation. We still have to engage in our normal animal activities, despite the heightened circumstances. Hannah directs me to a tiny half-bath off the kitchen, a closet that Adam converted. I leave both eagerly, because I need a couple of minutes alone, and reluctantly, because I don't want to miss an instant with Hannah and Adam and know that they will talk about me while I'm gone. As I sit on the toilet, separated from my birth parents by only a thin door, I feel embarrassed and ridiculous. Will they be able to hear me peeing? Will they listen to find out if I wash my hands after? Will they be curious or concerned if I take too long? I get up and search my face in the mirror to see if I look different from that last glimpse on the airplane, from how I've looked my entire life. The image reflected back at me does betray a sense of the journey that I am on, as if with these moment-to-moment discoveries I am evolving before my own eyes.

After poring over photographs for a while longer, I hear the front door open, and in come Lucy and Sam. Renee arrives soon after. We say an enthusiastic "hi!" to one another and hug. Meeting them feels strangely normal—"strangely normal" is shaping up into the oxymoronic catchphrase for the weekend— as we bypass introductions. Lucy has a couple of rings, necklaces and ear pierces and is wearing a short-sleeved T-shirt layered over a long-sleeved one and baggy jeans. She reminds me a bit of my sister—I tell her so, and she seems pleased, as I think Rachel would be. Sam is quirky, full of energy, so deadpan that he almost convinces me that he doesn't realize he is being funny. He seems focused and distracted simultaneously, as though he is concentrating very hard on something other than what or whomever is in front of him. Physically, he is a ten-year-old Adam. Renee is prettier than in the photographs, more delicate, with a light, precise manner about her. Now seventeen, she stands a couple of inches taller than I do, and I make a joke about Adam's long genes all going to her.

Lucy and Sam show me their rooms, pointing out highlights, such as Lucy's posters of Georgia O'Keeffe flower paintings and Sam's wooden dinosaur models that he built himself. He likes to create comic books, and shows me one with very complex drawings called "Power Pig," about a swine-turned-superhero. Both of them, particularly Sam, because he is younger, are eager to show off their interests and abilities to me, as though I am their older sister who has been away on a long trip. But while what I know about them through Hannah's and Adam's letters provides me with some framework, we don't have enough history for me to say, "Wow, Sam, you've done so much work on that Lego village!" or, "Lucy, do you still use those colored pencils I gave you?" So instead I murmur appreciatively, and sincerely. Hannah and Adam have already shown me Renee's room, and I comment on how nice the space and privacy must be in the converted attic. "It looks like a little studio up there," I say, "about the size of my apartment!" hoping to make her feel grown-up.

We all end up back in the living room, on the couch, the floor, the arm of a chair, and because the kids are home now, I pull out my photographs. I describe them as they get passed around—here I am at age four, in West Hampton over the summer, here's a recent one of my family, here's Chris, here are Vanni, Laurel and Cheryl, close friends from college. The Leyders consume my pictures as I did theirs, Hannah and Adam particularly interested in the ones of me as a child. One prompts Hannah to pull out a photograph of Renee at the same age, and we are all struck by the resemblance. Adam loves the one of Dad in Italy, saying that it corresponds to the descriptions of him from my letters, illustrating his personality, just as I hoped it would. "He seems like a wonderful man," Adam says, a bit poignantly, I think. When my limited supply is quickly depleted, Hannah and Adam say in unison, "Is this all you brought?" half-jokingly, as they make fun of their own endless stream of albums. "You could have brought a trillion pictures," Hannah adds, laughing at herself, "and it wouldn't have been enough." Even though their comment is light, I kick myself—despite all my meticulous planning, I didn't bring enough photographs. After our slow progression toward this weekend, I now feel that time is of the essence, as though this will be the sole opportunity for us to exchange information. Do I think that this visit will be the only one, that we'll have a reunion but not evolving places in one another's lives? I can't decide which I fear more—their presence or their absence.

We need to respond to anything, the slightest similarity, the slightest thought, analyzing minor similarities in great detail— "Oh, you like chocolate? I love chocolate!" "Do you prefer dark chocolate or milk chocolate?" "My father and I like bittersweet chocolate best." "My brother likes chocolate, though not as much, and he prefers milk chocolate. My father's sister, on the other hand . . ." Because we're so dry of contact, we absorb as much of one another as we can, spongelike. Nothing is insignificant in our process of filling in the outlines as completely as we can in this limited time face-to-face.

Living in the moment is taking nearly all my energy and concentration without much left over for reflection, and I easily slip into the here and now of their home life. As a rule, everyone takes off their boots upon entering the house to avoid tracking in snow from outside—so here we all are, padding around in our socks, immediately turning the situation informal and intimate. I ask if I can help Hannah prepare dinner, and she puts me to work chopping vegetables. She pours us each a glass of wine, and we chat as we cook, the others milling in and out of the kitchen, getting dishes to set the table, answering the telephone, asking questions. It's a family atmosphere that I'm used to: a lively group, all talking and laughing at once, a comfortable, casual chaos. I don't feel disruptive in the least, but rather that I simply add to what is already here.

They each have their own seat at the table, designated by a slightly different painted wooden napkin holder. I sit at the sixth place, the guest's place. After dinner, someone pulls out Pictionary from the overflowing shelves of games, and we have a rambunctious match. Sam often gets carried away after a turn is over and continues embellishing his scribbled clue, adding bugging-out eyes and dropping jaws to his figures as we repeatedly call him back. Then we have apple pie—one of the many products of Hannah's nervousness—for dessert, and retire to the living room with our tea to watch videos of Renee's and Lucy's *bat mitzvahs*, recorded in typically haphazard home-movie style.

Adam puts Sam to bed and Lucy heads up to her room to take a phone call from a friend. Chatting in the living room with us for a few minutes before going out, Renee, without missing a beat in the conversation, will suddenly cross the room to straighten something—adjust a stack of magazines, fluff a pillow, take a glass to the sink. I laugh to myself, because I have this same habit at my parents' house. Max and Rachel make fun of me, saying that the place is neater and cleaner after I've stopped by, calling me "Cinderella." After Renee leaves, Hannah, sitting with me on the couch, expresses concern about her daughter going away to college, considering her problem with homesickness. Having always thought of the tendency as a reaction to circumstance, now I wonder whether it could be inherited, considering that both Hannah and Renee, neither of whom lost parents in their childhoods, share it with me.

I can't decide if I feel more relaxed with the kids or alone with Hannah and Adam. Aside from enjoying my birth siblings' company, having them around diffuses tension, because there are three more people to pay attention to, to interact with; the focus isn't entirely on me, which is a relief. On the other hand, when the six of us have been together today, as pleasant as it has been, I have felt slightly self-conscious, too—I want the kids to like me, despite the fact that I am this new person thrown into the mix who is taking up a lot of their parents' time and energy and love. So there is also an element of relief to being alone with Hannah and Adam, alone with people whom I don't have to win over, and to letting them make me their focus without feeling guilty that I am monopolizing them.

I ask Hannah how she discusses sex with Renee and Lucy, and what her advice would be if either of them ever became pregnant. "I would support them in anything they decided," she says, her eyes rolling ceilingward as she thinks, hands neatly clasped around her mug, "but I probably would encourage them more to keep the baby or get an abortion than surrender the child for adoption." She sighs then, contemplating the pain of mistaken pregnancy. "I tell the girls that I became pregnant with you the single time that Adam and I didn't use birth control. That it takes only once." The cause and effect relationship between her lack of protection and my sitting here remains abstract. After all this time, the Susan Morgan part of me, the baby part, still is not completely out of exile, still remains somewhat unreachable to me.

"At dinner tonight, I found myself looking at you and then looking at Renee, Lucy and Sam," Hannah continues. "It was a combination of being familiar and unfamiliar at the same time.

283

Sitting across the table from you, I thought that these things—
your face, your hands—which I recognize only because they are
so similar to ours, would be truly familiar to me if I'd raised
you, if I'd looked at them every day." I realize that this scenario
is more conceivable for her, as she can imagine simply inserting
me into the life and family that she has already built. However,
as Adam wrote in his first letter, if Hannah had indeed kept
me, her life and family might have turned out very differently,
perhaps without these three other children, or even without
Adam. I glance at him now and again, sitting quietly in his armchair, watching us talk, occasionally contributing a comment,
asking or answering a question. Sometimes when there's a pause
in conversation, Adam will chuckle awkwardly and say, "So,
how ya doing?" And at times throughout the day I have caught
him staring at me, unsmiling, a cloudy look in his eyes.

I tell them about my talk with Max and Rachel, curious
about how they will respond to my brother's defensiveness.
"His reaction worries me, because I want him to like us,"
Hannah says. "But Sam is similar when we tell him something.
He feels left out, and wants things to remain the way he
thought they were." She takes a breath, looking off into the
middle distance as though in a reverie, thinking aloud. "It's
scary enough to contemplate meeting your father someday. Our
support group says that going through this process of getting
to know your birth child often brings you back to that young
woman doing something bad, with people judging you. All that
your father knows about me is that I gave up his precious
daughter. And so I continue to be that person when I think of

him." I remember reading that because a birth mother and adoptee's renewed relationship picks up where it was abruptly cut off, the two often revert back to where they were the last time they were together: the birth mother, to a place of confusion, fear and shame, the adoptee, to a place of disconnectedness and helplessness, and both to a place of loss. But while Hannah's reemergence has provoked these reactions in me in general, I haven't felt a specific need for her to give me all that she couldn't before—on the contrary, the idea makes me uncomfortable.

We didn't run into any of their friends today, but Hannah says that most of them know about me. "Adam and I told almost no one before we had told the kids, because we didn't want them to find out from someone else," she explains. "But once we told them, we could officially 'come out' as birth parents." Their closest friends know that I am here this weekend. Some of them have called to ask how the reunion is going, if they can bring something over, if they can do anything. But I'm glad I haven't had to meet any of them yet—the quiet, private tone feels right.

Sam calls from upstairs that he can't sleep. Hannah goes up to talk or read or sing a song, then comes back down. He calls again a few minutes later, sounding like he is caught in that vicious circle of his inability to fall asleep making him frustrated and even less able to fall asleep. As Adam goes up this second time, I recall having trouble falling asleep as a child, too. Sometimes I was restless and would find every excuse to call my father in, requesting glasses of apple juice, asking questions one

by one. Other times I was content to lie there, making shadow
puppets on the wall, drifting across the bridge of imagination
into dream. The soft illumination and muffled voices easing
their way into my bedroom from the kitchen and living room
soothed me. I felt secure in my parents' muted presence, just as
when we used to drive home from the beach late at night, and I
would lie in the backseat, watching the headlights of passing
cars making tracks on the ceiling, hearing from the radio up
front the soft staccato rhythms of the WINS news station jin-
gle, the low voice intoning, "You give us twenty-two minutes,
we'll give you the world."

Past midnight, Adam drives me to the Holiday Inn. Two
messages from Chris are waiting for me at the front desk,
"Please call A.S.A.P." Making my way up in the quietly whirring elevator, along the empty carpeted hallway, into the room
with the smoothed quilted bedspread and the plastic cups and
the rectangles of soap wrapped in paper, I am serene. The
silence rings in my ears, the space eases my joints. I can call
Chris without asking anyone, and I do. Unfortunately, he isn't
home, but I leave a message thanking him for checking on me,
telling him that the visit is going very well, that I will phone
him tomorrow night when I return to New York, that I love
him. Then, even though it's late, I call my parents. Mom
answers after the first ring, startled but awake, and yells for Dad
to pick up. On the line at the same time, they ask what meeting
the Leyders was like, what we did today, how I feel. By openly
discussing my experience with them, I feel less treasonous for
visiting this other family; my mother and father are still there,

they haven't changed or gone away. At one point, Mom asks, "So, are Hannah and Adam nice?" and I answer yes.

"Nicer than we are?" Dad banters without missing a beat.

"If at any point it starts to feel weird and you want to come home," Mom reassures me, "you just call us and we'll come get you."

We confirm our plan for dinner Monday night, they wish me good luck, and we tell one another "I love you" before hanging up.

I brush my teeth, wash my face and fall into the wide bed. Now, in the stillness of the climate-controlled hotel room, in the solitude between the crisp sheets, I can finally consider how I feel. How do I feel? I ask myself aloud, and then let out a small, tired chuckle as the question reminds me of my single support group experience with the cartoon facial expressions decorating the walls. I feel exhausted, physically and emotionally, I answer. Maybe the impact of this experience hasn't hit me yet. I don't feel elated, really. I think I feel calm. As my thoughts mumble out, I fall asleep.

Sunday, January 14

My nine-thirty wake-up call rouses me, and I realize after a second or two where I am. As at camp, when in the first moments of alertness my homesickness would wash over me, I now turn on my side, look out the window at the gray New Hampshire sky, and feel lonely.

I partially wish that I hadn't come yet. I want to start over, want that clean slate again, want the reunion still as my grail to quest for. We've already met, I've already said the things I've said and done the things I've done, and I no longer have the anticipation of the meeting happening. But I also wish that I were back home with this weekend already behind me. The time between being here in Hanover in a hotel bed now and being back at home in my own bed tonight seems an eternity, a swamp of effort and emotion to wade through before I can reach the other side. But I'm already in the middle, up to my waist in it, so there's no sense in doing anything but trudging on. More positively, I'm looking forward to the day ahead, as well, open to whatever it might bring.

Should I be trying harder? Am I making an impression? If so, what sense is my birth family getting of me? I worry whether they think I'm boring. I think back to yesterday, which seems so long ago, going over everything to check if I made any mistakes, and cringe as I recall our first moment in the airport. I went to Hannah first, planning to hug her and then Adam; but as I was hugging her, he came over and hugged us. It didn't occur to me at the time, but now I hope that he didn't feel excluded. Maybe I should have come to them together and hugged them both at once. I know I'm being overly analytical, but these little slips, like not bringing more photographs, gnaw at me.

While I'd appreciate more time alone, I want to call the Leyders before it gets too late in the morning. I can reflect all I want when I am back home, but for now, I'm here to drain these two days as dry as possible. Hannah answers, and I am relieved to hear that Renee and Lucy are still sleeping. I ask if she would pick me up in half an hour. When she arrives I am not quite ready, and so she sits at the little table by the window as I put on my sweater, gather my things. I feel a bit uncomfortable having her here, wishing that I had said forty-five minutes, that I had said I'd meet her in the lobby, wanting to be organized, prepared when I see her. But I'm ready soon enough.

We drive back to their house for waffles and pancakes, made from a nutty, whole-grain batter. We talk about when my flight takes off this evening, figuring out what time we'll have to drive to the airport, and discuss our afternoon plans.

"We could take Sarah on that walk to the frozen waterfall," Hannah says to Adam. "It's so beautiful up there."

He nods. "Yeah. Sounds great." The girls eventually make their way downstairs, prettily sleepy in their flannel pajamas and unruly hair, apologizing politely for rising so late. As we sit around the table together, I notice that we all have the same eyes. Although Sam's are blue and the other five pairs are green, all are light with long dark lashes. Hannah, Renee and Lucy have the exact color eyes that I do, olive green with a darker, almost navy circle outlining the iris. I'm glad that this is the trait we have most in common, as eyes are somehow more significant than aquiline noses or big ears or full lips. Windows to the soul?

After breakfast, Adam brings out pictures of his birth father and mother. "You look a little like her, I think," he says shyly, "especially in the cheekbones." Some pictures of her include Adam as a small boy—one that strikes me is of her holding him at age three or so, standing next to Shirley Smith, his future guardian, holding her own son, Mike. The photograph recalls ones of me with my mother Nancy, some taken scant months before her death, neither of us aware of what is going to happen. Pictures of the father whom Adam knew for only two weeks also reveal no indication of his fate. I recall Adam's description of his father as always wearing a "shit-eating grin" as I look at the elder Leyder, laughing or smirking in almost every picture.

Lucy and I accompany Renee to the trail as Sam goes with Hannah and Adam, and it is good to be together, the three girls. We discuss driving—Renee's recently acquired car (I take a picture of her, proudly positioned in the driver's seat), standard versus automatic, the drawback of living in New York City ("I didn't get my license until senior year of college," I sheepishly confess); music—Lucy prefers classic rock like Bob Marley and Jimi Hendrix, and both are fans of Ani DiFranco; college—Renee's relief about having her Williams application in, where else to apply if she is deferred; people I have interviewed for articles—they are most impressed by singer/songwriter Liz Phair, who, being an adoptee herself, was very interested in my story ("No way, Liz Phair asked you about *us?*").

But alone with the other children for the first time, I'm not sure how to refer to my birth parents. Directly addressing Hannah and Adam by their first names isn't confusing, but what should I call them when speaking with Renee and Lucy? Still "Hannah and Adam"? "*Your* mother and father"? Both ways sound impersonal, as though I am merely an adult friend of the family. But "*our* mother and father" doesn't sound right either, because they are not my parents in the same way. I end up resorting to "your mother and father," or alternately, the more casual, "your mom and dad," although neither feels exactly right.

The day is cold and clear. Bright sunlight reflects off the snow-covered path, ice pellets squeak underfoot. Hannah has brought her camera, too, and we all take pictures of one another along the walk—Sam stopping to climb in snowdrifts along the side and balancing large snow boulders on his head ("Look, you guys! Look! Take a picture!"), Lucy lying down to make angel impressions. At one point, she and I take pictures of each other at the same time, she posing with Hannah and Adam, I with Renee, and Sam rushing back and forth to be in both shots.

We reach the waterfall, stunning in its frozen motion. I think of Hannah being driven away from Staten Island Hospital almost twenty-seven years ago, time stopping for us at that moment, the image of young mother and infant child preserved until now. We ask some passersby to take pictures of the six of us together. As with the waitress in the coffee shop—was that only yesterday?—I wonder what these strangers think, supposing that they take us for a "normal" family. I am amused that there is so much more than meets the eye, and at the same time, comforted by the sense of belonging. Looking at the pictures later, I am jarred by the mood conveyed when one or two people happen not to be smiling in a photograph. Just like being caught blinking or scratching, it's easy enough not to smile on time, or to stop smiling too early. But in one of the shots, the four children are smiling, in a slightly unnatural, posed way but happily enough, and Hannah and Adam, who are both unsmiling, appear sad, searching. Perhaps I'm reading too much into the expressions, because in the next shot of the same pose, they are smiling along with us, and in a third, Hannah is camping it up, standing center with her arms spread, as if to say, "Hey, here's my brood!" But those first somber looks are captured, an accidental glimpse of a private instant.

We turn to head back, and Adam and I are gradually ahead of the others. As we have to walk single file because of the narrow path a heart-to-heart is awkward. Nevertheless, Adam launches into one, and I follow.

"You know, Sarah, I tend to worry about everything," he begins. "I worry how the visit's going, even while you're still here. Is it too hectic, I think, is Sarah getting enough time to be alone with each of us one-on-one? Are we being too open and familiar, or not enough? Should I have put out chips and salsa yesterday afternoon? You get the idea." As he chuckles self-consciously, I say that I completely understand, recalling myself this morning, worrying in my hotel room. Is this trait inherited, I wonder, did he pass it on to me through his genes? Or are we similar in this way because we are both adoptees? Or is it merely coincidental?

"I loved listening to you and Hannah talk last night and watching your face," Adam continues. "That was a miracle. You have such a beautiful, frequent smile, Sarah, and such a serious, sad face in repose." Touched, I thank him, thinking of catching his own unsmiling face last night, and all that it revealed.

He goes on to say that he finds himself missing me right now, already dreading my departure this evening. "I mean, now that I've finally met you, and can see you're a grown woman, it makes me realize your childhood is something gone. There's so much of your life that is lost. We can never catch up." It's true, I can tell them about my past, I can show them pictures of myself at various ages, but even so, they will never have known me as a toddler, a teenager. There's a gap that's impossible to fill completely. I look back at the receding waterfall. While our connection to one another was indeed frozen until now, our lives have progressed separately. So even though Adam would like to conjure spring to melt the ice, which has waited, immobile, for that warm touch to reanimate it, the water has continued to flow beneath the surface, perpetually changing in shape and structure.

All of this rattles around in my mind as I plod along, my breath coming out in steamy funnels, my feet crunching in Adam's larger footsteps an instant after he has made them. But I say nothing along these lines, opting instead to make encouraging noises about taking our relationship from here and how lucky we are to have found one another at all. I realize, as I did last night, that I have greater ease in being future- rather than past-oriented: for me, the loss is less palpable, because the decision to relinquish was theirs, while being relinquished was simply the fate that was handed to me; also, for me, this is an either-or situation, because the Leyders' raising me would have meant that I was someone else, someone who didn't even know the Saffians, let alone belong to their family, which is inconceivable. I try to see the circumstances in this positive light primarily for myself, because I'm not up for a heavy conversation, but I do believe that my optimism might help Adam feel less regretful and more grateful. And what else, really, do I have to offer him?

We go back to the house, eat leftovers from last night's dinner and hang out, chatting. We don't have to fill the day with activities to occupy ourselves, facing one another comes so naturally. The three kids play their instruments—the girls on piano, Renee classical, Lucy jazz, and Sam on trumpet—and I take pictures. Sam has a remarkably good ear, automatically harmonizing when he sings along with whatever song is playing, even if he's never heard it. My friends have often mocked me for doing this, but, like Sam, I almost can't help hearing the harmony. I comment on the Leyders' dinner set, all handmade by Hannah—large and small plates, mugs, pitchers. Down in her studio, she invites me to select some pieces to take home. I choose a pair of candlesticks and a small box with a lid, and she wraps them in newspaper. She asks if she can give me something for my parents, as well, but I decline, saying that it is generous of her, but that I will show them mine instead, as I am unsure how they would feel receiving a gift from her.

"What about naming me Susan," I ask when we're back upstairs, sitting at the table again. "Was I named after anyone in your family?"

"No, I just liked it," Hannah says. "You know, it's so strange, and so difficult, to give your child a name knowing that the people who end up raising her probably won't keep it." I try to imagine how it must feel not to be able to give your child anything, that nothing of you, the birth mother, will carry over.

But in getting to know Hannah, I'm realizing how much she has indeed given me, in subtler ways—her love of the outdoors and exercise, her non-materialistic ethics, the earthy strength imbuing her femininity that I strive to emulate.

We are all surprised when the time comes to pile into the car and go to the airport. Arriving early, we stand in the lobby and chat as we wait, and when my boarding is announced, everyone seems loath to say goodbye. I hug each of them, asking Sam and Lucy to send me drawings, and Renee to let me know about colleges. Hannah and Adam shrug at the immensity of what we've just been through and ask, "So what happens now?"

"I don't know," I say honestly, "I've never done this before, either." Adam wonders whether when they happen to come to down to New York, they can maybe call and see me? "Maybe," I answer. I feel as if I've consumed a large and sumptuous meal and am not yet ready for another one. I still need to digest a bit, to sort out all the aromas and textures and flavors.

After one last farewell, I walk through the metal detector, which promptly lets off a loud beep. I turn back to the Leyders and laugh, thinking that the flight staff doesn't care that I just had a reunion with my birth parents, they want to make sure that I'm not carrying any weapons aboard. I take off my watch and go through silently this time, collect my belongings off the conveyor belt, give a small final wave to my birth family, and disappear through the door.

Back in New York by eight o'clock, I am struck by a song Sam sang yesterday, an altered version of "Show Me the Way to

Go Home," which Renee taught to him once during a car trip. The lyrics were ridiculously verbose, substituting "alcoholic beverage" for "drink," "cerebellum" for "head," "perambulate" for "roam," "habitual abode" for "home." I think now that "show me the way to go home" is the very plea I am making, but to whom? Going to Hanover was returning home, in a sense, even though I had never been there before. Coming back to my apartment at the end of the weekend is returning home, to where I currently live, to a place that is familiar. And tomorrow evening, going to my parents' house will be returning home as well, to the place where I grew up, the place that school forms used to term my "permanent address." But while still in the midst of determining what exactly home is, I am already certain that it is more than a mere habitual abode. As I walk through my little studio, studying the red Buddha painting in the living room, the books on the shelves, the clawed feet of the old-fashioned bathtub, I recall returning from camp at the end of each summer and noticing details that I normally overlooked out of habit. Our apartment always seemed to have shrunk while I was away, because I had grown, physically and otherwise. But tonight is more significant: I was only away for one night, but it is as though I have traveled in time.

Perhaps I have traveling on my mind when I go to the video store and rent *Apollo 13*, at a loss for what else to do. I make popcorn and watch the movie in a daze. When it's over, I unpack methodically, and then decide that it's late enough to call Chris in California, that he'll be home. With my phone still out of order,

I head back out to what has become my regular pay phone, on the corner of Bleecker Street outside the Grand Union supermarket, bundled up in preparation for a long conversation. At Chris' "Hello?" I start to sob for the first time all weekend. Crying this hard is a relief, as if something long pent up—over the weekend, over these three years, over my entire life—is being released at last. But I am also crying because when Chris asks me, "How do you feel?" all I can pinpoint is a void, and that makes me sad— my lack of emotion in itself provokes an emotion.

"I thought I'd rush to tell you everything, but I'm too tired and overwhelmed to do that yet."

"I understand."

This is the first time in a while that I have not wanted to share with him immediately, not needed his input to help me determine how I feel. I will tell him about the weekend over time, but not in the automatic and unabridged way to which I have grown accustomed. Now I clearly see the experience as personal and all my own.

After we hang up, I return home and climb into bed. I remember looking at the Leyders' first photographs in August 1993 and concluding that they were just pictures of people. Yes, a reunion with my birth parents is a profound experience, but ultimately, they are just people, I am just a person, we are just meeting. What we do together is unremarkable: chop vegetables, pad around the house in our socks, watch home movies, take walks. Maybe that is exactly what is so wonderfully remarkable about it.

I'd mused on the reunion my entire life, even before I knew who my birth parents were or that they existed. Occasionally, I

297

felt curious, and, more rarely, I felt quite alone, as though I didn't belong anywhere. But mostly I found solace in the unknown. So when the Leyders first contacted me, I resented them for denying me that mystery. When we were getting to know one another through our letters, there was still this event that we were building up to. Now that it's in the past rather than the future, part of me feels empty. I had hoped that I would feel fuller from meeting them. Perhaps eventually I will gain that sense of wholeness, but immediately post-reunion, I still long for it. Despite how much I thought over the weekend that the experience was changing me, now that it has occurred, I am disappointed as well as comforted when I realize that I am also the same.

298

Monday, January 15

It's midnight, and I'm lying on the couch in my parents' living room. Everyone is in bed, the house is quiet. I wonder whether the others are lying there, pondering, or if I am the only one still awake. My coming here tonight, on the heels of the trip to Hanover, reassured us all that this is my family, that this is where I belong. My sense of security here is not because the time with the Leyders fell short of my expectations—although I am unclear what my expectations were, exactly, I think our reunion surpassed them. But the experience wouldn't have been complete if I couldn't have shared it with my family. Perhaps that was what the void was last night, a feeling of being in limbo, of having had this experience but not yet reconnected with my family, and thus, not yet fully returned.

As I approached my parents' brownstone this evening, I recalled the morning when I had come here after receiving a phone call from a woman saying that she was my birth mother. I remembered how surprised I had been that the stoop, the tree in front of their house, everything had seemed somewhat altered. Walking down the block three years later, I understood that after Hannah's phone call I had felt changed, and so the world around me appeared changed, too. This evening, as well, the stoop, the tree, the light beckoning from the kitchen windows, looked a bit different, again, because I was seeing them through different eyes.

I had been concerned about my parents being hurt, and worried that they wouldn't show me if they were. But the most important element of this evening was that they each told me they were proud. When I first arrived, I walked into the living room where Dad was, and he immediately took me in his arms and hugged me tightly. "I'm so proud of you, Saraleh," he said softly in my ear. "It was very courageous, to do something that must have been so hard. I'm so proud of you, and I love you very much." That meant everything to me.

Aperture

In March 1997, I took another trip to Hanover. Recalling my painstaking specifications on the first visit to my birth family a little over a year earlier, I noticed the equally conscious adjustments I made the second time around. Now I was eager to witness the road connecting my home to theirs concretely as well as philosophically: while I had flown in January 1996, this time I headed north by bus, houses growing larger as we approached and then receding behind us, wind whipping in through the open door colder with each stop, trees turning to naked black silhouettes as the fields became powdery with snow, yellow afternoon giving way to blue dusk. I stayed for three nights as compared to my previous single night, and at the Leyders' house instead of a hotel, coming down to breakfast in my pajamas along with the other kids. Friday night, as I lay in Lucy's bed—she had doubled up with Renee, who was home from Williams for spring break—gazing up at the glow-in-the-dark star and comet stickers decorating the ceiling, I wondered how

Hannah felt, lying in her own bed with Adam in the next room, having her four children under the same roof for the first time.

I met friends of the family throughout the weekend. Watching Sam's Hebrew class participate in the Shabbat service at temple on Friday evening, I occasionally glanced to the side and caught Lucy's friends sitting in a cluster a few seats away, peering at me inquisitively, and then, upon making eye contact, quickly returning their attention to their prayer books. Saturday, a couple of Renee's high school friends, also on vacation from college, came over to watch a movie with us. My last evening in Hanover, out to dinner at a restaurant, people stopped by our table now and then to say hello. Everyone whom I met was already familiar with our circumstances, no explanation was necessary. I felt ready for these steps forward, and took them decisively and with ease. How far we had come from being two disembodied voices on the telephone. But the more we learned about one another, the more we could see how much there still was to know.

Hannah wrote in her first letter, dated February 8, 1993, that finding me was like coming to "the end of a very long and torturous journey." Giving me up set the journey in motion—for them, into a life of having relinquished a child, and for me, into a life of having been relinquished and then adopted. But giving me up also eventually led to a search, and calling me began a third phase, that of getting to know one another through correspondence.

Meeting provoked yet another journey, which we will perhaps always be on—that of figuring out how we fit into one another's lives. After our reunion, Adam wrote, "In one of your early letters, you speculated whether what we wanted out of a reunion was 'closure.' My God. What's the opposite of 'closure'? 'Aperture'?" Our reunion was indeed an opening, in posing a new question: now that we "know" one another, now that we have met face-to-face, where do we go from here?

Thus the odyssey is an all-encompassing continuum, reunion a form of *re-adoption*—of that original child, family, self, which had previously existed in shadow. On the bus ride back to New York from this second visit to Hanover, as I looked out the window at the moving landscape, it struck me that I was finally coming to terms with an idea already clear to many—that we are not born entirely formless, like so much clay waiting to be molded by our environments into people with identities. I turned my hands palm-side up and examined their lines, realizing that perhaps more than our physical traits—the color of our hair and eyes, the size of our noses and feet, whether we have hitchhiker's thumbs and attached earlobes—is predestined. *Who we are*, in the larger sense—our likes and our dislikes, what makes us sad and what brings us joy, how we relate to others and how we reflect in moments alone, how we exist both in the world and in our heads and hearts—can be partially inherited, as well. I leaned back in the seat and closed my eyes, looking inside to recognize Susan Morgan, that formerly latent aspect of myself, as she materialized from the vapor. In transit on the road between the Leyders and the Saffians, I thought that perhaps just as one can have many children, one can, in varying degrees, also have many parents, many families—and even many selves, or discrete but complementary parts that make up the whole.

Resources

ORGANIZATIONS

American Adoption Congress (AAC)

(202) 483–3399. 1000 Connecticut Ave., NW, Suite 9, Washington, DC 20036. The largest national adoption reform organization. AAC's membership includes adoptees, birth parents, adoptive parents and professionals working for open records and openness in adoption practice. It publishes a quarterly newsletter with articles on current issues and holds national and regional conferences with workshops offering emotional support, search information and legislative strategies. (*Also see On-line Resources, below.*)

International Soundex Reunion Registry (Soundex)

(702) 882–7755. P.O. Box 2312, Carson City, NV 89702. One of the two largest adoption registries in the United States, Soundex was founded in 1975 for the purpose of facilitating mutual consent reunions of all kinds. Adoptees and birth parents register by submitting a form with all known relevant information

about themselves and the other party, which is then entered into databases and cross-referenced until a match is made. There is no fee to register, and all voluntary contributions are tax-deductible.

Adoptee Liberty Movement Association (ALMA)

(212) 581–1568. P.O. Box 154, Washington Bridge Station, New York, NY 10033. The other major adoption registry in the United States, with chapters around the country. Adoptees and birth parents are entered into databases, which are cross-checked regularly, and if a match is made, ALMA facilitates a reunion. It also assists in legal searches through workshops and one-on-one consulting, and is active in the fight against closed records. All services are "free" to members, who have paid a registration fee and annual dues.

Adoption Crossroads/Council for Equal Rights in Adoption (CERA)

(212) 988–0110. 356 E. 74th Street, Suite 2, New York, NY 10021. Joe Soll, C.S.W. Support network and registry, in favor of open records. Offers walk-in "rap groups," "Healing Weekend" retreats, and search advice and assistance. One may either become a member or pay per service, and all contributions and fees are tax-deductible. Also has chapters in New York State, New Jersey, Connecticut and Vermont.

ON-LINE RESOURCES

American Adoption Congress (AAC):
http://www.american-adoption-cong.org/

RESOURCES

Adoptees Resources Home Page:
http://psy.ucsd.edu/~jhartung/adoptees.html
e-mail: hartung@crl.ucsd.edu

Jeff Hartung, Administrator. Newsletter offering extensive information on laws, free search advice and assistance and links to many other websites.

Adoption: A Gathering:
link through http://www.weblab.org
e-mail: gathering@weblab.org

Suki Jones, Director. Forum inviting all members of the triad to share thoughts and stories, ask questions and give advice. Includes a resource guide.

AIML (Adoptees Internet Mailing List)'s U.S. Adoption Laws by State:
http://www.webreflection.com/aiml/uslaws.html

Compiled by Carol Komissaroff and updated by Rosemarie Ventura and Dana Kressierer. Summary of current adoption laws, listed by state, covering United States Records Access Laws as of 1991, with amendments up to the present. There are also links to websites and bulletin boards where one can find further information and post queries.

Adoptee/Birth Parent Search Support Forum:
http://www.adopting.org/ffcwnr.html

Birth Registry for Separated Families:
http://www.janyce.com/genebirth/gene.html

BirthQuest:
http://www.access.digex.net/~vqi/top.html
Database dedicated to searching adoptees, birth parents,
adoptive parents and siblings. $20 registration "donation."

BOOKS

Brodzinsky, David M., and Marshall D. Schechter, eds. *The Psychology of Adoption* (New York: Oxford University Press, 1990)

Edelman, Hope. *Motherless Daughters: The Legacy of Loss* (Reading, MA: Addison-Wesley, 1994)

Gediman, Judith S., and Linda P. Brown. *Birth Bond: Reunions Between Birth Parents and Adoptees—What Happens After* (Far Hills, NJ: New Horizon Press, 1989)

Homes, A. M. *In a Country of Mothers* (New York: Knopf, 1993)

Lifton, Betty Jean. *Twice Born: Memoirs of an Adoptive Daughter* (New York: Penguin, 1977)

_____. *Lost and Found: The Adoption Experience* (New York: HarperCollins, 1988)

_____. *Journey of the Adopted Self: A Quest for Wholeness* (New York: Basic Books, 1994)

Moorman, Margaret. *Waiting to Forget: A Mother Opens the Door to Her Secret Past* (New York: W. W. Norton, 1996)

Schaefer, Carol. *The Other Mother: A Woman's Love for the Child She Gave Up for Adoption* (New York: Soho Press, 1991)

Sorosky, Arthur D., Annette Baran, and Reuben Pannor. *The Adoption Triangle* (San Antonio, TX: Corona, 1989)

Strauss, Jean A. *Birthright: The Guide to Search and Reunion for Adoptees, Birth Parents and Adoptive Parents* (New York: Penguin, 1994)

Waldron, Jan L. *Giving Away Simone* (New York: Times Books, 1995)

Acknowledgments

For helping me to find the statue within the block of marble, I thank my editors, Linda Kahn, Jo Ann Miller and Gail Winston, as well as my agent and friend Tina Bennett, with her inimitable blend of chutzpah, sensitivity and tireless interest. And for his unflagging patience, precision and eleventh-hour calm, I thank my project editor, Richard Fumosa.

Profound gratitude for sage teachers and advisers Michael Scammell, Fenton Johnson, Le Anne Schreiber, Richard Locke, Mary Catherine Bateson and Faith Lamb Parker.

Deep appreciation for good friends Vanni Kassarjian, Barbara Bashlow Gross, Laurel Watts, Nikki Levy, Timothy Murphy and David Bennahum, my doppelgänger.

Much gratefulness to Karen Avenoso, Malcolm Gladwell, Christopher Smith, Bailey Foster, and Tori Rowan for their significant support.

Most crucially, with love and wonderment, I thank—

my birth family, particularly my birth parents, for letting me tell our story and incorporate their honest, eloquent words in the process

my parents, Marvin and Kathy Saffian, and my brother and sister, Max and Rachel, for their joyful pride and trust in me

and Christopher Wilcha, for his boundless giving, tenderness and humor.